MATHEMATICAL MODELS IN ENVIRONMENTAL POLICY ANALYSIS

MATHEMATICAL MODELS IN ENVIRONMENTAL POLICY ANALYSIS

Edited by
L.A. Petrosjan and V.V. Zakharov

Translated from the Russian by Y.M. Donets

NOVA SCIENCE PUBLISHERS, INC.
COMMACK, NEW YORK

Assistant Vice President/Art Director: Maria Ester Hawrys
Graphics: Frank Grucci
Editorial Production: Susan Boriotti
Office Manager: Annette Hellinger
Acquisitions Editor: Tatiana Shohov
Book Production: Ladmila Kwartirof, Christine Mathosian,
                Joanne Metal and Tammy Sauter
Circulation: Iyatunde Abdullah, Cathy DeGregory and
              Annette Hellinger

*Library of Congress Cataloging–in–Publication Data
available upon request*

ISBN 1-56072-515-X
*© 1997 Nova Science Publishers, Inc.
  6080 Jericho Turnpike, Suite 207
  Commack, New York 11725
  Tele. 516-499-3103 Fax 516-499-3146
  E-Mail: Novascience@earthlink.net*

Printed in the United States of America

Contents

PREFACE

The ideas and models discussed in this book are not presented as "solution" to environmental problems. They are merely examples of contributions that can be made by mathematicians to facilitate rational environmental policy making. Obviously, mathematicians alone can not achieve much. There must be cooperation with other disciplines in order to supply environmental policy makers with good data and technique. We based our research on interdisciplinary science which may be named mathematical ecology.

Mathematical ecology as a science can be traced back to the early twentieth century. Its emergence was stimulated by scholarly works of an outstanding mathematician V. Volterra and his contemporaries A. Lotka and V. Kostitsin. The further development of mathematical ecology was the focus of research efforts made by G. F. Gauze, A. N. Kolmogorov, H. Odum, Y. M. Svirezhev, R. A. Poluektov et al. The deepest penetration of mathematical methods is observed in investigations of biological population dynamics that are central to the issues of ecology and population genetics.

Today man's capability to materially affect the processes occurring in biosphere is comparable to the energy of natural origin. For this reason, the interactions of man and biosphere have become the focus of much theoretical and empirical research. The most challenging issues of economy and social development are closely allied to those of environmental pollution, climate evolution, sustained existence of ecosystems, depletion of natural resources, etc. In view of environmental effect and pollution, ecology has assumed a new significance. Ecology is the science of interrelationships among plant and animal organisms and their relation to environment. The subject matter of ecology includes populations of organisms, biological species, communities, ecosystems and biosphere in general. A special line of investigation is human ecology which is the study of general relationships between nature and society. For this reason, ecology substantially differs from other sciences in that it has no unified basis which, as in the case of other sciences, can be likened to a powerful trunk of the tree capable to produce more specialized avenues of investigation. Conversely, the interlacing of such sciences as botany, zoology, climatology, physical demography, soil science, biochemistry, microbiology, applied mathematics, sociology, population geography, and economics forms the powerful trunk of ecology.

To solve ecological problems, mathematicians have to develop methods for constructing and examining mathematical models of ecological processes. The framework for development of such methods is provided by fundamental research in control theory, game theory, systems theory, etc. This monograph is designed to bring to the attention of mathematicians, ecologists, economists and biologists the need to develop mathematical models and techniques capable of solving ecological problems. The monograph is organized as follows. Chapter I contains classical models for biological community performance, size control optimization problems for species in communities, issues of ecological system stability, and conflict control models for population dynamics. Chapter II presents air pollution models and methods for solving problems of emission control and optimal lay-out of industrial enterprises which serve as emission sources. Chapter III highlights the major results of application of the game-theoretic approach to the models constructed in Chapter II. Interest coordination models are constructed for the interacting parties using restricted natural resources; resource rationing techniques and penalty optimization methods are proposed; "fish wars" and coordination of conservation measures are discussed. Chapter IV deals with hierarchical development control systems for closed ecological systems. Consideration is being given to the systems modeled by hierarchical games, the diamond-shaped control systems with additional relations, and the dynamic stability of ecological solutions. Chapter V is devoted to multicriteria optimization problems of control. Multicriteria model is constructed for development of a closed ecosystem. Optimal control methods are presented for multicriteria systems. The method of constructing Pareto-optimal sets is provided for the problem of approaching several target points. Chapter VI deals with evolutionary games and their related existence and stability issues of evolution strategies for populations and species. Chapter VII discusses the CO_2 emission control model and the environmental policy coordination method with side payments.

When considering dynamic models the special attention is given to the problem of dynamic stability (time-consistency) of the optimal solutions concerning environmental policy. Unfortunately this is not a common aspect in modern mathematical ecology.

It is a pleasure to thank K. Kondratjev for valuable comments. In addition we thank Y. Donets for translation, E. Ekimova, N. Savischenko, E. Legnina, A. Cherkasova, A. Kovshov for the significant help they have given us over the period of design of this book. The book was written under the financial support of the Russian Basic Researchs Foundation.

Chapter 1

MATHEMATICAL MODELS FOR POPULATION DYNAMICS

In mathematics, efforts have long been made to model the dynamics of isolated biological populations and communities comprising the interacting populations of various species. One of the models for isolated population growth was proposed in 1798:

$$dN/dt = \mu N,$$

where N is the population size and; μ is the difference between the birth and death rates. The solution of this equation $N(t) = N(0)e^{\mu t}$ for $\mu > 0$ increases without bound. However, the effect of unbounded exponential growth of population is not observed in nature, where the resources supporting this growth are limited. The population size in a given environment is generally bounded by a certain quantity K, referred to as the carrying capacity: $N(t) \to K$ as $t \to \infty$. The models allowing (to some extent) for this fact emerged later. For example, in 1825 . B. Gompertz examined the model describing the "Saturation" effect:

$$dN/dt = -\mu N \ln (N/K)/\ln K.$$

Experiments on animals, however, showed that the saturation sets in faster than it follows from the solution

$$N(t) = K e^{\ln(N(0)/K)e^{-\mu t/\ln K}}.$$

of this equation.

Finally, in 1938 Ferhulst proposed a simple and clear model which adequately described biological population dynamics:

$$dN/dt = \mu N(K - N)/K.$$

The in-depth study of models for biological communities comprising several populations of distinct species is contained in Volterra [4]. For example, the interaction dynamics in the community made up of two biological populations is described by the system of differential equations

$$dN_1/dt = N_1(\varepsilon_1 + \gamma_1 N_2), \qquad dN_2/dt = N_2(\varepsilon_2 + \gamma_2 N_1),$$

where ε_i are coefficients of natural population growth (or death); γ_i are interspecific interaction coefficients. Depending on the choice of coefficients the model describes either the struggle of species for a common resource or a predator-prey type interaction when one species serves as food for the other. Although some authors focus their attention on construction of various models, V. Volterra concentrated on the in-depth study of the models constructed for biological communities. It is the opinion of many scientists that the present-day mathematical ecology derives from Volterra's book. In his epilogue to the Russian edition of this book, Y. M. Svirezhev writes that "Volterra's study is undoubtedly the theory of biological communities constructed exactly as a mathematical theory".

In mathematical ecology, one of the main issues is the problem of ecosystem stability. By "stability" is usually meant the maintenance of a species size level in a given biological community, the absence of fluctuations in the size of populations in a community, etc. For the community, the stability measure is taken to be its diversity. This approach is based on the assumption that a wider set of species can more adequately respond to changes in environment, maintaining the number of species unaffected and reducing changes in the species size level. Ecologists tend to use the information measure of species diversity

$$D = -\sum_{i=1}^{n} p_i \ln p_i, \qquad p_i = N_i/N, \qquad N = \sum_{i=1}^{n} N_i,$$

where n is the number of species in a community and N_i is the size of the i-th species. Clearly this approach suggests that the community stability is governed by the magnitude of D. It is well known that D attains a maximum if $p_i = 1/n$, i.e., when all species are equal in number. This, however, is contrary to facts of life because in nature we generally find dominant species. The chief limitation of this approach is that the information measure of stability takes no account of intracommunity interactions. The information measure can be adequately applied to communities which are in the early stages of development with poor interactions.

Mathematical theory of stability deals with mathematical models of real objects, not with real objects themselves. Although the notion of dynamical system stability has several definitions, the principal among them is that of stability in Liapunov's sense.

Suppose the species interaction dynamics is described by the system of differential equations

$$dN_i/dt = f_i(N_1, N_2, \ldots, N_n), \qquad i = 1, 2, \ldots, n, \qquad (*)$$

whose right-hand sides satisfy the conditions which guarantee the existence and uniqueness of a continuously differentiable solution starting at the time $t = t_0$ from the point $N^0 = (N_1^0, N_2^0, \ldots, N_n^0)$.

Equilibrium or stationary state is taken to be a point N^* in the phase space such that $f_i(N_1^*, N_2^*, \ldots, N_n^*) \equiv 0$ for all $i = 1, 2, \ldots, n$.

D e f i n i t i o n 1. The solution $N = N^*$ of system $(*)$ is called Liapunov stable if for every $\varepsilon > 0$ at a given $t_0 \geq 0$ there is $\delta > 0$ such that for

$$\sum_{i=1}^{n}(N_i^0 - N_i^*)^2 < \delta$$

there is

$$\sum_{i=1}^{n}\left(N_i(t, N_1^0, N_2^0, \ldots, N_n^0, t_0) - N_i^*\right)^2 < \varepsilon$$

at $t \geq t_0$.

Here $N_i(t, N_1^0, N_2^0, \ldots, N_n^0, t_0)$ $(i = 1, 2, \ldots, n)$ is a solution of system $(*)$ with initial data $N_1^0, N_2^0, \ldots, N_n^0, t_0$. Furthermore, if

$$\sum_{i=1}^{n}\left(N_i(t, N_1^0, N_2^0, \ldots, N_n^0, t_0) - N_i^*\right)^2 \to 0$$

as $t \to +\infty$, then the solution $N = N^*$ is called asymptotically stable.

The function $V(N_1, N_2, \ldots, N_n)$, given in the phase space of system $(*)$, is called positive definite (negative definite) if:

1) $V(N_1^*, N_2^*, \ldots, N_n^*) = 0$;

2) $V(N_1, N_2, \ldots, N_n) > 0$ $(V(N_1, N_2, \ldots, N_n) < 0)$ for $N \neq N^*$

D e f i n i t i o n 2. The derivative of the function $V(N_1, N_2, \ldots, N_n)$ along the trajectory

$$N(t) = (N_1(t, N_1^0, N_2^0, \ldots, N_n^0, t_0), N_2(t, N_1^0, N_2^0, \ldots, N_n^0, t_0), \ldots,$$

$$N_n(t, N_1^0, N_2^0, \ldots, N_n^0, t_0))$$

in terms of the system $(*)$ is defined to be

$$\frac{d}{dt}V(N(t)) = \sum_{i=1}^{n} \frac{\partial V}{\partial N_i} f_i = W(N_1, N_2, \ldots, N_n).$$

This leads us to the following theorems.

Theorem 1. If the system of differential equations $(*)$ is such that it is possible to select a positive definite function V whose derivative W is computed in terms of system $(*)$ and satisfies the inequality $W \leq 0$, then the equilibrium is stable.

Theorem 2. The equilibrium N^* of system $(*)$ is called asymptotically stable if the conditions of Theorem 1 are satisfied and, moreover, the function W is negative definite.

The essentials of the mathematical theory of stability are discussed more comprehensively in [14]. The stability of ecosystems is closely related to the optimal control of such systems because the human interference with the biological community performance must be such that its effect on the ecosystem would allow for stability of the system equilibria. This leads us to the system control problem aimed at transferring this system from one stable state to another. For this reason, the present chapter deals with the ecosystem control optimization problems along with the stability issues.

1.1   Coexistence of Two Biological Species

Following V. Volterra, we assume that, where the amount of available food is unbounded, the size levels of two species N_1 and N_2 have positive constant coefficients of growth ε_1 and ε_2.

In reality the amount of food, and hence the growth coefficients, decreases as the populations increase in number. This may be reflected by the growth coefficients represented as $\varepsilon_1 - \gamma_1 F(N_1, N_2)$ and $\varepsilon_2 - \gamma_2 F(N_1, N_2)$, where γ_1, γ_2 are positive constants characterizing the food demand on the part of each of the species; $F(N_1, N_2)$ is the rate of food consumption. Suppose the function $F(N_1, N_2)$ becomes zero when $N_1 = 0$ and $N_2 = 0$, and monotonically increases in each of its variables.

The population development dynamics can be described by the system of differential equations

$$dN_1/dt = N_1(\varepsilon_1 - \gamma_1 F(N_1, N_2)),$$

$$dN_2/dt = N_2(\varepsilon_2 - \gamma_2 F(N_1, N_2)). \tag{1.1}$$

We rewrite (1.1) in the form

$$d\ln N_1/dt = \varepsilon_1 - \gamma_1 F(N_1, N_2),$$

$$d\ln N_2/dt = \varepsilon_2 - \gamma_2 F(N_1, N_2). \tag{1.2}$$

Eliminating the function $F(N_1, N_2)$ from (1.2), we obtain

$$\gamma_2 \frac{d\ln N_1}{dt} - \gamma_1 \frac{d\ln N_2}{dt} = \varepsilon_1\gamma_2 - \varepsilon_2\gamma_1,$$

or

$$\frac{d\ln\left(N_1^{\gamma_2}/N_2^{\gamma_1}\right)}{dt} = \varepsilon_1\gamma_2 - \varepsilon_2\gamma_1.$$

The solution of this equation becomes

$$\frac{N_1^{\gamma_2}}{N_2^{\gamma_1}} = \frac{\left(N_1^0\right)^{\gamma^2}}{\left(N_2^0\right)^{\gamma_1}} = e^{(\varepsilon_1\gamma_2 - \varepsilon_2\gamma_1)t}, \tag{1.3}$$

where $N_1^0 = N_1(0), N_2^0 = N_2(0)$.

It can be easily shown that the solution of system (1.1) with positive initial data are bounded on a finite time interval. Indeed, we may select the value N_1', such that $F(N_1', 0) > \varepsilon_1/\gamma_1$. Furthermore, if the solution $N_1(t)$ attains the value N_1', then

$$F(N_1, N_2) > F(N_1', 0) > \varepsilon_1/\gamma_1,$$

and hence dN_1/dt (see (1.1)) becomes less than zero, which renders further growth in $N_1(t)$ impossible. A similar reasoning applies to $N_2(t)$.

We now turn to expression (1.3). Suppose $\varepsilon_1/\gamma_1 > \varepsilon_2/\gamma_2$. The relation $N_1^{\gamma_2}/N_2^{\gamma_1}$ then increases infinitely, i.e. $\lim_{t\to\infty}(N_1^{\gamma_2}/N_2^{\gamma_1}) = +\infty$. Hence, because of the boundedness of N_1 and N_2, we have that $N_2(t) \to 0$.

This means that the second population, for which the value of ε_i/γ_i is smaller, decreases in number tending to zero, while the first population number tends to the value determined from the equation $\varepsilon_1 - \gamma_1 F(N_1, 0) = 0$. This confirms the intuitive inference that the species which has a smaller coefficient of natural growth and is more sensitive to food shortage tends to disappear.

We shall now consider the case where one of the species is a predator while the other is a prey. The predator is assumed to feed on the prey only. We adopt a simple hypothesis: the prey growth coefficient is equal to $\varepsilon_1 - \gamma_1 N_2$, while the predator growth coefficient is equal to $\gamma_2 N_1 - \varepsilon_2$.

Here N_1 is the prey population size; N_2 is the predator population size; ε_1 is the natural growth rate for the prey; γ_1 is the rate at which the predator consumes the prey; ε_2 is the predator death rate in the absence of the prey; γ_2 is the rate at which the predator turns the prey biomass into its own biomass. The population size dynamics in the predator-prey system is then described by the system of differential equations

$$dN_1/dt = N_1(\varepsilon_1 - \gamma_1 N_2),$$

$$dN_2/dt = N_2(\gamma_2 N_1 - \varepsilon_2). \tag{1.4}$$

We now multiply the first equation by γ_2 and add to the second equation multiplied by γ_1:

$$\gamma_2 dN_1/dt + \gamma_1 dN_2/dt = \varepsilon_1 \gamma_2 N_1 - \varepsilon_2 \gamma_1 N_1. \tag{1.5}$$

Next, we multiply the first equation by ε_2/N_1 and add to the second equation multiplied by ε_1/N_2:

$$\frac{\varepsilon_2}{N_1}\frac{dN_1}{dt} + \frac{\varepsilon_1}{N_2}\frac{dN_2}{dt} = -\varepsilon_2 \gamma_1 N_2 + \varepsilon_1 \gamma_2 N_1. \tag{1.6}$$

From (1.5) and (1.6) we get

$$\gamma_2\frac{dN_1}{dt} + \gamma_1\frac{dN_2}{dt} = \varepsilon_2\frac{d\ln N_1}{dt} + \varepsilon_1\frac{d\ln N_2}{dt}.$$

Integration yields

$$N_1^{-\varepsilon_2} e^{\gamma_2 N_1} = C N_2^{\varepsilon_1} e^{-\gamma_1 N_2}, \tag{1.7}$$

where $C = N_1^{0-\varepsilon_2} e^{\gamma_2 N_1^0} / \left(N_2^{0\varepsilon_1} e^{-\gamma_1 N_2^0}\right)$.

Equation (1.7) describes the family of closed curves centered at the point $(N_1^*, N_2^*) : N_1^* = \varepsilon_2/\gamma_2, N_2^* = \varepsilon_1/\gamma_1$. Examining the behavior of these curves, V. Volterra came to an important conclusion about periodicity of fluctuations in the population size and stability of an equilibrium (N_1^*, N_2^*). It turns out that N_1^* and N_1^* are respectively the average values of N_1 and N_2 in the fluctuation period. Indeed, let us rewrite the equations (1.4) as

$$\frac{d\ln N_1}{dt} = \varepsilon_1 - \gamma_1 N_2, \qquad \frac{d\ln N_2}{dt} = -\varepsilon_2 + \gamma_2 N_1.$$

We now integrate both parts of the equation over the time interval equal to one fluctuation period. By periodicity, we get

$$0 = \varepsilon_1 T - \gamma_1 \int_0^T N_2 dx, \qquad 0 = -\varepsilon_2 T + \gamma_2 \int_0^T N_1 dx,$$

Finally we have

$$N_1^* = \frac{\varepsilon_2}{\gamma_2} = \frac{1}{T} \int_0^T N_1 dt, \qquad N_2^* = \frac{\varepsilon_1}{\gamma_1} = \frac{1}{T} \int_0^T N_2 dt.$$

These relations are the expression of the law of conservation of average values which is stated as follows. The average (during a period T) values for the predator and prey sizes are independent of initial conditions and equal to equilibrium numbers.

We now suppose that, in a predator-prey system, individuals of both species are artificially annihilated. Let us discuss the question of how such annihilation of individuals affects their average numbers if it is carried out in proportion to these numbers with the proportionality coefficients α_1 and α_2 for the prey and predator, respectively. Under the above assumptions, system (1.4) can be expressed as

$$dN_1/dt = N_1(\varepsilon_1 - \alpha_1 - \gamma_1 N_2), \qquad \alpha_1 > 0,$$

$$dN_2/dt = N_2(-\varepsilon_2 - \alpha_2 + \gamma_2 N_1), \qquad \alpha_2 > 0. \tag{1.8}$$

We assume that $\alpha_1 < \varepsilon_1$, i.e. the prey annihilation coefficient is less than its natural growth coefficient. In this case we also observe periodic fluctuations in their numbers. Let us compute the average values

$$\frac{1}{T} \int_0^T N_1(t) dt = \frac{\varepsilon_2 + \alpha_2}{\gamma_2}, \qquad \frac{1}{T} \int_0^T N_2(t) dt = \frac{\varepsilon_1 - \alpha_1}{\gamma_1}.$$

Thus, if $\alpha_1 < \varepsilon_1$, then the average prey population grows in numbers while the average predator population decreases.

We shall now consider the case where the prey annihilation coefficient is greater than its natural growth coefficient, i.e. $\alpha_1 > \varepsilon_1$. Then $\varepsilon_1 - \alpha_1 - \gamma_1 N_2 < 0$ for any $N_2 > 0$, and hence the solution of the first equation in (1.8) is bounded above by the exponentially decreasing function $N_1(t) \leq N_1^0 e^{(\varepsilon_1 - \alpha_1)t}$, that is $N_1(t) \to 0$ as $t \to \infty$. From a certain time $\bar{t}$, at which $\gamma_2 N_1(\bar{t}) - \alpha_2 - \varepsilon_2 = 0$, the solution of the second equation in (1.8) also starts to decrease and tends to zero as $t \to \infty$.

Thus, in the case $\alpha_1 > \varepsilon_1$ both species disappear.

1.2   Generalized Volterra Models of the Predator-Prey Type

Clearly the first models constructed by V. Volterra could not allow for all interactions in a predator-prey system, because they were largely simplified with respect to real conditions. For example, if the number of predators N_2 is equal to zero, then it follows from the equations (1.4) that the prey population infinitely grows in number, which is contrary to facts of life. These models, however, are valuable in that they provided a framework for rapid development of mathematical ecology.

Many investigations focused on modifications of the predator-prey system and contributed to construction of more general models allowing for a real situation in nature.

In 1936 A. N. Kolmogorov suggested that the following system of equations be used to describe the predator-prey system dynamics:

$$dN_1/dt = N_1 g_1(N_1, N_2), \qquad dN_2/dt = N_2 g_2(N_1, N_2),$$

where g_1 decreases as predators grow in numbers, while g_2 increases as preys grow in numbers.

The above system of differential equations was general enough to adequately represent for the actual population behavior and provided a means for qualitatively analyzing its solutions.

More recently, Kolmogorov studied thoroughly a less general model [21]

$$dN_1/dt = g_1(N_1)N_1 - L(N_1)N_2, \qquad dN_2/dt = g_2(N_1, N_2)N_2. \qquad (1.9)$$

Similar models are discussed in [51], [57].

Special cases of system (1.9) have been the focus of much research. The table given below list special cases of the functions $g_1(N_1), L(N_1), g_2(N_1, N_2)$ used in such models (see [58]).

We now consider the model which allows for intraspecific competition among individuals of the prey [45]:

$$dN_1/dt = \varepsilon_1 N_1 - \gamma_1 N_1 N_2 - \gamma N_1^2,$$

$$dN_2/dt = k\gamma_1 N_1 N_2 - \varepsilon_2 N_2. \qquad (1.10)$$

Here intraspecific competition is taken into account by addendum γN_1^2. In this model, the prey population fails to increase in size to infinity where there is no predator. As is easy to see, its size is bounded by a constant $\varepsilon_1/\gamma, \gamma > 0$.

Predatory-Prey Community Models.

$g_1(N_1)$	$L(N_1)$	$g_2(N_1, N_2)$	Authors
ε_1	$\alpha_{12}N_1$	$\varepsilon_2 + \alpha_{21}N_1$	Volterra
$\varepsilon_1 - \alpha_1 N_1$	$\alpha_{12}N_1$	$\varepsilon_2(1 - e^{-\gamma N_1})$	Gauze
ε_1	$\alpha_{12}N_1$	$\varepsilon_2 - a_{21}\dfrac{N_2}{N_1}$	Pislow
ε_1	$\dfrac{\alpha N_1}{1 + \alpha h N_1}$	$\varepsilon_2 - a_{21}\dfrac{N_2}{N_1}$	Holling
ε_1	$b(1 - e^{-\gamma N_1})$	$\varepsilon_2 - a_{21}\dfrac{N_2}{N_1}$	Ivlev
ε_1	$\dfrac{\alpha(N_1)N_1}{1 + \alpha(N_1)h N_1}$	$\varepsilon_2 - a_{21}\dfrac{N_2}{N_1}$	Royama
$1 - \dfrac{N_1}{K_1}$	$\dfrac{\alpha N_1}{1 + \alpha h N_1}$	$1 - \dfrac{N_2}{K_1}N_1.$	Shimazu
$\varepsilon_1 - \alpha_1 N_1$	$\alpha_{12}(1 - e^{\gamma N_1})$	$\varepsilon_2(1 - a_{21}e^{-\mu N_1})$	May

System (1.10) has a unique nontrivial equilibrium (N_1^*, N_2^*):

$$N_1^* = \frac{\varepsilon_2}{k\gamma_1}, \qquad N_2^* = \frac{\varepsilon_1 k \gamma_1 - \varepsilon_2 \gamma}{k\gamma_1^2}.$$

Since N_1 is bounded, then $N_1^* = \varepsilon_2/(k\gamma_1) \leq \varepsilon_1/\gamma$. This inequality ensures nonnegativity of N_2^*.

Let us show that the trajectory $N(t) = (N_1(t), N_2(t))$, emanating from the point (N_1^0, N_2^0), such that $0 < N_1 \leq \frac{\varepsilon_1}{\gamma}, N_2 > 0$, approaches the point (N_1^*, N_2^*) as $t \to \infty$. To prove this, we consider the following function:

$$V(N_1, N_2) = N_1^*\Big(\frac{N_1}{N_1^*} - \ln\frac{N_1}{N_1^*} - 1\Big) + \frac{1}{k}N_2^*\Big(\frac{N_2}{N_2^*} - \ln\frac{N_2}{N_2^*} - 1\Big).$$

Each of the parenthetical expressions is nonnegative and can be equal to zero only if $N_1 = N_1^*$ or $N_2 = N_2^*$. Thus, $V(N_1, N_2) > 0$ at all points $N = N(N_1, N_2) > 0$, except an equilibrium, and $V(N_1, N_2) = 0$ only at the point (N_1^*, N_2^*).

Expressing ε_1 and ε_2 in terms N_1^* N_2^*, we transform system (1.10):

$$\varepsilon_2 = k\gamma_1 N_1^*, \varepsilon_1 = \gamma_1 N_2^* + \varepsilon_2 \gamma/(k\gamma_1).$$

We have

$$dN_1/dt = \gamma_1 N_1(N_2^* - N_2) + N_1\gamma(N_1^* - N_1),$$
$$dN_2/dt = k\gamma_1 N_2(N_1 - N_1^*). \tag{1.11}$$

The derivative of the function $V(N_1, N_2)$ is calculated with respect to time along the trajectory of system (1.11):

$$\frac{dV}{dt} = N_1^* \Big(\frac{1}{N_1^*} - \frac{1}{N_1}\Big)\Big[\gamma_1 N_1(N_2^* - N_2) + N_1\gamma(N_1^* - N_1)\Big] +$$

$$+ \frac{1}{k}N_2^*\Big(\frac{1}{N_2^*} - \frac{1}{N_2}\Big)\Big[k\gamma_1 N_2(N_1 - N_1^*)\Big] = -\gamma(N_1^* - N_1)^2.$$

Thus, by system (1.11), the derivative of function V is negative at all points except a straight line $N_1 = N_1^*$ (for $\gamma > 0$). This line contains only the whole trajectory $N^*(t) = N^* = (N_1^*, N_2^*)$. Indeed, by (1.10), $\frac{dN_1}{dt}|_{(N_1^*, N_2)} \neq 0$, $\frac{dN_2}{dt}|_{(N_1^*, N_2)} = 0$ holds for every point of the straight line (N_1^*, N_2), where $N_2 \neq N_2^*$. Hence, if at some time $\bar{t}$ $N_1(\bar{t}) = N_1^*$, $N_2(\bar{t}) = N_2 \neq N_2^*$, then for $t = \bar{t} + \Delta t$ ($\Delta t > 0$) we have $N_1(\bar{t} + \Delta t) \neq N_1^*$, i.e. the trajectory leaves the straight line $N_1 = N_1^*$ at the time $\bar{t} + \Delta t$. Thus, the function V decreases along the trajectory of system (1.10) that is different from the equilibrium, and hence $N(t) \to N^*$ as $t \to \infty$. The last reasoning suggests that the equilibrium is asymptotically stable for $\gamma > 0$.

If $\gamma = 0$, then $\frac{dV}{dt} \equiv 0$. This implies that the equilibrium is stable, but not asymptotically stable.

1.3   Trophic Functions and Their Impact on Stability of a Predator-Prey System

Let $L = L(N_1)$ be the function describing consumption of prey by one predator in a unit time. The function $L(N_1)$ is called a trophic function of predator.

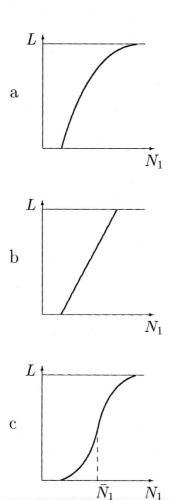

Fig. 1.

In the previously examined systems, trophic functions were constants (except Kolmogorov's model). Experimental studies show that these functions generally belong to one of the three types. Functions of the first type (Fig.1,a) - monotonically increasing with a gradually decreasing derivative - are typical for vertebrates and some species of predatory fishes. Functions of the second type (Fig.1, b) are linear in a particular interval and have a well-defined saturation threshold. These are typical for filtrate predators (e.g.,mollusks). Functions of the third type (Fig.1, c) are typical for the predators capable of conducting a goal-oriented search for prey.

D e f i n i t i o n 2. The function $L(N)$ is called convex if for any two points $N^{(1)}$ and $N^{(2)}$ such that $N^{(1)} \neq N^{(2)}$ the inequality

$$L(N^{(1)}\lambda + N^{(2)}(1 - \lambda)) \geq \lambda L(N^{(1)}) + (1 - \lambda)L(N^{(2)})$$

holds for all $\lambda \in [0, 1]$. If the inverse inequality is true, then the function is called concave.

We shall now consider the following system of differential equations describing predator-prey interactions with the trophic functions $L(N_1)$:

$$dN_1/dt = \varepsilon_1 N_1 - L(N_1)N_2,$$

$$dN_2/dt = kL(N_1)N_2 - \varepsilon_2 N_2, \tag{1.12}$$

where $k > 0$.

A nontrivial equilibrium for this system is the point (N_1^*, N_2^*), whose coordinates satisfy the conditions

$$L(N_1^*) = \varepsilon_2/k, \quad N_2^* = (k\varepsilon_1/\varepsilon_2)N_1^*.$$

Since the function $L(N_1)$ monotonically increases, the positive stationary point (N_1^*, N_2^*) is unique.

The characteristic equation for the system (1.12) linearized in the neighborhood of the point (N_1^*, N_2^*) is

$$\lambda^2 - \lambda\varepsilon_1\left(1 - \frac{L'(N_1^*)N_1^*}{L(N_1^*)}\right) + \varepsilon_1\varepsilon_2\frac{L'(N_1^*)N_1^*}{L(N_1^*)} = 0$$

Denoting $\alpha = L'(N_1^*)N_1^*/L(N_1^*)$, we rewrite the characteristic equation as follows:

$$\lambda^2 - \lambda\varepsilon_1(1 - \alpha) + \varepsilon_1\varepsilon_2\alpha = 0.$$

The roots of the equation are

$$\lambda_{1,2} = \frac{\varepsilon_1(1 - \alpha)}{2} \pm \frac{1}{2}\sqrt{\varepsilon_1^2(1 - \alpha)^2 - 4\varepsilon_1\varepsilon_2\alpha}$$

If $\varepsilon_1^2(1 - \alpha)^2 - 4\varepsilon_1\varepsilon_2\alpha \geq 0$, then the stationary point is a node ($\lambda_1\lambda_2 > 0$) or a saddle ($\lambda_1\lambda_2 < 0$). If, however, $\varepsilon_1^2(1 - \alpha)^2 - 4\varepsilon_1\varepsilon_2\alpha < 0$, then the stationary point is a focus ($1 \neq \alpha$) or a center ($1 = \alpha$).

Let us consider the equation

$$\alpha^2 - 2(\frac{\varepsilon_1 + 2\varepsilon_2}{\varepsilon_1})\alpha + 1 = 0,$$

whose roots are

$$\alpha_{1,2} = \frac{\varepsilon_1 + 2\varepsilon_2 \pm 2\sqrt{\varepsilon_2(\varepsilon_1 + \varepsilon_2)}}{\varepsilon_1}.$$

The stationary point now becomes a focus or a center if

$$\alpha_1 < L'(N_1^*)N_1^*/L(N_1^*) < \alpha_2,$$

and it becomes a node or a saddle if

$$L'(N_1^*)N_1^*/L(N_1^*) \le \alpha_1 \quad \text{or} \quad L'(N_1^*)N_1^*/L(N_1^*) \ge \alpha_2.$$

Equilibrium stability is ensured if $1 - \alpha < 0$ or, in view of the value of α,

$$L'(N_1^*)N_1^* > L(N_1^*). \tag{1.13}$$

We now consider the function $L(N_1)/N_1$, describing a relative proportion of prey consumed by predator. The condition for this function to increase at the point N_1^* is provided by positiveness of its derivative, that is

$$L'(N_1^*)/N_1^* - L(N_1^*)/(N_1^*)^2 > 0.$$

The last inequality is equivalent to (1.13). This means that the equilibrium is stable when a relative proportion of prey consumed by predator increases in the neighborhood of the point N_1^*. For the trophic function of the first type

$$L(N_1^2)/N_1^2 < L(N_1^1)/N_1^1,$$

where $N_1^2 > N_1^1 > 0$. This follows from the trophic function convexity. Thus, for the communities with the trophic function of the first type (Fig.1,a) the relative proportion of prey consumed by predator decreases, and hence such a community has no stability.

For the trophic function of the third type the equilibrium is stable if $N_1 < \overline{N}_1$, where $\overline{N}_1$ is the point of inflection for this function (Fig.1, c). This follows from the fact that the trophic function is concave in the interval $[0, \overline{N}_1]$, and hence the relative proportion of prey consumed by predator increases.

The form of the trophic function substantially affects stability of a predator-prey system. However, there are also other factors affecting stability, e.g., environmental conditions, the possibility for a prey to develop some defense strategy, changes in the natural prey growth rate governed by size, etc. To allow for these factors, we need to investigate more complex systems.

1.4   Models for n-species Interactions

For the most part the models for interactions in biological communities are constructed by describing interactions in terms of differential equations for the size of species $N_i(t)$. Clearly there are nonnegative solutions that have a biological meaning.

Dynamic equations for a community (where no account is taken of the population age composition) generally become

$$dN_i/dt = F_i(N_1, N_2, \ldots, N_n; t), \qquad i = 1, 2, \ldots, n, \qquad (1.14)$$

where the functions F_i describe the rate at which populations fluctuate in size depending on a species interaction structure and species numbers.

We suppose that the functions F_i are explicitly independent of time and system (1.14) is isolated. Then the equation $N_i = 0$ implies

$$F_i(N_1, \ldots, N_{i-1}, 0, N_{i+1}, \ldots, N_n) = 0$$

and F_i can be represented as

$$F_i(N_1, N_2, \ldots, N_n) = N_i G_i(N_1, N_2, \ldots, N_n),$$

where G_i stand for generalized growth coefficients. In the simple case, these functions become

$$G_i(N_1, N_2, \ldots, N_n) = \varepsilon_i - \sum_{i=1}^{n} \gamma_{ij} N_j,$$

resulting in

$$dN_i/dt = N_i(\varepsilon_i - \sum_{j=1}^{n} \gamma_{ij} N_j), \qquad i = 1, 2, \ldots, n. \qquad (1.15)$$

In modern literature on mathematical ecology, models of the form (1.15) are usually called Volterra. Here ε_i is the natural growth rate for the i-th species in the absence of other species; the coefficients of γ_{ij} account for the nature of interactions between the i-th and the j-th species ($i \neq j$); γ_{ij} are intraspecific interaction indices. The matrix $\Gamma = \|\gamma_{ij}\|$ is commonly known as a community matrix or an interaction matrix. The coefficients γ_{ii} of matrix Γ affect the natural population growth rate for the i-th species in the absence of other species. If $\gamma_{ii} > 0$, then we are dealing with intraspecific competition or self-limiting of the i-th species in size. The impact of the j-th species on the i-th species is specified by the product $\gamma_{ij}N_iN_j$ subject to the hypothesis of "encounters and equivalents". The essence of this hypothesis is as follows.

We suppose that the number of encounters between individuals of the species i and j in a time dt is equal to $m_{ij}N_iN_jdt$. The result of these encounters is that the i-th species have declined in number by the magnitude $p_{ij}m_{ij}N_iN_jdt$, where p_{ij} indicates the proportion of individuals of the i-th species annihilated during the encounter ($0 \leq p_{ij} \leq 1$). On the other hand, the j-th species have grown in number by the magnitude $p_{ij}m_{ij}N_iN_jdt$ with some proportionality coefficient referred to as the equivalent. In this manner the biomass of the i-th species is immediately transformed into that of the j-th species.

As noted before, only nonnegative solutions of system (1.15) have the biological meaning. Moreover, the models under study fail to adequately describe the community dynamics where the number of species is close to zero, because species may now disappear under the action of random factors that are not reflected in equations.

Denote by R_+^n a positive orthant of the n-dimensional Euclidean space R^n. In what follows we examine stability of the equilibrium $N^* \in R_+^n$.

The equilibrium of system (1.15) $N^* = (N_1^*, N_2^*, \ldots, N_n^*)$ must satisfy the system of equations

$$N_i\Big(\varepsilon_i - \sum_{j=1}^{n} \gamma_{ij}N_j\Big) = 0, \qquad i = 1, 2, \ldots, n.$$

If $N^* > 0$, then this equilibrium is a solution of the system of equation

$$\sum_{j=1}^{n} \gamma_{ij}N_j = \varepsilon_i, \qquad i = 1, 2, \ldots, n, \tag{1.16}$$

or, in matrix form,

$$\Gamma N = \varepsilon, \tag{1.17}$$

where $\varepsilon = (\varepsilon_1, \varepsilon_2, \ldots, \varepsilon_n)$.

In terms of system (1.15), V. Volterra examined two subclasses of such systems, namely: conservative and dissipative.

We shall identify some quantity $\alpha_i > 0$ with the average biomass of individuals of the i-th species. The total community biomass then is $\overline{M} = \sum_{i=1}^{n} \alpha_i N_i$. In

terms of the trajectories of system (1.15), the total community biomass follows
the equation

$$dM/dt = \sum_{i=1}^{n} \alpha_i \varepsilon_i N_i - \sum_{i=1}^{n} \alpha_1 \sum_{j=1}^{n} \gamma_{ij} N_i N_j.$$

If one is successful in selecting positive coefficients α_i in such a way that the
quadratic form

$$\chi = \sum_{i,j=1}^{n} \alpha_i \gamma_{ij} N_i N_j \equiv 0,$$

then the system (1.15) is called conservative. If, however, the quadratic form
χ is positive definite, the system is called dissipative.

Conservative systems are thus typified by the unbounded growth in the
total biomass of community, where the dissipative systems feature the growth
in the total biomass impeded by species interactions.

For the conservative system, the following equation must hold

$$\gamma_{ij} = 0, \qquad \alpha_i \gamma_{ij} + \alpha_j \gamma_{ji} = 0, \qquad i,j = 1,2,\ldots,n.$$

Thus, the coefficients γ_{ij} and γ_{ji} are opposite in sign or are simultaneously
equal to zero.

V. Volterra showed that, for the conservative system (1.15), it is necessary
and sufficient that the following conditions be satisfied:

1) $\gamma_{ii} = 0$, $i = 1,2,\ldots,n$;

2) $\gamma_{ij} = \gamma_{ji} = 0$ or $\gamma_{ij}\gamma_{ji} < 0$ with $i \neq j$;

3) $\gamma_{i_1 i_2}\gamma_{i_3 i_4} \cdots \gamma_{i_{m-1} i_m} = (-1)^m \gamma_{i_2 i_1}\gamma_{i_4 i_3} \cdots \gamma_{i_m i_{m-1}}$ for any permutation of
indices $i_1, i_2, \ldots, i_m$ from $\{1,2,\ldots,n\}$.

System (1.15) can be rewritten as

$$dN_i/dt = -N_i \sum_{j=1}^{n} \gamma_{ij}(N_j - N_j^*), \qquad i = 1,2,\ldots,n, \qquad (1.18)$$

where $N^* = (N_1^*, N_2^*, \ldots, N_n^*)$ is a nontrivial equilibrium, i.e. $N_i^* > 0$, $i = 1,2,\ldots,n$.

We shall now consider the function

$$V(N_1, N_2, \ldots, N_n) = \sum_{i=1}^{n} \alpha_i(N_i - N_i^* \ln N_i) \qquad (1.19)$$

and calculate the derivative of this function along the trajectory of system
(1.18):

$$dV/dt = -\sum_{i=1}^{n} \alpha_i(N_i - N_i^*) \sum_{j=1}^{n} \gamma_{ij}(N_j - N_j^*),$$

or

$$dV/dt = - \sum_{i,j=1}^{n} \alpha_i \gamma_{ij} (N_i - N_i^*)(N_j - N_j^*).$$ (1.20)

If the system is conservative, then expression (1.20) is identically zero. The function $V(N)$ is Liapunov's function for system (1.18) and attains a minimum at the point N^*. Since the derivative of the function $V(N)$ is identically zero for all $N \in R_+^n$, the equilibrium is stable (but not asymptotically stable).

In his analysis of conservative systems, V. Volterra showed the existence in the case of nonsingularity of the matrix Γ for an even n of the first integral

$$(e^{N_1}/N_1^{q_1})^{\alpha_1} (e^{N_2}/N_2^{q_2})^{\alpha_2} \ldots (e^{N_n}/N_n^{q_n})^{\alpha_n} = \text{const},$$

where $q = (q_1, q_2, \ldots, q_n)$ is a solution of system (1.16). From this it follows that for $q > 0$ the number of all species is bounded from above and below by positive constants. Moreover, if $N(0) \neq N^*$, then at least one species has undamped fluctuations in size. Here the mean values

$$\frac{1}{t} \int_0^t N_i(\tau) d\tau \xrightarrow[t \to \infty]{} N_i^*.$$

This property is called the law of asymptotic means.

In dissipative systems, the quadratic form χ is positive definite. From this it follows that all $\gamma_{ii} > 0$, i.e. all species must be self-limiting. This means that the classes of conservative and dissipative systems are not intersecting. Another important condition for dissipativity is that the determinant of matrix Γ is nonzero; hence it immediately follows that the solution of system (1.17) is unique. Finally, the last necessary condition is that all principal minors of matrix Γ are positive.

If the solution of system (1.17) is positive, then the first integral of system (1.15) becomes

$$(e^{n_1}/n_1)^{\alpha_1 N_1^*} \ldots (e^{n_n}/n_n)^{\alpha_n N_n^*} = c \exp\{- \int_0^t \chi(N_1^* - N_1, \ldots, N_n^* - N_n) d\tau\},$$

where $n_i = N_i/N_i^*$, $c > 0$. As noted by V. Volterra, $N(t) \to N^*$ as $t \to \infty$ for any initial values of $N(0) \in R_+^n$, because the quadratic form χ is positive definite.

If we consider the function $V(N_1, N_2, \ldots, N_n)$ of the form (1.19), then on the trajectories of the dissipative system we obtain $dV/dt \leq 0$ for all $N(t)$

from the region R_+^n, with the equality $dV/dt = 0$ holding for $N(t) = N^*$ only. This means that $N(t) \to N^*$ as $t \to \infty$, and the equilibrium is stable for any initial values from R_+^n, i.e. the domain of asymptotic stability is the entire nonnegative orthant. This also explains the inferences made by V. Volterra.

We shall now consider a biological community composed of n species, in which species j consumes species $j-1$ [45]. The interaction dynamics is given by the system of differential equations

$$dN_1/dt = N_1(\varepsilon_1 - \gamma_{11}N_1 - \gamma_{12}N_2),$$

$$dN_i/dt = N_i(-\varepsilon_i + \gamma_{i,i-1}N_{i-1} - \gamma_{i,i+1}N_{i+1}), \qquad (1.21)$$

$$\gamma_{n,n+1} = 0, \ i = 2,3,\ldots,n,$$

where $\varepsilon_i, \gamma_{ii} > 0$, $\gamma_{ij} = -\gamma_{ji}$, $i,j = 1,2,\ldots,n$. Obviously this system is neither conservative nor dissipative. Self-limitation is lacking in all species but the first one.

An equilibrium for this system is the point in the phase space satisfying the following system of equations

$$\gamma_{11}N_1 + \gamma_{12}N_2 = \varepsilon_1, \qquad \gamma_{i,i-1}N_{i-1} - \gamma_{i,i+1}N_{i+1} = \varepsilon_i,$$

$$\gamma_{n,n+1} = 0, \qquad i = 2,3,\ldots,n.$$

Equations (1.21) may now be written in the form

$$dN_1/dt = -N_1(\gamma_{11}(N_1 - N_1^*) + \gamma_{12}(N_2 - N_2^*)),$$

$$dN_i/dt = N_i(\gamma_{i,i-1}(N_{i-1} - N_{i-1}^*) - \gamma_{i,i+1}(N_{i+1} - N_{i+1}^*)), \qquad (1.22)$$

$$\gamma_{n,n+1} = 0, \qquad i = 1,2,\ldots,n.$$

Compute the derivative of the function $V(N_1, N_2, \ldots, N_n)$ on the trajectories of system (1.22)

$$dV/dt = -\alpha_1(\gamma_{11}(N_1 - N_1^*) + \gamma_{12}(N_1 - N_1^*)(N_2 - N_2^*) +$$

$$+ \sum_{i=1}^{n} \alpha_i(N_i - N_i^*)(\gamma_{i,i-1}(N_{i-1} - N_{i-1}^*) - \gamma_{i,i+1}(N_{i+1} - N_{i+1}^*)).$$

Select coefficients α_i as follows

$$\alpha_1 = 1 \qquad \alpha_{i+1} = \alpha_i \gamma_{i,i+1}/\gamma_{i+1}, \qquad i = 1,2,\ldots,n-1.$$

Considering that $\gamma_{ij} = -\gamma_{ji}$, we obtain

$$dV/dt = -\gamma_{11}(N_1 - N_1^*)^2.$$

Show that the set $V^* = \{N : N_1 = N_1^*, \ N > 0\}$ contains no trajectory of system (1.22) except the rest point $N = N^*$. Indeed, suppose the opposite is true, namely: there exists a trajectory $N(t)$, which is lying entirely in the set V^* and does not coincide with N^*. Since $N_1(t) = N_1^*$, we have $dN_1(t)/dt \equiv 0$. Hence it follows that $N_2(t) \equiv N_2^*$ and $dN_2(t)/dt \equiv 0$. In a similar way we obtain $N_i(t) \equiv N_i^*$, $i = 3, 4, \ldots, n$.

Thus, for the above community of the predator-prey type one can draw inferences about the asymptotic stability of a positive equilibrium at large, i.e. for any initial values of $N(0) > 0$ the evolution proceeds in such a way that $N(t) \xrightarrow[t \to \infty]{} N^*$ subject to $N^* > 0$.

1.5 An Ecological Niche and Equations of Competition

Although the coefficient γ_{ij} of the community matrix Γ have already been interpreted in terms of the hypothesis of "encounters and equivalents", they also have another conceptual interpretation using the notion of an ecological niche and competition.

Let there be given a space X of environmental factors that are vitally important for community populations. Vital factors may be interpreted to mean the quantity and species composition of food, living conditions, relief, rate of use of natural resources by man, etc. The ecological niche is taken to be a region of space X in which a species can exist and outside of which it cannot exist.

In actual practice, ecological niches are generally overlapping. Many species coexist in the same area and consume the same resource. If the resource is in short supply, we have competition events, and the ecological niche becomes vital to the structure of competitive interaction.

Ecological niches are usually examined by employing the Gauze principle of competition elimination which eliminates the possibility of coexistence for two species with the same ecological niches, i.e. the niches may only be partially overlapping.

We shall define a niche in terms of the notion of a resource and consumption function.

We suppose that the resource consumed by populations in a community is characterized by the vector $x \in X$, and its volume is bounded by a magnitude $K(x)$. The function $K(x)$ is usually called a resource spectrum. Consumption of the resource by species i is characterized by a preference function $f_i(x)$, also known as a consumption function. The function $f_i(x)$ may also describe a probability density for consumption of resource x by species i. The most preferable resource corresponding to a maximum value of the function f_i is usually called the center of niche.

Let $N_i(t)$ be the size (biomass) of population i at the time t. Then the product $f_i(x)N_i(t)$ describes the volume of resource x, being consumed by species i. The difference $K(x) - \sum_{i=1}^{n} f_i(x)N_i(t)$ suggests that the populations consuming resource x can coexist. If this difference is sufficiently large, then the population may increase in size obeying the law $dN_i/dt = \varepsilon_i N_i$, $i = 1, 2, \ldots, n$.

We suppose that the population growth is affected by the relative depletion of resource at the point x that is equal to

$$[K(x) - \sum_{i=1}^{n} f_i(x)N_i(t)]/K(x).$$

In this case the size dynamics of population i is described by the equation

$$\frac{dN_i}{dt} \equiv \frac{\varepsilon_i N_i}{K(x)} \Big[K(x) - \sum_{i=1}^{n} f_i(x)N_i(t) \Big]. \tag{1.23}$$

Denote $K_i = \int_X K(x)f_i(x)dx$. The expression for K_i is interpreted to mean the total volume of resources consumed by species i and is called the niche capacity. Multiplying equation (1.23) by $f_i(x)K(x)$ and integrating over the entire resource space X, we obtain

$$\frac{dN_i}{dt} = \varepsilon_i N_i \Big(1 - \sum_{j=1}^{n} \frac{a_{ij}}{K_i} N_j \Big), \tag{1.24}$$

where $a_{ij} = \int_X f_i(x)f_j(x)dx$ are the coefficients of competition. Denoting $\gamma_{ij} = \varepsilon_i a_{ij}/K_i$, $i, j = 1, 2, \ldots, n$, we may write equation (1.24) in the form

$$\frac{dN_i}{dt} = N_i \Big(\varepsilon_i - \sum_{j=1}^{n} \gamma_{ij} N_j \Big). \tag{1.25}$$

System (1.25)is dissipative, because with $\alpha_i = K_i/\varepsilon_i$, $i = 1, 2, \ldots, n$, the quadratic form

$$\sum_{i,j=1}^{n} \alpha_i \gamma_{ij} N_i N_j = \int_X \sum_{i,j=1}^{n} f_i(x) N_i f_j(x) N_j dt = \int_X \left[\sum_{i=1}^{n} f_i(x) N_i\right]^2 > 0$$

for all $N \neq 0$.

Thus, if there exists a positive solution of system $\Gamma N = \varepsilon$ with coefficients from (1.25), then it is an equilibrium that is globally asymptotically stable in a positive orthant R_+^n.

We shall now consider communities with consumption functions of the Gaussian type [45]

$$f_i(x) = \frac{1}{\sqrt{2\pi\sigma_i^2}} \exp\left[\frac{-(x - x_i)^2}{2\sigma_i^2}\right],$$

where $x \in (-\infty, +\infty)$; x_i is a center of niche; σ_i^2 is a normal distribution variance. Denote by d_{ij} a distance between x_i and x_j. The competition coefficients then become

$$a_{ij} = \frac{1}{\sqrt{2\pi}\sigma_i\sigma_j} \int_{-\infty}^{+\infty} \exp\left[-\frac{x^2}{2\sigma_i^2} - \frac{(x - d_{ij})^2}{2\sigma_j^2}\right] dx =$$

$$= \frac{1}{\sqrt{2T(\sigma_i^2 + \sigma_j^2)}} \exp\left[-\frac{d_{ij}^2}{2(\sigma_i^2 + \sigma_j^2)}\right].$$

If all distributions have the same variance $\sigma^2 = \sigma_i^2$ and $x_1 < x_2 < x_3 < \ldots < x_n$, then $d_{ij} = |i - j|d$,

$$a_{ij} = \frac{1}{1\sigma\sqrt{\pi}} \exp\left[-\frac{(i - j)^2 d^2}{4\sigma^2}\right].$$

The competition coefficients can be written as

$$a_{ij} = a^{(i-j)2}, \qquad a = \left(2\sigma\sqrt{\pi}\right)^{-1-(i-j)2} \exp\left(\frac{d^2}{4\sigma}\right).$$

Then we obtain the competition matrix

$$A = \begin{pmatrix} 1 & a & a^4 & \ldots & a^{(n-1)^2} \\ a & 1 & a & \ldots & a^{(n-2)^2} \\ a^4 & a & 1 & \ldots & a^{(n-3)^2} \\ \vdots & \vdots & \vdots & \ddots & \vdots \\ \alpha^{(n-1)^2} & \alpha^{(n-2)^2} & \alpha^{(n-3)^2} & \ldots & 1 \end{pmatrix}.$$

The quantity d/σ is usually used to characterize the density of species packing in a community or the proximity measure for ecological niches. Note that the matrix A is kept dissipative even for all sufficiently small values of d/σ (for an arbitrarily dense packing of species). Therefore a positive equilibrium is asymptotically stable for any density of species packing. The rate of convergence in system perturbations to equilibrium is characterized by the minimum eigenvalue of matrix A . For a sufficiently large n $\lambda_{min} \approx 1 - 2a + 2a^4 - 2a^9 + 2a^{16} - \ldots$, for sufficiently small values d/σ yields

$$\lambda_{min} \approx 4\sqrt{\pi}(\sigma/d)\exp(-\pi\sigma^2/d^2).$$

Hence it follows that although for a high density of packing λ_{min} is kept positive and asymptotic stability is formally retained, the time of return of the system from a perturbed state $N(0)$ to an equilibrium sharply increases.

1.6   Balance Equations in Ecology. Bringing an Ecological System to a Stable Equilibrium

In ecology, balance equations describe flows of biomass and energy between principal components of terrestrial systems in terms of the law of conservation of mass and energy. Flows of mass and energy are schematically shown in Fig.2.

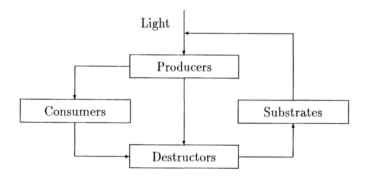

Fig. 2.

Components of a community are defined as follows.

Producers with biomass $x_i(i = 1, 2, \ldots, m)$ are predominantly green plants capable of transforming light energy into their own biomass and feeding on simple substances, i.e. substrates whose biomass will be c_k $(k = 1, 2, \ldots, r)$. Basically, substrates are the products of vital activities of consumers. Consumers with biomass y_j $(j = 1, 2, \ldots, n)$ are the animals feeding on producers and other organisms.

The equation accounting for a mass balance in the ecosystem is

$$\frac{dx_i}{dt} = (F_x^i - D_x^i)x_i - \sum_{j=1}^{n} u_{ij}y_j + \sum_{k=1}^{p} w_{ik}c_k + R_x, \qquad i = 1, 2, \ldots, m;$$

$$\frac{dy_j}{dt} = (F_y^j - D_y^j)y_i - \sum_{r=1}^{n} v_{jr}y_r \qquad j = 1, 2, \ldots, n;$$

$$\frac{dc_k}{dt} = \sum_{j=1}^{n} V_{kj}y_j - \sum_{i=1}^{m} w_{ki}x_i, \qquad k = 1, 2, \ldots, r,$$

where F_x^i, F_y^j are natural growth coefficients; D_x^i, D_y^j are death coefficients; u_{ij} is the rate at which the biomass of the i-th producer is consumed by an individual of the j-th consumer; w_{ik} is the rate at which the biomass of the k-th substrate is transformed into that of the i-th producer; v_{jr} is the rate at which the j-th consumer is consumed by the r-th; V_{kj} is the rate at which the k-th substrate is produced by the j-th consumer; w_{ki} is the rate at which the k-th substrate is consumed by the i-th producer; R_x describes light transformation.

By and large this system adequately describes balance relations in terrestrial ecosystems. On the other hand, it suffers from excess generality and hence cannot be applied to specific systems. For this reason, to concretely define the model by properly choosing the coefficients that are generally the functions of the components of a given ecosystem.

Under reasonably natural assumptions about the growth and death coefficients and the rates of biomass transformation, (e.g., as shown in [45]) we may transform ecological balance equations to a Volterra system, thereby establishing the possibility for construction of Volterra models on the basis of a more general reasoning than the hypothesis of "encounters and equivalents".

Let us consider the control problem for Volterra's system

$$dN_i/dt = N_i(\varepsilon_i - \sum_{j=1}^{n} \gamma_{ij}N_j) + u_i, \tag{1.26}$$

where the control vector $u = (u_1, u_2, \ldots, u_n)$ is selected from an admissible control set U.

Let us suppose that, in system (1.26), for $u \equiv 0$ there is a positive stable equilibrium N^*. Now consider the following problem: find a control vector $u \in U$, such that system (1.26) is changed to a stable equilibrium $\overline{N}^* > 0$.

We have thus stated the problem of transferring an ecological system to a new regime which maintains the size of populations at a given level.

Admissible controls are now taken to be of the form

$$u = CN, \tag{1.27}$$

where $C = \mathrm{diag}\{c_i\}$.

System (1.26) may be written as

$$dN_i/dt = N_i \sum_{j=1}^{N} \gamma_{ij}(N_j^* - N_j) + u_i.$$

Replace control u_i by its expression from (1.27):

$$dN_i/dt = N_i(\sum_{j=1}^{n} \gamma_{ij}(N_j^* - N_j) + c_i). \tag{1.28}$$

Now find c_i, assuming that system (1.28) has an equilibrium $\overline{N}^*$. To this end, the parenthetical expression must be zero for $N = \overline{N}^*$. From this it follows that

$$c_i = \sum_{j=1}^{n} \gamma_{ij}(\overline{N}_j^* - N_j^*). \tag{1.29}$$

Thus, if in system (1.26) the control is chosen to be of the form (1.27) with coefficients (1.29), then the system assumes a new equilibrium $\overline{N}^*$, and stable at that, provided the equilibrium N^* has been stable, because the control leaves the coefficients of the community matrix unaffected.

In the case of a dissipative system, for any $N(0) \in R_+^n$ the trajectory of system (1.26) under the chosen control may reach the point $\overline{N}^*$ because of the asymptotic stability of this equilibrium. Thus, in the case of a dissipative system, the control (1.27) with coefficients (1.29) solves the problem of changing system (1.26) from any initial state $N(0) \in R_+^n$ to a specified stationary state $\overline{N}^*$.

When it comes to a conservative system, the equilibrium is stable, but not asymptotically stable; therefore the system experiences stable fluctuations in size, and the control (1.27) fails to solve the problem of transferring the system to a stationary state.

We shall now consider Liapunov's function for the conservative system (1.28), where $\alpha_i = 1$, $i = 1, 2, \ldots, n$, in the form

$$V(N) = \sum_{i=1}^{n} (N_i - \overline{N}_i^* \ln N_i)$$

and compute the derivative of this function along the trajectory

$$dV/dt = - \sum_{i,j=1}^{n} \gamma_{ij}(N_i - \overline{N}_i^*)(N_j - \overline{N}_j^*). \tag{1.30}$$

Since this system is conservative, the derivative of the function V along the system trajectory is equal to zero.

We shall add to the right-hand side of (1.30) the addandum $- \sum_{i=1}^{n} \Delta\gamma_i(N_i - \overline{N}_i^*)^2 < 0$, $\Delta\gamma_i > 0$. Then dV/dt becomes negative everywhere except the point $\overline{N}^*$.

We replace the control $u = CN$ by selecting

$$u = CN + \text{diag}\{\delta_i N_i\}(\overline{N}^* - N), \tag{1.31}$$

where $\delta_i > 0$, and substitute it into system (1.26). Computing the derivative of the function V along the trajectory of system (1.26) with control (1.31), we obtain

$$dV/dt = - \sum_{i=1}^{n} \delta_i(N_i - \overline{N}_i^*)^2 < 0.$$

The equilibrium of system (1.26) under control (1.31) thus becomes asymptotically stable, and hence the control (1.31) solves the problem of transferring the conservative system (1.26) to a prescribed stable equilibrium $\overline{N}^*$.

We shall now consider the control problem for the community whose population is composed of n species. Here species j consumes species $j - 1$ and is self-limiting. The stability issue for this system has been discussed in section 4 of the present chapter.

The community dynamics is given by the equations

$$dN_1/dt = N_1(\varepsilon_1 - \gamma_{11}N_1 - \gamma_{12}N_2),$$

$$dN_i/dt = N_i(-\varepsilon_i + \gamma_{i,i-1}N_{i-1} - \gamma_{i,i+1}N_{i+1}), \tag{1.32}$$

$$\gamma_{n,n+1} = 0, \qquad i = 2, 3, \ldots, n,$$

where $\varepsilon, \gamma_{ij} > 0$, $\gamma_{ij} = -\gamma_{ji}$, $i, j = 1, 2, \ldots, n$.

Suppose we need to transfer the system from the point $N(0) \in R_+^n$ to a stable equilibrium, where $N_1 = N_1^*$. Because of the self-limitation of the first species, we assume that $N_1^* < \varepsilon_1/\gamma_{11}$.

First we consider the case where $n = 3$. Let us introduce the control $u_3 = c_3 N_3$ into system (1.32):

$$dN_1/dt = N_1(\varepsilon_1 - \gamma_{11}N_1 - \gamma_{12}N_2),$$

$$dN_2/dt = N_2(-\varepsilon_2 + \gamma_{21}N_1 - \gamma_{23}N_3), \tag{1.33}$$

$$dN_3/dt = N_3(-\varepsilon_3 + \gamma_{32}N_2) + u_3.$$

The equilibrium N^* must satisfy the system of equations

$$\varepsilon_1 - \gamma_{11}N_1 - \gamma_{12}N_2 = 0,$$

$$-\varepsilon_2 + \gamma_{21}N_1 - \gamma_{23}N_3 = 0, \tag{1.34}$$

$$-\varepsilon_3 + \gamma_{32}N_2 + c_3 = 0.$$

Let us express N_2 and N_3 in terms of N_1:

$$N_2 = (\varepsilon_1 - \gamma_{11}N_1)/\gamma_{12}, \qquad N_3 = (-\varepsilon_2 + \gamma_{21}N_1)/\gamma_{23}. \tag{1.35}$$

Setting $N_1 = N_1^*$ and substituting into (1.35), we obtain

$$N_2^* = (\varepsilon_1 - \gamma_{11}N_1^*)/\gamma_{12}, \qquad N_3^* = (-\varepsilon_2 + \gamma_{21}N_1^*)/\gamma_{23}. \tag{1.36}$$

The value of control u_3 can be found from (1.34)

$$u_3 = \left(\varepsilon_3 - \gamma_{32}\frac{\varepsilon_1 - \gamma_{11}N_1^*}{\gamma_{12}}\right) N_3. \tag{1.37}$$

Since $N_1^* < \varepsilon_1/\gamma_{11}$, $N_2^* > 0$. If N_3^* is to be positive, it is essential that $N_1^* > \varepsilon_2/\gamma_{21}$. In this case, system (1.33) with control (1.37) has an asymptotically stable positive equilibrium (N_1^*, N_2^*, N_3^*).

If $N_1^* < \varepsilon_2/\gamma_{21}$, then the N_3^* derived in (1.36) is negative, and hence we need something more than a mere introduction of control u_3 into system (1.32).

Let us consider the controlled system

$$dN_1/dt = N_1(\varepsilon_1 - \gamma_{11}N_1 - \gamma_{12}N_2) + u_1,$$

$$dN_2/dt = N_2(-\varepsilon_2 + \gamma_{21}N_1 - \gamma_{23}N_3) + u_2, \tag{1.38}$$

$$dN_3/dt = N_3(-\varepsilon_3 + \gamma_{32}N_2) + u_3,$$

where $u_i = c_i N_i$. The stationary point of system $N^* > 0$ must satisfy the equations

$$\varepsilon_1 - \gamma_{11} N_1 - \gamma_{12} N_2 + c_1 = 0,$$

$$-\varepsilon_2 + \gamma_{21} N_1 - \gamma_{13} N_3 + c_2 = 0,$$

$$-\varepsilon_3 + \gamma_{32} N_2 + c_3 = 0.$$

Let $N_1^* < \varepsilon_2/\gamma_{21}$. Expressing N_2 and N_3 via N_1 and substituting $N_1 = N_1^*$, we obtain

$$N_2^* = \frac{\varepsilon_1 - \gamma_{11} N_1^* + c_1}{\gamma_{12}},$$

$$N_3^* = \frac{-\varepsilon_2 + \gamma_{21} N_1^* + c_2}{\gamma_{13}}.$$

Since $N_1^* < \varepsilon_1/\gamma_{11}$, $N_2^* > 0$ for any $c_1 \geq 0$. Set $c_1 = 0$. From the condition $N_3^* \geq 0$ we obtain

$$c_2 > \varepsilon_2 - \gamma_{21} N_1^*. \tag{1.39}$$

The value of c_3 must be taken the same as in (1.37). Then the equilibrium $N^* \in R_+^n$ of system (1.38) is found to be the point with coordinates

$$N_1^*, \quad N_2^* = \frac{\varepsilon_1 - \gamma_{11} N_1^*}{\gamma_{12}}, \quad N_3^* = \frac{-\varepsilon_2 + \gamma_{21} N_1^* + c_2^*}{\gamma_{13}},$$

where c_2^* satisfies (1.39). The control in system (1.38) is:

$$u_1 = 0, \quad u_2 = c_2^* N_2, \quad u_3 = \left(\varepsilon_3 - \gamma_{32} \frac{\varepsilon_1 - \gamma_{11} N_1^*}{\gamma_{12}} \right) N_3. \tag{1.40}$$

Thus, depending on the sign of expression $\varepsilon_2 - \gamma_{21} N_1^*$, in order to transfer system (1.32) (n=3) from the initial state $N(0) \in R_+^n$ to a positive stable equilibrium, in which N_1 assumes the value N_1^*, we need to use control (1.37) for system (1.33) and control (1.40) for system (1.38).

The results are now easily generalized to the case $n > 3$. System (1.32) with control $u = (u_1, u_2, \ldots, u_n)$ then becomes

$$dN_1/dt = (\varepsilon_1 - \gamma_{11} N_1 - \gamma_{12} N_2) + u_1,$$

$$dN_i/dt = (-\varepsilon_i + \gamma_{i,i-1} N_{i-1} - \gamma_{i,i+1} N_{i+1}) + u_i, \tag{1.41}$$

$$i = 2, 3, \ldots, n, \quad \gamma_{n,n+1} = 0.$$

The control $u = CN$, where $C = \text{diag}\{c_i^*\}$, $c_1^* = 0$; $c_n^* = \varepsilon_n - \gamma_{n,n-1} N_n^*$; $c_i^* = 0$, if $N_{i-1}^* > \varepsilon_i/\gamma_{i,i-1}$, $c_i^* > \varepsilon_i - \gamma_{i,i-1} N_{i-1}^*$, if $N_{i-1}^* \leq \varepsilon_i/\gamma_{i,i-1}$, $i = 2, 3, \ldots, n-1$, transfers system (1.41) from any initial state $N(0) \in R_+^n$ to a stable equilibrium with a specified value N_1^*. In this case the other coordinates of equilibrium are determined from the formulas

$$N_2^* = \frac{\varepsilon_1 - \gamma_{11} N_1^*}{\gamma_{12}},$$

$$N_i^* = \frac{c_{i-1}^* - \varepsilon_{i-1} + \gamma_{i-1,i-2} N_{i-2}^*}{\gamma_{i-1,i}}, \qquad i = 3, 4, \ldots, n.$$

We shall consider the optimal control problem for a community, where a resource is supplied thereto from outside, and each species consumes the previous one in the case $n = 3$ [47]. For example, the community may be composed of a farm crop, crop-destroying insects, and a predator feeding on these insects. An external resource can be taken to be a fertilizer or irrigation water.

The community dynamics is given by the equations

$$dN_0/dt = Q - \gamma_0 N_0 N_1,$$

$$dN_1/dt = N_1(\varepsilon_1 + \gamma_{10} N_0 - \gamma_{12} N_2),$$

$$dN_2/dt = N_2(-\varepsilon_2 + \gamma_{21} N_1 - \gamma_{23} N_3), \qquad (1.42)$$

$$dN_3/dt = N_3(-\varepsilon_3 + \gamma_{32} N_2),$$

where Q is the rate of supply of a resource N_0; N_1, N_2, N_3 are the species biomass, and the coefficients $\gamma_0, \gamma_{ij} > 0$ are such that there exist an asymptotically stable positive equilibrium.

Suppose we wish to raise the level of crop yield, i.e. the biomass N_1. In this case we will use chemical and biological methods of pest control. The first method is to apply or spread insecticides over fields, while the second is to encourage a parasite species (predator) to grow in biomass. The control parameter is taken to be the rate of supply of an external resource (application of fertilizers). Let us introduce the controls u_2 and u_3 into system (1.42):

$$dN_0/dt = Q - \gamma_0 N_0 N_1,$$

$$dN_1/dt = N_1(\varepsilon_1 + \gamma_{10} N_0 - \gamma_{12} N_2),$$

$$dN_2/dt = N_2(-\varepsilon_2 + \gamma_{21} N_1 - \gamma_{23} N_3) - u_2, \qquad (1.43)$$

$$dN_3/dt = N_3(-\varepsilon_3 + \gamma_{32} N_2) + u_3,$$

where $u_2 = c_2 N_2$, $u_3 = c_3 N_3$. The quantity $c_2 \geq 0$ is the rate of insecticide application, while $c_3 \geq 0$ is the relative rate of artificial increase in predator biomass. The control parameters are Q, c_2, c_3.

The functional for problem (1.43) is taken to be

$$J = k_1 N_1^* - k_0 Q - k_2 c_2 N_2^* - k_3 c_3 N_3^*. \tag{1.44}$$

Here k_1 is the unit cost of the first species biomass; k_0 is the cost of applying a resource at the unit rate; k_2 is the cost of applying insecticides at the unit rate; k_3 is the unit output cost of predator biomass; N_1^*, N_2^*, N_3^* are the biomass of species when system (1.43) is in equilibrium.

We assume that control impacts are all bounded from above: $Q \le \overline{Q}$, $c_2 \le \bar{c}_2$, $c_3 \le \bar{c}_3$. Let us state the following problem: find the values of parameters Q, c_2 and $_3$, which ensure existence and stability of a community at the maximum value of the functional (1.44).

The equilibrium of system (1.43) is taken as

$$N_1^* = Q/(\gamma_0 N_0^*), \qquad N_2^* = (\varepsilon_3 - c_3)/\gamma_{32},$$

$$N_0^* = (\gamma_{12} N_2^* - \varepsilon_1)/\gamma_{10}, \qquad N_3^* = (\gamma_{21} N_1^* - \varepsilon_2 - c_2)/\gamma_{32}, \tag{1.45}$$

and is determined via parameters Q, c_2, c_3. If the N^* is to be positive, it is necessary that the following inequalities hold

$$0 \le c_3 < \varepsilon_3, \qquad 0 \le c_2 < \gamma_{21} N_1^* - \varepsilon_2, \qquad 0 < \gamma_{12} N_2^* - \varepsilon_1. \tag{1.46}$$

Expressing Q, c_2, c_3 via N_0^*, N_2^*, N_3^* by (1.45)

$$Q = \gamma_0 N_0^* N_1^*, \qquad c_2 = \gamma_{21} N_1^* - \gamma_{23} N_3^* - \varepsilon_2, \qquad c_3 = -\gamma_{32} N_2^* + \varepsilon_3 \tag{1.47}$$

and substituting these expressions into (1.44), we obtain

$$J = k_1 N_1^* - k_0 N_0^* N_1^* - k_2 \gamma_{21} N_1^* N_2^* + (k_3 \gamma_{32} + k_2 \gamma_{23}) N_2^* N_3^* + k_2 \varepsilon_3 N_3^* - k_3 \varepsilon_3 N_3^*$$

In view of (1.46), (1.47), the constraints for N_i^* can be written as $N_i^* > 0, \gamma_{21} N_1^* - \gamma_{23} N_3^* - \varepsilon_2 \ge 0$.

The problem is finally formulated as follows: find

$$J = k_1 N_1^* - k_0 N_0^* N_1^* - k_2 \gamma_{21} N_1^* N_2^* +$$

$$+ (k_3 \gamma_{32} + k_2 \gamma_{23}) N_2^* N_3^* + k_2 \varepsilon_3 N_3^* - k_3 \varepsilon_3 N_3^* \to \max \tag{1.48}$$

subject to

$$\gamma_0 N_0^* N_1^* \le \overline{Q}, \qquad 0 \le \gamma_{21} N_1^* - \gamma_{23} N_3^* - \varepsilon_2 \le \bar{c}_2,$$

$$-\gamma_{32} N_2^* \le \bar{c}_3 - \varepsilon_3, \qquad N_i^* \ge 0, \qquad i = 1, 2, 3. \tag{1.49}$$

Let $\overline{N}^*$ be a solution of problem (1.48), (1.49). If $c_3 = -\gamma_{32}\overline{N}_2^* + \varepsilon_3 > 0$, then extermination of crop pests will be accomplished by increasing the number of parasite species, i.e. using the biological method of pest control. If, however, $c_2 = \gamma_{21}\overline{N}_1^* - \gamma_{23}\overline{N}_3^* - \varepsilon_3 > 0$, then the chemical method of pest control is adopted. If c_2 and c_3 are simultaneously greater than zero, then the pest control method is called mixed.

1.7 Control of Generalized Lotka-Volterra Systems

We shall consider a generalized Lotka - Volterra system of the form

$$dN_i/dt = g(N_i)\left(\epsilon_i - \sum_{j=1}^{n} \gamma_{ij} f_j(N_j)\right), \quad i = 1, 2, \ldots, n, \qquad (1.50)$$

where the functions g_i, f_i are continuously differentiable and satisfy the following conditions:

1) $f_i(0) = 0$;
2) $df_i/dN_i > 0$;
3) $g_i(0) = 0$;   (1.51)
4) $g_i(N_i) > 0$ when $N_i > 0$.

We replace variables in equation (1.50)

$$y_i = f_i(N_i), \qquad i = 1, 2, \ldots, n. \qquad (1.52)$$

Under condition 2), for $N_i \geq 0$ there exist single-valued inverse functions $N_i = f_i^{-1}(y_i)$, $i = 1, 2, \ldots, n$. From (1.51) it follows that the functions f_i^{-1} satisfy the following conditions:

1) $f_i^{-1}(0) = 0$;
2) $\partial f^{-1}(y_i)/\partial y_i > 0$ for $y_i \geq 0$. In view of replacement of the variables (1.52), equation (1.50) becomes

$$dy_i/dt = \Psi_i(y_i)(\epsilon_i - \sum_{j=1}^{n} \gamma_{ij} y_j), \qquad i = 1, 2, \ldots, n, \qquad (1.53)$$

where

$$\Psi_i(y_i) = \left(\frac{\partial f^{-1}(y_i)}{\partial y_i}\right)^{-1} g_i(f_i^{-1}(y_i)).$$

Obviously,

1) $\Psi_i(0) = 0$;

2) $\Psi_i(y_i) > 0$ for $y_i > 0$.

Let y^* be a positive equilibrium of system (1.53). Then we write (1.53) as

$$dy_i/dt = \Psi_i(y_i) \sum_{j=1}^{n} \gamma_{ij}(y_j^* - y_j) \tag{1.54}$$

and consider the control problem for system (1.54). For this purpose, we add a control to the right-hand side, i.e. consider the system

$$dy_i/dt = \Psi_i(y_i) \sum_{j=1}^{n} \gamma_{ij}(y_j^* - y_j) + u_i, \tag{1.55}$$

where $u = (u_1, u_2, \ldots, u_n)$ is the vector of control impacts selected from the admissible control set U.

We show that the function

$$V(y) = \sum_{i=1}^{n} \alpha_i \int_{y_i^*}^{y_i} \frac{x - y_i^*}{\Psi_i(x)} dx$$

is Liapunov's function for system (1.54). In fact, since

$$\frac{\partial V}{\partial y_i} = \alpha_i \frac{y_i - y_i^*}{\Psi_i(y_i)}, \qquad i = 1, 2, \ldots, n,$$

the function V has a unique extremum that is attained at a point $y = y^*$ such that $V(y^*) = 0$. The Hessian of the function V at the point y^* is

$$H(V) = \left\| \frac{\partial^2 V}{\partial N_i \partial N_j} \right\| = \text{diag}\{\frac{\alpha_i}{\Psi_i(y_i^*)}\};$$

it is a positive definite matrix, because $\Psi_i(y_i^*) > 0$. Thus, the global minimum of the function $V(y) > 0$ is attained at the point $y = y^*$, while $V'(y) < 0$ for $y > 0$, $y \neq y^*$.

We assume that system (1.55) is to be transferred from the state $y > 0$ to a stable equilibrium $\bar{y}^* > 0$. Now suppose that system (1.53) is dissipative and $\alpha_i = 1$, $i = 1, 2, \ldots, n$. The control $u = (u_1, u_2, \ldots, u_n)$, where

$$u_i = \Psi_i(y_i) \sum_{j=1}^{n} \gamma_{ij}(\bar{y}_j^* - y_j^*), \tag{1.56}$$

solves the stated problem.

Indeed, computing the derivative of the function

$$V = \sum_{i=1}^{n} \int_{\bar{y}_i^*}^{y_i} \frac{x - \bar{y}_i^*}{\Psi_i(y_i)} dx \qquad (1.57)$$

by system (1.55) with control (1.56), we obtain

$$\frac{dV}{dt} = \sum_{i=1}^{n} \frac{y_i - \bar{y}_i^*}{\Psi_i(y_i)} \left(\sum_{j=1}^{n} \Psi_i(y_i)\gamma_{ij}(y_j^* - y_j) + \right.$$

$$\left. + \Psi_i(y_i) \sum_{j=1}^{n} \gamma_{ij}(y_j^* - y_j^*) \right) = -\sum_{i=1}^{n}\sum_{j=1}^{n}(y_i - y_i^*)\gamma_{ij}(y_j - \bar{y}_j^*) =$$

$$= -(y - \bar{y}^*)\Gamma(y - \bar{y}^*) > 0.$$

If system (1.53) is conservative, then stable periodic oscillations are set up in system (1.55) with control (1.56). The equilibrium $\bar{y}^*$ is stable, but not asymptotically stable. We select the control

$$u_i = \Psi_i(y_i) \left(\sum_{i=1}^{n} \gamma_{ij}(\bar{y}_j^* - y_j^*) + \delta_i(\bar{y}_i^* - y_i) \right), \qquad (1.58)$$

where $\delta_i > 0$, $i = 1, 2, \ldots, n$.

Let us compute the derivative of the function (1.57) in terms of trajectories of (1.55) with control of the form (1.58):

$$\frac{dV}{dt} = \sum_{i=1}^{n} \frac{y_i - \bar{y}_i^*}{\Psi_i(y_i)} \left(\sum_{j=1}^{n} \Psi_i(y_i)\gamma_{ij}(y_j^* - y_j) + \right.$$

$$\left. + \Psi_i(y_i) \sum_{j=1}^{n} \gamma_{ij}(\bar{y}_j^* - y_j^*) + \Psi_i(y_i)\delta_i(\bar{y}_i^* - y_i) \right) =$$

$$= -\sum_{i=1}^{n}\sum_{j=1}^{n}(y_i - \bar{y}_i^*)\gamma_{ij}(y_j - \bar{y}_j^*) - \sum_{i=1}^{n}\delta_i(\bar{y}_i^* - y_i)^2 =$$

$$= -\sum_{i=1}^{n}\delta_i(\bar{y}_i^* - y_i)^2 < 0. \qquad (1.59)$$

The inequality holds at all points $y \neq \bar{y}^*$. Thus, the case of a conservative system, control (1.58) solves the problem of transferring system (1.55) from any position $\bar{y} > 0$ to an equilibrium $\bar{y}^*$, such that by (1.59) this equilibrium is asymptotically stable.

1.8 Conflict Control Model for Dynamics of Two Species

This section deals with the conflict control model for dynamics of a community composed of two species. Passage from the control problem for dynamics of a community, which has only one subject of control, to the problem with several subjects of control, each of which pursues his own objectives, constitutes a natural approximation of the model to an actual situation where market mechanisms are involved in exploitation of natural resources. Similar problems have been long and fruitfully discussed in literature, especially concerning with what is called "fish wars" [60]. Here we shall restrict our consideration to a dynamic model of two species and two subjects of control. The reader may easily generalize the example under consideration to the case of any number of species and any number of subjects of control.

Following the terminology of game theory we shall refer to the subjects of control as players.

Let the changes in biomass of two species be described by the following system of differential equations

$$\dot{N}_1 = N_1(\epsilon_1 - \gamma_{11}N_1 - \gamma_{12}N_2) - u_1 - v_1,$$

$$\dot{N}_2 = N_2(\epsilon_2 - \gamma_{21}N_1 - \gamma_{22}N_2) - u_2 - v_2, \qquad (1.60)$$

$$N_1(0) = N_1^0, \qquad N_2(0) = N_2^0,$$

where $u = (u_1, u_2)$ is the control vector for Player 1 and $v = (v_1, v_2)$ is the control vector for Player 2.

Let us state the players objectives. Suppose that in a unit time player i's fixed costs are equal to $a_i > 0$, and the costs of catching species are proportional to the squares of controlled variables with positive coefficients c_{i1} and c_{i2}, respectively. The tax on catch of unit biomass of species j is equal to $k_j > 0$. The selling price for unit biomass of species j is equal to $p_j > 0$. Also, suppose that at each time the players incur expenses in the form of payments that are proportional to a deviation of the current state of system (1.60) from the equilibrium $(\overline{N}_1, \overline{N}_2)$ of this system in an unperturbed state (i.e. for $u \equiv 0, v \equiv 0$). In this case, player i incurs expenses with a coefficient $m_i > 0$. Thus, if during a period $[0, T]$ the players are catching species at the rates $u(t)$ and

$v(t)$ respectively, then the expenses incurred by Player 1 in this period are

$$J_1(u,v) = \int\limits_0^T \Big(m_1((N_1 - \overline{N}_1)^2 + (N_2 - \overline{N}_2)^2) + a_1 +$$

$$+ (k_1 - p_1)u_1 + c_{11}u_1^2 + (k_2 - p_2)u_2 + c_{12}u_2^2\Big)\,dt,$$

and those incurred by Player 2 are

$$J_2(u,v) = \int\limits_0^T \Big(m_2((N_1 - \overline{N}_1)^2 + (N_2 - \overline{N}_2)^2) + a_2 +$$

$$+ (k_1 - p_1)v_1 + c_{21}v_1 + (k_2 - p_2)v_2 + c_{22}v_2^2\Big)\,dt.$$

We assume that the players seek to minimize their expenses by employing open-loop controls.

First we consider the players noncooperative behavior. The optimality principle is taken to be a Nash equilibrium. Recall that the pair of open-loop controls $(u^0(t), v^0(t))$ is called a Nash equilibrium if the following conditions hold for any admissible open-loop controls $u(t), v(t)$ used by the players

$$J_1(u^0(t), v^0(t)) \le J_1(u(t), v^0(t)),$$

$$J_2(u^0(t), v^0(t)) \le J_2(u^0(t), v(t)).$$

We now suppose that Player 2 choses his open-loop control $v^0(t)$, to be optimal, i.e. it forms with control $u^0(t)$ a Nash equilibrium. Then it is clear that the control $u^0(t)$ must supply a minimum to the functional $J_1(u, v^0)$ along the trajectories of system (1.60). In this case the control $u^0(t)$ must satisfy the necessary conditions of Pontryagin's minimum principle.

Let us write out the Hamiltonian for Player 1

$$H_1 = m_1((N_1 - \overline{N}_1)^2 + (N_2 - \overline{N}_2)^2) + a_1 + (k_1 - p_1)u_1 +$$

$$+ c_{11}u_1^2 + (k_2 - p_2)u_2 + c_{12}u_2^2 +$$

$$+ \lambda_{11}(N_1(\epsilon_1 - \gamma_{11}N_1 - \gamma_{12}N_2) - u_1 - v_1^0) +$$

$$+ \lambda_{12}(N_2(\epsilon_2 - \gamma_{21}N_1 - \gamma_{22}N_2) - u_2 - v_2^0),$$

where the conjugate variables λ_{11} and λ_{12} satisfy the system of equations

$$\dot{\lambda}_{11} = -\frac{\partial H_1}{\partial N_1} = -2m_1(N_1 - \bar{N}_1) - \lambda_{11}(\epsilon_1 - 2\gamma_{11}N_1 - \gamma_{12}N_2) + \lambda_{12}\gamma_{21}N_2,$$

$$\dot{\lambda}_{12} = -\frac{\partial H_1}{\partial N_2} = -2m_1(N_2 - \bar{N}_2) - \lambda_{12}(\epsilon_2 - \gamma_{21}N_1 - 2\gamma_{22}N_2) + \lambda_{11}\gamma_{12}N_1,$$

with boundary conditions $\lambda_{11}(T) = \lambda_{12}(T) = 0$. The minimum of the Hamiltonian is attained at the values of control $u(t)$ such that for each $t \in [0, T]$ the fulfillment of conditions

$$\frac{\partial H_1}{\partial u_1} = 0, \qquad \frac{\partial H_1}{\partial u_2} = 0.$$

Alternatively

$$\frac{\partial H_1}{\partial u_1} = k_1 - p_1 + 2c_{11}u_1 - \lambda_{11} = 0,$$

$$\frac{\partial H_2}{\partial u_2} = k_2 - p_2 + 2c_{12}u_2 - \lambda_{12} = 0.$$

Hence, by the convexity of the integrand, we obtain an optimal value for Player 1's control

$$u_1^0(t) = \frac{\lambda_{11} - (k_1 - p_1)}{2c_{11}},$$

$$u_2^0(t) = \frac{\lambda_{12} - (k_2 - p_2)}{2c_{12}}. \tag{1.61}$$

In a similar manner, it can be shown that a Nash-equilibrium open-loop control for Player 2 can be computed from the formulas

$$v_1^0(t) = \frac{\lambda_{21} - (k_1 - p_1)}{2c_{21}},$$

$$v_2^0(t) = \frac{\lambda_{22} - (k_2 - p_2)}{2c_{22}}, \tag{1.62}$$

where λ_{21} and λ_{21} satisfy the system of differential equations

$$\dot{\lambda}_{21} = -2m_2(N_1 - \bar{N}_1) - \lambda_{21}(\epsilon_1 - 2\gamma_{11}N_1 - \gamma_{12}N_2) + \lambda_{22}\gamma_{21}N_2,$$

$$\dot{\lambda}_{22} = -2m_2(N_2 - \bar{N}_2) - \lambda_{22}(\epsilon_2 - \gamma_{21}N_1 - 2\gamma_{22}N_2) + \lambda_{21}\gamma_{12}N_1$$

with boundary conditions $\lambda_{21}(T) = \lambda_{22}(T) = 0$.

Thus, to find for players the pair of open-loop controls forming a Nash equilibrium in the dynamic game of interest, we need to solve the system of differential equations

$$\dot{N}_1 = N_1(\epsilon_1 - \gamma_{11}N_1 - \gamma_{12}N_2) - \frac{\lambda_{11} - (k_1 - p_1)}{2c_{11}} - \frac{\lambda_{21} - (k_1 - p_1)}{2c_{21}},$$

$$\dot{N}_2 = N_2(\epsilon_2 - \gamma_{21}N_1 - \gamma_{22}N_2) - \frac{\lambda_{12} - (k_2 - p_2)}{2c_{12}} - \frac{\lambda_{22} - (k_2 - p_2)}{2c_{22}},$$

$$\dot{\lambda}_{11} = -2m_1(N_1 - \overline{N}_1) - \lambda_{11}(\epsilon_1 - 2\gamma_{11}N_1 - \gamma_{12}N_2) + \lambda_{12}\gamma_{21}N_2,$$

$$\dot{\lambda}_{12} = -2m_1(N_2 - \overline{N}_2) - \lambda_{12}(\epsilon_2 - \gamma_{21}N_1 - 2\gamma_{22}N_2) + \lambda_{11}\gamma_{12}N_1,$$

$$\dot{\lambda}_{21} = -2m_2(N_1 - \overline{N}_1) - \lambda_{21}(\epsilon_1 - 2\gamma_{11}N_1 - \gamma_{12}N_2) + \lambda_{22}\gamma_{21}N_2,$$

$$\dot{\lambda}_{22} = -2m_2(N_2 - \overline{N}_2) - \lambda_{22}(\epsilon_2 - \gamma_{21}N_1 - 2\gamma_{22}N_2) + \lambda_{21}\gamma_{12}N_1,$$

with initial boundary conditions $N_1(0) = N_1^0$, $N_2(0) = N_2^0$, $\lambda_{11}(T) = \lambda_{12}(T) = \lambda_{21}(T) = \lambda_{22}(T) = 0$. Then we substitute the resulting solution into the formulas (1.61) and (1.62) and calculate the values of the Nash-equilibrium open-loop controls $u^0(t)$ and $v^0(t)$.

We shall now consider the players' cooperative behavior. In cooperation, the players are aiming to minimize total expenses. With this aim in mind the players acting as one player jointly decide on their controls. In this case, the problem reduces to that of an optimal single-criterion control

$$J(u, v) = J_1(u, v) + J_2(u, v).$$

The Hamiltonian becomes

$$H = (m_1 + m_2)((N_1 - \overline{N}_1)^2 + (N_2 - \overline{N}_2)^2) + (k_1 - p_1)(u_1 + v_1) +$$

$$+ c_{11}u_1^2 + c_{21}v_1^2 + (k_2 - p_2)(u_2 + v_2) + c_{12}u_2^2 + c_{22}v_2^2 +$$

$$+ \lambda_1(N_1(\epsilon_1 - \gamma_{11}N_1 - \gamma_{12}N_2) - u_1 - v_1) +$$

$$+ \lambda_2(N_2(\epsilon_2 - \gamma_{21}N_1 - \gamma_{22}N_2) - u_2 - v_2).$$

Optimality conditions for control variables are in the form

$$\frac{\partial H}{\partial u_1} = \frac{\partial H}{\partial u_2} = \frac{\partial H}{\partial v_1} = \frac{\partial H}{\partial v_2} = 0.$$

Hence we derive the formulas for computing the optimal control values

$$u_1^* = \frac{\lambda_1 - (k_1 - p_1)}{2c_{11}},$$

$$u_2^* = \frac{\lambda_2 - (k_2 - p_2)}{2c_{12}}, \tag{1.63}$$

$$v_1^* = \frac{\lambda_1 - (k_1 - p_1)}{2c_{21}},$$

$$v_2^* = \frac{\lambda_2 - (k_2 - p_2)}{2c_{22}}.$$

where the values of λ_1 and λ_2 are obtained from the solution of the system of differential equations

$$\dot{N}_1 = N_1(\epsilon_1 - \gamma_{11}N_1 - \gamma_{12}N_2) - \frac{\lambda_1 - (k_1 - p_1)}{2c_{11}} - \frac{\lambda_1 - (k_1 - p_1)}{2c_{21}},$$

$$\dot{N}_2 = N_2(\epsilon_2 - \gamma_{21}N_1 - \gamma_{22}N_2) - \frac{\lambda_2 - (k_2 - p_2)}{2c_{12}} - \frac{\lambda_2 - (k_2 - p_2)}{2c_{22}},$$

$$\dot{\lambda}_1 = -\frac{\partial H_1}{\partial N_1} = -2(m_1 + m_2)(N_1 - \overline{N}_1) - \lambda_1(\epsilon_1 - 2\gamma_{11}N_1 - \gamma_{12}N_2) +$$

$$+ \lambda_2\gamma_{21}N_2,$$

$$\dot{\lambda}_2 = -\frac{\partial H_1}{\partial N_2} = -2(m_1 + m_2)(N_2 - \overline{N}_2) - \lambda_2(\epsilon_2 - \gamma_{21}N_1 - 2\gamma_{22}N_2) +$$

$$+ \lambda_1\gamma_{12}N_1,$$

with initial boundary conditions

$$N_1(0) = N_1^0, \qquad N_2(0) = N_2^0, \qquad \lambda_1(T) = \lambda_2(T) = 0.$$

For the thus obtained controls $u^*(t) = (u_1^*(t), u_2^*(t))$ and $v^*(t) = (v_1^*(t), v_2^*(t))$ the inequality

$$J(u^*(t), v^*(t)) \leq J(u(t), v(t))$$

holds for any admissible open-loop controls of players. Hence,

$$J(u^*(t), v^*(t)) = J_1(u^*(t), v^*(t)) + J_2(u^*(t), v^*(t)) \leq$$

$$\leq J_1(u^0(t), v^0(t)) + J_2(u^0(t), v^0(t)),$$

where $(u^0(t), v^0(t))$ is a Nash equilibrium.

In conditions of noncooperative behavior the expenses incurred by the players are respectively $J_1(u^0(t), v^0(t))$ and $J_2(u^0(t), v^0(t))$. In conditions of cooperation, however, the savings in expenses arising from players' cooperation are to be divided among the players. Thus, in the example of cooperative model, the players expenses are respectively $\xi_1 + J_1(u^0, v^0)$ and $\xi_2 + J_2(u^0, v^0)$, where

$$\xi_1 \geq 0, \qquad \xi_2 \geq 0, \qquad \xi_1 + \xi_2 = J(u^*, v^*) - J(u^0, v^0).$$

Some issues of the theory of Volterra systems have been set forth in this chapter with emphasis on control problems for such systems.

In our opinion, application of the results of the optimal control theory to the biological systems may enable ecologists to obtain further insight into mechanisms of human impact on ecosystems and find optimal ways of exploiting such systems. Those who wish to take a close look at the present day theory of Volterra systems may refer to such books as [4, 42, 45, 46].

Chapter 2

DYNAMIC MODEL FOR AIR POLLUTION

Although the issues of atmospheric diffusion have long been studied, the results of such studies have been only recently applied to the problems of air pollution.

The late 1920s witness the emergence of an important notion, namely: in many instances the transfer of heat and moisture in the ground level atmosphere can be approximated by the occurrence of passive impurities and these processes can be investigated in terms of the same differential equations.

The relationship between the results of investigations of atmospheric impurity diffusion and the patterns of heat and moisture transfer in the ground level air reveals itself in the solution of the corresponding problems. Thus, the Green functions obtained from the solution of differential equations for heat and moisture transfer are the distribution functions of impurities spreading in the air from the source under certain boundary conditions.

Establishment of the form of equations describing atmospheric diffusion was of great importance. To describe the process of atmospheric diffusion, use was made of parabolic differential equations that are a generalization of the well-known Fik equation. L. V. Keller was among those who initially suggested that Fik's equation should be used for this purpose. The original literatures on atmospheric diffusion outlined two approaches to the ground-level spread of impurities. One approach derives from the work accomplished by A. Robers and is based on the solution of the turbulent diffusion equation with constant coefficients. The other approach has been developed by O. Setten and employs formulas to determine the concentration of impurities from a source obtained statistically.

The investigations in these areas are reviewed in A. S. Monin and A. M. Jaglom [31], G. Chenadi [50], etc.

Domestic studies are centered largely around turbulent diffusion equations with variable coefficients. This line of investigation seems to be universal, because it enables one to solve problems for a variety of sources, environmental features, and boundary conditions.

New requirements for methods of investigating atmospheric diffusion appeared in the course of time. It became necessary to investigate turbulent flows at high attitudes and study such issues as air scattering of impurities at significant distances from sources, and allowance for a great number of parameters. Stages of evolution of such research methods are shown,e.g. in M. E. Berland [2]. Atmospheric diffusion, as applied to environmental issues, has been extensively studied in G. I. Marchuk [25, 26].

This chapter focuses on industrial emission assessment, optimal layout of new industrial enterprises, assessment of emission from operating enterprises with regard to emission standards for ecologically significant zones, and control of vehicle emissions.

2.1 Equations of Air Impurities Transfer and Diffusion

Following the Euler technique, the air flow at the time t is characterized by the velocity field, i.e. by the component values of the velocity vector at all possible points of Cartesian rectangular space. To study the phenomena of turbulent diffusion (i.e. the spread of impurities in a turbulent flow), the Lagrange method of describing motions is more convenient to use, because here the trajectories of sufficiently small air volume elements are used in place of point velocities. If the air volume elements differ in chemical composition, i.e. they contain foreign matters other than air, then the flow is said to contain a certain impurity. If an impurity is introduced merely at some points of a turbulent flow, then diffusion will cause the impurity to spread over the entire volume occupied by the air flow.

The impurity generally appears in the flow as a gaseous additive or a great number of small solid matters. In this case it is characterized by the Euler field of volume concentration $q(t, x, y, z)$. We consider the transfer phenomenon in the absence of diffusion. In this case, the impurity concentration in the air volume element remains intact, and hence along the trajectories of this volume element the equality $dq/dt = 0$ holds identically or

$$\frac{\partial q}{\partial t} + v_1 \frac{\partial q}{\partial x} + v_2 \frac{\partial q}{\partial y} + v_3 \frac{\partial q}{\partial z} = 0, \tag{2.2}$$

where v_1, v_2, v_3 are components of the air flow velocity $v(x, y, z)$.

It is well known that for the lowest atmospheric layer there is what is called the equation of continuity [25]

$$\frac{\partial v_1}{\partial x} + \frac{\partial v_2}{\partial y} + \frac{\partial v_3}{\partial z} = 0, \tag{2.2}$$

or

$$\operatorname{div} v = 0, \quad v = (v_1, v_2, v_3).$$

In view of (2.2), we have

$$\operatorname{div} vq = v_1 \frac{\partial q}{\partial x} + v_2 \frac{\partial q}{\partial y} + v_3 \frac{\partial q}{\partial z} + q \operatorname{div} v = v_1 \frac{\partial q}{\partial x} + v_2 \frac{\partial q}{\partial y} + v_3 \frac{\partial q}{\partial z},$$

Equation (2.2) then may be written as

$$\frac{\partial q}{\partial t} + \operatorname{div} vq = 0. \tag{2.3}$$

In what follows we assume that the condition (2.2) always holds. Moreover, we assume that

$$v_3 = 0$$

when

$$z = 0, \qquad z = H.$$

Equation (2.3) can be generalized. Thus, if during transfer of impurity its part settles or ceases to exist, then equation (2.1) becomes

$$dq/dt = -\sigma q,$$

$$\frac{\partial q}{\partial t} + \operatorname{div} vq + \sigma q = 0. \tag{2.4}$$

If at some point in space there is an impurity emitter whose intensity and location are described by the function $f(x, y, z, t) = Q\delta(r - r_0)$, where $\delta(r - r_0)$ is the δ-function satisfying the condition

$$\int_G \varphi(r)\delta(r - r_0)\, dr = \begin{cases} \varphi(r_0), & r_0 \in G, \\ 0, & r_0 \bar{\in} G, \end{cases}$$

then the transfer of impurity in the absence of diffusion is described by

$$\frac{dq}{dt} = f. \tag{2.5}$$

In view (2.4) and (2.5), the equation of transfer in the presence of the impurity emitter becomes

$$\frac{dq}{dt} + \text{div } vq + \sigma q = f. \tag{2.6}$$

Suppose equation (2.6) is given in a region G of a Cartesian three-dimensional space with side cylindrical surface and bases $z = 0$ and $z = H$.

Let us add to the equation the initial boundary conditions

$$q = q_0 \text{ at } t = t_0, \tag{2.7}$$

$$q = q_S \text{ on } S \text{ for } v_n < 0, \tag{2.8}$$

where q_0 and q_S are the given functions and v_n is the projection of vector v onto the external normal to the side surface S.

Multiplying equation (2.6) by q and integrating over the time interval $0 \leq t \leq T$ and region G, we obtain

$$\int\limits_0^T \int\limits_G \frac{q^2}{2} \, dG \, dt + \int\limits_0^T \int\limits_G \text{div} \frac{vq^2}{2} \, dG \, dt + \sigma \int\limits_0^T \int\limits_G q^2 \, dG \, dt = \int\limits_0^T \int\limits_G fq \, dG \, dt.$$

Using the Ostrogradskii-Gauss formula

$$\int\limits_G \text{div} \frac{vq^2}{2} \, dG = \int\limits_S v_n \frac{q^2}{2} \, dS,$$

we obtain

$$\int\limits_G \frac{q_T^2}{2} \, dG + \int\limits_0^T dt \int\limits_S \frac{v_n^+ q_S^2}{2} \, dS + \sigma \int\limits_0^T dt \int\limits_G q^2 \, dG =$$

$$= \int\limits_G \frac{q_0^2}{2} \, dG - \int\limits_0^T dt \int\limits_S \frac{v_n^- q_s^2}{2} \, dS + \int\limits_0^T dt \int\limits_G fq \, dG, \tag{2.9}$$

where

$$v_n^+ = \begin{cases} v_n, & v_n > 0, \\ 0, & v_n < 0, \end{cases}$$

$$v_n^- = v_n - v_n^+.$$

We now consider the uniqueness of the solution of problem (2.6)–(2.8). To equation (2.6) with boundary conditions (2.7), (2.8) let there correspond two solutions q_1 and q_2, that do not coincide on a set of nonzero measure. Let $w = q_1 - q_2$ and consider the problem

$$\frac{dw}{dt} + \text{div } vw + \sigma w = 0;$$

$$w = 0 \text{ at } t = 0; \qquad w = 0 \text{ on } S, \qquad \text{if } v_n < 0.$$

For the function w identity (2.9) becomes

$$\int\limits_G \frac{w_T^2}{2} \, dG + \int\limits_0^T dt \int\limits_S \frac{v_n^+ w^2}{2} \, dS + \sigma \int\limits_0^T dt \int\limits_G w^2 \, dG = 0 \qquad (2.10)$$

Expression (2.10) is identical only if $w = 0$, i.e. $q_1 = q_2$. We have thus proved the uniqueness of the solution.

Here we have merely outlined the proof of uniqueness for the solution of problem (2.6)–(2.8). In what follows, without going into theoretical details, we assume that the conditions which ensure the uniqueness of the solution are all satisfied.

Although the above model of impurity spread adequately accounts for the essence of the process, it idealizes to some extent the physical picture which is much more complex. It is well known that the impurity spreads out in the air forming a complex concentration distribution away from its source. This is because the atmosphere is a turbulent medium in which vortices (small-scale fluctuations) are formed spontaneously. The physics of fluctuation effects is well understood. The simplest theory which enables one to derive equations for average concentrations implies representation of the function q as the sum of the averaged $\bar{q}$ and the fluctuation component q', i.e. $q = \bar{q} + q'$, in which case the q' rapidly varies with time and is a small variable as compared to $\bar{q}$. As shown in [26], the equations for average impurity concentrations are

$$\frac{\partial q}{\partial t} + \text{div } vq + \sigma q = \frac{\partial}{\partial z} \nu \frac{\partial q}{\partial z} + \mu \Delta q + f, \qquad (2.11)$$

where Δ is the Laplace operator; $\nu \geq 0$ and $\mu \geq 0$ are respectively the horizontal and vertical diffusion coefficients computed experimentally, with initial boundary conditions

$$q = q_S \text{ on } S, \qquad v_n < 0; \qquad (2.12)$$

$$\frac{\partial q}{\partial z} = \alpha q \text{ with } z = o; \qquad \frac{\partial q}{\partial z} = 0 \text{ with } z = z_H. \qquad (2.13)$$

Problem (2.11)–(2.13) also has a unique solution.

The investigation techniques for the impurity spreading can be first conveniently examined by referring to the simplest examples [25]. We shall consider merely a diffusion statement of the problem, where $v \equiv 0$,

$$\sigma q = \mu \frac{d^2 q}{dx^2} + Q\delta(x - x_0) \qquad (2.14)$$

in infinite medium $-\infty < x < \infty$, where Q is the capacity of the emission source located at the point $x = x_0$. Boundary conditions are taken to be the boundedness condition for solution over the entire region, while the source function f is taken to be the function $f = Q\delta(x - x_0)$, where $Q \geq 0$ is a constant. For n sources located at the points $x_1, x_2, \ldots, x_n$, the function f takes the form

$$f = \sum_{i=1}^{n} Q_i(t)\delta(x - x_i),$$

where $Q_i \geq 0$ is the i-th source capacity. If the emission intensity is the function of time, then f takes the form

$$f = \sum_{i=1}^{n} Q_i(t)\delta(x - x_i).$$

For the mobile source problem, one has to use the function

$$f = \sum_{i=1}^{n} Q_i(t)\delta(x - x_i(t)).$$

We shall now consider problem (2.14) by reducing it to an equivalent form which contains no δ-function. To this end, we integrate the equation in the ε-neighborhood of the point x_0

$$\sigma \int_{x_0 - \varepsilon}^{x_0 + \varepsilon} q \, dx = \mu \frac{dq}{dx}\Big|_{x_0 + \varepsilon} - \mu \frac{dq}{dx}\Big|_{x_0 - \varepsilon} + Q,$$

using the δ-function property

$$\int_{x_0 - \varepsilon}^{x_0 + \varepsilon} \delta(x - x_0) \, dx = 1.$$

Letting ε for zero, we obtain

$$\mu \frac{dq}{dx}\Big|_{x_0 + \varepsilon} - \mu \frac{dq}{dx}\Big|_{x_0 - \varepsilon} + Q = 0. \qquad (2.15),$$

Let us consider two regions denoting their relevant solutions as q_- and q_+, i.e. we consider two problems:

$$\mu\frac{d^2q_+}{dx^2} - \sigma q_+ = 0, \qquad q_+ = 0 \text{ as } x \to \infty; \qquad (2.16)$$

$$\mu\frac{d^2q_-}{dx^2} - \sigma q_- = 0, \qquad q_- = 0 \text{ as } x \to -\infty. \qquad (2.17)$$

With $x = x_0$, the solutions of problems (2.16), (2.17) are related by (2.15). By assuming that the solution of the problem is continuous at all points, including $x = x_0$, we obtain

$$q_+ = q_- \text{ at } x = x_0. \qquad (2.18)$$

The solutions of problem (2.16), (2.17) become

$$q_+ = C_+ \exp[-\sqrt{\sigma/\mu}(x - x_0)],$$

$$q_- = C_- \exp[-\sqrt{\sigma/\mu}(x_0 - x)].$$

Substituting these solutions in (2.15) and (2.18), we obtain $C_+ = C_- = Q/(2\sqrt{\mu\sigma})$. Finally, the solution of problem (2.14) may be written as

$$q(x) = \frac{Q}{2\sqrt{\tau\mu}} \begin{cases} \exp[-\sqrt{\frac{\sigma}{\mu}}(x - x_0)], & x \geq x_0, \\ \exp[-\sqrt{\frac{\tau}{\mu}}(x_0 - x)], & x < x_0 \end{cases}.$$

Hence it follows that diffusion results in the solution that is exponentially and symmetrically decreasing in both directions away from the point $x = x_0$.

We shall now consider a more complex situation, where the air velocity is nonzero, i.e. the impurity spreading is described by the equation

$$v\frac{dq}{dx} + \sigma q = \mu\frac{d^2q}{dx^2} + Q\delta(x - x_0),$$

$v > 0, -\infty < x < +\infty$. As in the preceding case, we have two problems:

$$\mu\frac{d^2q_+}{dx^2} + v\frac{dq_+}{dx} - \sigma q_+ = 0, \qquad q_+ = 0 \text{ as } x \to \infty; \qquad (2.19)$$

$$\mu\frac{d^2q_-}{dx^2} + v\frac{dq_-}{dx} - \sigma q_- = 0, \qquad q_- = 0 \text{ as } x \to -\infty. \qquad (2.20)$$

Solutions to (2.19) and (2.20) may be represented as

$$q_+ = C_+ \exp\left[-\left(\sqrt{\frac{\sigma}{\mu} + \frac{v^2}{4\mu^2}} - \frac{v}{2\mu}\right)(x - x_0)\right], \qquad x \geq x_0, \qquad (2.21)$$

$$q_- = C_- \exp\left[-\left(\sqrt{\frac{\sigma}{\mu} + \frac{v^2}{4\mu^2}} - \frac{v}{2\mu}\right)(x_0 - x)\right], \qquad x \le x_0, \qquad (2.22)$$

Substituting (2.21) and (2.22) in (2.15) and (2.18), yields
$C_+ = C_- = C = Q/\sqrt{4\sigma\mu + v^2}$. The solutions of the problem then become

$$q(x) = \frac{Q}{\sqrt{4\sigma\mu + v^2}} \begin{cases} \exp\left[-\left(\sqrt{\frac{\sigma}{\mu} + \frac{v^2}{4\mu^2}} - \frac{v}{2\mu}\right)(x - x_0)\right], & x \ge x_0, \\[4mm] \exp\left[-\left(\sqrt{\frac{\sigma}{\mu} + \frac{v^2}{4\mu^2}} - \frac{v}{2\mu}\right)(x_0 - x)\right], & x < x_0. \end{cases}$$

2.2   Dual Diffusion Problem

In the preceding section we have considered the equation of atmospheric impurity transfer which enables one to obtain distribution of average impurity
concentration in a given area. In many practical problems, however, one has to
consider adjoined equations of diffusion, e.g., in the enterprise siting problem
with regard to a permissible pollution level [26].

Let L be a linear operator in the Hilbert function space satisfying the
necessary smoothness conditions. The scalar product of two functions from
this space is determined as follows:

$$(g, h) = \int_0^T dt \int_G hg \, dG,$$

where $[0, T]$ is the range of the variable t and G is the range of space variables.
     We consider the equation

$$Lg = f, \qquad (2.23)$$

where g and f are the given elements of the Hilbert space. To the operator L
let there correspond an adjoint operator L^* determined from the condition

$$(g, Lh) = (h, L^*g). \qquad (2.24)$$

Setting in this equation $h = q, g = q^*$, we obtain

$$(q^*, Lq) = (q, L^*q^*),$$

or, in view of (2.23),

$$(q^*, f) = (q, L^* q^*).$$

Suppose we have

$$L^* q^* = p, \tag{2.25}$$

where p is the function which remains to be defined. Condition (2.24) then becomes

$$(q^*, f) = (q, p). \tag{2.26}$$

Problem (2.25) is called the dual of problem (2.23) with (2.26) as the duality condition for the problems being considered.

We shall now formulate adjoint equations for our problem. Let us consider the turbulent diffusion equation

$$\frac{\partial q}{\partial t} + v_1 \frac{\partial q}{\partial x} + v_2 \frac{\partial q}{\partial y} + v_3 \frac{\partial q}{\partial z} + \sigma q = \frac{\partial}{\partial t} \nu \frac{\partial q}{\partial z} + \mu \Delta q + f, \tag{2.27}$$

with initial boundary conditions

$$q = q_0 \text{ at } t = t_0, \qquad q = 0 \text{ on } S,$$

$$\frac{\partial q}{\partial z} = \alpha q \text{ on } z = 0, \qquad \frac{\partial q}{\partial z} = 0 \text{ with } z = H, \tag{2.28}$$

$$q(0, x, y, z) = q(T, x, y, z) = q_0(x, y, z)$$

We assume that $v_3 = 0$ when $z = 0$, $z = H$.

We shall now consider in the Hilbert space a subset φ of functions that are periodic in the interval $[0, T]$ and satisfy equation (2.27) as well as initial boundary conditions (2.28).

The scalar product of functions from φ is determined as

$$(g, h) = \int\limits_0^T \int\limits_G g h \, dG.$$

Equation (2.27) may be rewritten as

$$Lq = f,$$

$$L = \frac{\partial}{\partial t} + v_1 \frac{\partial}{\partial x} + v_2 \frac{\partial}{\partial y} + v_3 \frac{\partial}{\partial z} + \sigma - \frac{\partial}{\partial z} \nu \frac{\partial}{\partial} - \mu \Delta.$$

We rewrite the left part of identity (2.24) for the functions from the space φ:

$$(g, Lh) = \int\limits_0^T dt \int\limits_G g\left(\frac{\partial h}{\partial t} + v_1\frac{\partial h}{\partial y} + v_2\frac{\partial h}{\partial z} + \right.$$

$$\left. + v_3\frac{\partial h}{\partial z} + \sigma h - \frac{\partial}{\partial z}\nu\frac{\partial h}{\partial z} - \mu\Delta h\right) dG. \tag{2.29}$$

Integrating by parts and using Ostrogradskii-Gauss formulas, we obtain

$$\int\limits_0^T dt \int\limits_G g\frac{\partial h}{\partial t} dG = \int\limits_G g_T h_T \, dG - \int\limits_G g_0 h_0 \, dG - \int\limits_0^T dt \int\limits_G h\frac{\partial g}{\partial t} dG,$$

$$\int\limits_0^T dt \int\limits_G g\left(v_1\frac{\partial h}{\partial x} + v_2\frac{\partial h}{\partial y} + v_3\frac{\partial h}{\partial z}\right) dG = \int\limits_0^T dt \int\limits_S v_n g h \, dS -$$

$$- \int\limits_0^T dt \int\limits_G h\left(v_1\frac{\partial g}{\partial x} + v_2\frac{\partial g}{\partial y} + v_3\frac{\partial g}{\partial z}\right) dG,$$

$$\int\limits_0^T dt \int\limits_G g\frac{\partial}{\partial z}\nu\frac{\partial h}{\partial z} dG = \int\limits_0^T dt \int\limits_{S_H} \nu\left(g\frac{\partial h}{\partial z} - h\frac{\partial g}{\partial z}\right) dS -$$

$$- \int\limits_0^T dt \int\limits_{S_0} \nu\left(g\frac{\partial h}{\partial z} - h\partial g\partial z\right) dS + \int\limits_0^T dt \int\limits_G h\frac{\partial}{\partial z}\nu\frac{\partial g}{\partial z} dG,$$

$$\mu\int\limits_0^T dt \int\limits_G g\Delta h \, dG = \mu\int\limits_0^T dt \int\limits_S \left(g\frac{\partial h}{\partial n} - h\frac{\partial g}{\partial n}\right) dS -$$

$$- \mu\int\limits_0^T dt \int\limits_G h\Delta g \, dG,$$

where v_n is the projection of the velocity vector onto the external normal to the lateral surface; S_H and S_0 are the respective curves of intersection for the lateral surface of cylinder and the top $z = H$ and the bottom face $z = 0$.

Next, by the periodicity of the functions g and h and under the boundary conditions, (2.29) can be transformed to the form

$$(g, Lh) = \int\limits_0^T dt \int\limits_G h\left(-\frac{\partial g}{\partial t} - v_1\frac{\partial g}{\partial x} - v_2\frac{\partial g}{\partial y} - -v_3\frac{\partial g}{\partial z} + \sigma g - \frac{\partial}{\partial z}\nu\frac{\partial g}{\partial z} - \mu\Delta g\right) dG.$$

Denoting

$$-\frac{\partial}{\partial t} - v_1\frac{\partial}{\partial x} - v_2\frac{\partial}{\partial y} - -v_3\frac{\partial}{\partial z} + \sigma - \frac{\partial}{\partial z}\nu\frac{\partial}{\partial z} - \mu\Delta = L^*,$$

we obtain the identity $(g, Lh) = (h, L^*g)$.

We define the dual problem as follows:

$$g = q^*,$$

$$-\frac{\partial q^*}{\partial t} - v_1\frac{\partial q^*}{\partial x} - v_2\frac{\partial q^*}{\partial y} - v_3\frac{\partial q^*}{\partial z} + \sigma q^* - \frac{\partial}{\partial z}\nu\frac{\partial q^*}{\partial z} - \mu\Delta g^* = p,$$

$$q^* = q_0^* \text{ at } t = t_0, \qquad q^* = 0 \text{ on } S,$$

$$\frac{\partial q^*}{\partial z} = \alpha q^* \text{ on } z = 0, \qquad \frac{\partial q^*}{\partial z} = 0 \text{ with } z = H;$$

$$q^*(0, x, y, z) = q^*(T, x, y, z).$$

Here the function p is selected to suit the form of the functional in the primal problem. For example, the functional may be taken to be the harmful impurity concentration g averaged over some region $G_0 \subset G$ and the time interval $[0, T]$

$$J = \int\limits_0^T dt \int\limits_{G_0} q \, dG.$$

Considering the duality condition $(g, f) = (h, p)$ and selecting the function p as

$$p = \begin{cases} 1, & (x, y, z) \in G_0, \\ 0, & (x, y, z) \overline{\in} G_0, \end{cases}$$

we then have $J = (q, f)$, or, by the dual formula,

$$J = (q^*, f). \tag{2.30}$$

Thus, two ways are possible for computing the functional J. One way is to solve the primal problem and compute the functional values by a proper choice of the function p. The other way is to use the dual problem with the known source function f. The question of choosing a proper way depends on specific conditions of the problem and optimization objectives. For example, if the problem is to optimize the values of the functional J by a proper choice of the function f or its parameters describing the location and intensity of pollution sources, then to solve this problem it is worthwhile to use the adjoint equation and representation of the functional J in the form (2.30).

E x a m p l e 1 [26]. Suppose the impurity spread is described by the simplest diffusion equation

$$\frac{\partial q}{\partial t} + \sigma q - \mu\frac{\partial^2 q}{\partial x^2} = Q\delta(x - x_0); \qquad (2.31)$$

$q = 0$ at $t = 0$.

We are required to determine an area $w \subset G = (-\infty; +\infty)$, where the source with emission intensity Q may be located so that the emission level at a given point of the area $G : x = \xi$ at the time $t = \tau_1$ does not exceed a given constant c, i.e. $J = q(\xi, \tau_1) \leq c$. The functional J can be represented as $J = \int_0^T dt \int_G pq \, dG$, where $p = \delta(x - \xi)\delta(t - \tau_1)$.

Binary representation of the functional yields

$$J = \int_0^T dt \int_G f q^*(x_0, t) \, dt, \qquad (2.32)$$

Here q^* is a solution of the adjoint equation

$$-\frac{\partial q^*}{\partial t} + \sigma q^* - \mu\frac{\partial^2 q^*}{\partial x^2} = \delta(x - \xi)\delta(t - \tau_1); \qquad (2.33)$$

$q^* = 0$ at $t = T$. In (2.32), we make a replacement of the variable $t = T - t$, $t \in [0, T]$. In this case the operator of the obtained problem coincides with the operator of problem (2.31).

It is known that the solution of problem (2.33) may be obtained in the form

$$q^*(\tilde{t}, x) = \int_0^{\tilde{t}} \int_{-\infty}^{+\infty} \tilde{q}(x - \eta, \tilde{t} - \tau)\delta(\eta - \xi)\delta(T - \tau - \tau_1) \, d\eta \, d\tau, \qquad (2.34)$$

where $\tilde{q}$ is the fundamental solution of problem (2.33)

$$\tilde{q}(t, x) = \frac{\Theta(t)}{2\sqrt{\mu\pi t}} \exp\left[-\left(\sigma t + \frac{x^2}{4\mu t}\right)\right], \qquad (2.35)$$

$$\Theta(t) = \begin{cases} 1, & t > 0, \\ 0, & t \leq 0. \end{cases}$$

Substituting (2.35) into (2.34) and returning to the variable t, we obtain

$$q^*(t, x) = \begin{cases} \dfrac{1}{2\sqrt{\mu\pi(\tau_1 - t)}} \exp\left[-\sigma(\tau_1 - t) - \dfrac{(x - \xi)^2}{4\mu(\tau_1 - t)}\right], & t \in [0, \tau_1), \\ 0, & t \in [\tau_1, T]. \end{cases}$$

Hence

$$J(x) = \frac{Q}{2\sqrt{\mu\pi}} \int\limits_0^{\tau_1} \frac{1}{\sqrt{\tau_1 - t}} \exp\left[-\sigma(\tau_1 - t) - \frac{(x - \xi)^2}{4\mu(\tau_1 - t)}\right] dt. \qquad (2.36)$$

The area where the source with emission capacity Q can be located is determined from condition $J(x) \le c$. On selecting $x_0 \in w = \{x : J(x) \le c\}$, the impurity spread is described by the solution of problem (2.31) which, in view of (2.35), becomes

$$q(t, x) = \frac{Q}{2\sqrt{\mu T}} \int\limits_0^t \frac{1}{\sqrt{t - \tau}} \exp\left\{-\left[\sigma(t - \tau) + \frac{(x - x_0)^2}{4\mu(t - \tau)}\right]\right\} d\tau.$$

E x a m p l e 2 [26]. Let the impurity transfer be described by the equation

$$\frac{\partial q}{\partial t} + v\frac{\partial q}{\partial x} + \sigma q - \mu\frac{\partial^2 q}{\partial x^2} = Q\delta(x - x_0);$$

$$q = 0 \text{ at } t = 0, \qquad q \to 0 \text{ as } t \to \pm\infty.$$

The source of harmful impurity must be located at a point x_0 such that

$$|x_0 - \xi_1| = \min_{x \in G} |x - \xi_1|, \qquad q(\tau_1, \xi_1) < 0,$$

i.e. at the time τ_1 the emission should not exceed at the point ξ_1 a constant $c > 0$, in which case the point x_0 is nearest the point ξ_1.

The functional of the primal problem is

$$J = \int\limits_0^T dt \int\limits_{-\infty}^{+\infty} pq\, dx = q(\tau_1, \xi_1),$$

i.e. $p = \delta(x - \xi_1)\delta(t - \tau_1)$. The dual problem then is

$$-\frac{\partial q^*}{\partial t} - v\frac{\partial q^*}{\partial t} + \sigma q^* - \mu\frac{\partial^2 q^*}{\partial x^2} = p; \qquad (2.37)$$

$$q^* = 0 \quad t = T, \qquad q^* \to 0 \quad x \to \pm\infty.$$

Based on the duality conditions, we obtain the dual representation of the functional

$$J = \int\limits_0^T dt \int\limits_{-\infty}^{+\infty} fq^*\, dx = Q\int\limits_0^T q^*(t, x_0)\, dt. \qquad (2.38)$$

The fundamental solution of the operator of problem (2.37) can be obtained by the Fourier transform

$$F[q] = \int\limits_{-\infty}^{+\infty} q(t, x) e^{i\xi x} \, dx.$$

Let us apply the Fourier transform to the equation

$$-\frac{\partial q}{\partial t} - v\frac{\partial q}{\partial x} + \sigma q - \mu\frac{\partial^2 q}{\partial x^2} = \delta(t - \tau_1)\delta(x - \xi).$$

Obtain the equation

$$-\frac{\partial}{\partial t}F[q] - (iv\xi - \sigma + \mu\xi^2)F[q] = \delta(t - \tau_1),$$

whose solution is the function

$$F[q](t, \xi) = \Theta(t)\exp\{-(iv\xi + \sigma + \mu\xi^2)t\}$$

Using the inverse Fourier transform yields the fundamental solution

$$q(t, x) = \frac{\Theta(t)}{2\sqrt{\mu\pi t}}\exp\left\{-\left[\sigma t + \frac{(x + vt)^2}{4\mu t}\right]\right\}.$$

Replacing the variables $t = T - t - \tau_1$ and $x = x - \xi_1$ and considering (2.34), we obtain the solution of problem (2.37). The functional (2.38) then becomes

$$J = \frac{Q}{2\sqrt{\mu\pi}}\int\limits_0^{\tau_1}\exp\left\{-\left[\sigma(\tau_1 - \tau) + \frac{(x_0 - \xi_1 + v(\tau_1 - \tau))^2}{4\mu(\tau_1 - \tau)}\right]\right\}d\tau.$$

Another application of dual equations is provided by the problem of emission from the source moving on a plane.

E x a m p l e 3. Let the impurity spread be described by the equation

$$\frac{\partial q}{\partial t} + v_1\frac{\partial q}{\partial x} + v_2\frac{\partial q}{\partial y} + \sigma q - \mu\Delta = \sum_{i=1}^n Q_i\delta(r - r_1)\delta(t - \tau_1);$$

$$q \to 0 \text{ as } |r| \to \infty; \quad q(T, x, y) = q(0, x, y) = 0.$$

Here the area G is the whole plane; $r = (x, y)$; Q_i is the emission capacity of the source at the time τ_i when it is at the point $r_i = (x_i, y_i)$, $0 \le \tau_i < T$, $i = 1, 2, \ldots, n$.

The functional will be taken to be the pollution level at the point r_T at the time T.

The dual of problem (2.39) is

$$-\frac{\partial q^*}{\partial t} - v_1 \frac{\partial q^*}{\partial x} - v_2 \frac{\partial q^*}{\partial y} + \sigma q^* - \mu \Delta q^* =$$

$$= \delta^*(r - r_T)\delta(t - T); \; .$$

$$q^* \to 0 \text{ as } |r| \to \infty; \qquad q^*(0, x, y) = q^*(T, x, y) = 0.$$

To solve the primal and dual problems, we may represent q and q^* as follows:

$$q = \sum_{i=1}^{n} q_i, \qquad q^* = \sum_{i=1}^{n} q_i^*,$$

where q_i is a solution of the problem

$$\frac{\partial q_i}{\partial t} + v_i \frac{\partial q_i}{\partial y} + \sigma q_i - \mu \Delta q_i = Q_i \delta(r - r_i)\delta(t - t_i); \qquad (2.40)$$

$$q_i = 0 \text{ at } t = 0; \qquad q_i \to 0 \text{ as } |r| \to \infty,$$

while q_i^* is a solution of the dual of problem (2.40)

$$\frac{\partial q_i^*}{\partial t} - v_1 \frac{\partial q_i^*}{\partial x} - v_2 \frac{\partial d_i^*}{\partial x} + \sigma q_i^* - \mu \Delta q_i^* = \delta(r - r_T)\delta(t - T), \qquad (2.41)$$

$$q_i^* = 0 \text{ at } t = T; \qquad q_i^* \to 0 \text{ as } |r| \to \infty.$$

Let the functional of the primal problem (2.40) be

$$J_i = q_i(r_T, T), \qquad (2.42)$$

and let its dual representation be

$$J_i = Q_i q_i^*(r_i, \tau_i). \qquad (2.43)$$

Solution of problems (2.40) and (2.41) can be obtained by analogy with the one-dimensional case of the preceding problem. Note that in the derivation of the formulas given below it is assumed that $v_1 = \text{const } v_2 = \text{const}$. To solve the primal and dual problems we have the following formulas:

$$q_i = \begin{cases} \dfrac{Q_i}{4\pi\mu(t - \tau_i)} \exp\left\{ -\sigma(t - \tau_i) - \dfrac{[y - y_i - v_2(t - \tau_i)]^2}{4\mu(t - \tau_i)} - \right. \\ \left. - \dfrac{[x - x_i - v_1(t - \tau_i)]^2}{4\mu(t - \tau_i)} \right\}, & t \in (\tau_i, T), \\ 0, & t \in [0, \tau_i], \end{cases}$$

$$q_i^* = \begin{cases} \dfrac{1}{4\pi\mu(T - t)} \exp\left\{ -\sigma(T - t) - \dfrac{[x - x_T - v_1(T - t)]^2}{4\mu(T - t)} - \right. \\ \left. - \dfrac{[y - y_T - v_2(T - t)]^2}{4\mu(T - t)} \right\}, & t \in [0, T), \\ 0, & t = T. \end{cases}$$

Considering that $J = \sum\limits_{i=1}^{n} J_i$, we obtain

$$J = \sum_{i=1}^{n} \frac{Q_i}{4\pi\mu(T - \tau_i)} \exp\left\{ -\left[\sigma(T - \tau_i) + \right.\right.$$

$$+ \frac{(x_T - x_i - v_1(T - \tau_i))^2 + (y_T - y_i - v_2(T - \tau_i))^2}{4\mu(T - \tau_i)} \bigg]\bigg\}.$$

This expression does not depend on which of the representations of the functional J_i is used, (2.42) or (2.43).

Although the above examples employ a large number of simplifying assumptions, they adequately describe the possibilities for dual equations to solve the problems of location of harmful impurity sources. Efficient application of dual equations is largely determined by correct statement of the problem and a proper choice of the functional for the primal problem and its dual representation. It is application of dual representation of the functional that permits a significant reduction in computations, because it obviates the need for multiple solution of the primal problem.

2.3   Optimization of Location of Industrial Enterprises

This problem arises in planning of economic development of areas with a clearly defined economic structure. In general, such areas are densely populated and have the recreation and other environmentally significant zones. Of course, these factors impose special restrictions on the location of enterprises.

Suppose we need to determine a construction site for a new enterprise so that its emissions would conform with sanitary standards for specified environmentally significant zones. The source of harmful impurity is located at a point $r_0 = (x_0, y_0, z_0)$ and its emission capacity is equal to Q. In this case the equation describing the impurity transfer is

$$\frac{\partial q}{\partial t} + v_1 \frac{\partial q}{\partial x} + v_2 \frac{\partial q}{\partial y} + v_3 \frac{\partial q}{\partial z} + \sigma q =$$

$$= \frac{\partial}{\partial z} \nu \frac{\partial q}{\partial z} + \mu \Delta q + Q \delta(r - r_0) \qquad (2.44)$$

with initial boundary conditions

$$q = q_0 \text{ at } t = 0; \qquad (2.45)$$

$$\partial q \partial z = \alpha q \text{ with } z = 0,$$

$$\partial q / \partial z = 0 \text{ with } z = H, \qquad q = 0 \text{ on } S. \qquad (2.46)$$

We impose on the solution the necessary conditions of smoothness and periodicity

$$q(T, r) = q(0, r).$$

We are required to determine an area $w \in G$, where the source of harmful impurity can be located so that emission concentration in environmentally significant zones $G_k (k = 1, 2, \ldots, m\}$ would conform with a specified sanitary standard c.

The functionals are taken to be the concentration value averaged over time and zones G_k

$$J_k = \frac{1}{T} \int\limits_0^T dt \int\limits_{G_k} q \, dG.$$

These functionals must satisfy the constraints

$$J_k \leq c, \qquad k = 1, 2, \ldots, m. \qquad (2.47)$$

This problem can be solved by exhausting the values r_0 in the region G, but this process is rather tedious. In practice, such exhaustion can be accomplished in a goal-oriented manner by taking into account air flows and using statistical methods. Both ways require substantial computations and are difficult even for present-day computers to implement. Application of dual equations, however, enables one to obviate numerous difficulties in finding solutions, because for each of the zones G_k one has to solve only once the corresponding dual problem. We shall now examine this algorithm.

First we determine areas w_k that are suitable for the siting of an emission source and take into account constraints (2.47) for the corresponding value k. The area W then can be obtained by intersection of the areas $w_k : w = \bigcap_{k=1}^{m} w_k$. To determine each of the areas, we shall formulate the corresponding dual problem and select functionals. The functional of the primal problem may be written as

$$J_k = \int_G \int_0^T dt\, p_k q \, dG,$$

where

$$p_k = \begin{cases} \dfrac{1}{T}, & r \in G_k, \\ 0, & r \overline{\in} G_k, \quad k = 1, 2, \dots, m. \end{cases}$$

The dual of problem (2.44)–(2.46) is

$$-\frac{\partial q^*}{\partial t} - v_1 \frac{\partial q^*}{\partial y} - v_3 \frac{\partial q^*}{\partial z} + \sigma q = \frac{\partial}{\partial z} \nu \frac{\partial q^*}{\partial z} + \mu \Delta q^* + p_k, \qquad (2.48)$$

$$q^* = q_T^* \text{ at } t = T, \qquad q^*(T, r) = q^*(0, r) = 0; \qquad (2.49)$$

$$\frac{\partial q^*}{\partial z} = \alpha q^* \text{ with } z = 0, \qquad \frac{\partial q^*}{\partial z} = 0 \text{ with } z = H, \qquad q^* = 0 \text{ on } S. \quad (2.50)$$

The dual representation of the functional J_k becomes

$$J_k = Q \int_0^T q_k^*(t, r_0) \, dt,$$

where $q_k^*(t, r)$ is a solution of problem (2.48)-(2.50).

Employment of dual representation of the functional makes possible determination of the area

$$w_k = \{ r = (x, y, z) \in G : Q \int_0^T q_k^*(t, r) \, dt \le c \}$$

for each $k = 1, 2, \dots, m$.

If the intersection $w = \bigcap_{k=1}^{m} w_k$ is nonempty, then the source can be sited at one of the points in the area w. Evidently such possibility always exists.

Suppose the area w is nonempty. Consider the minimax problem: evaluate $r_0 = (x_0, y_0, h) \in G$ for the expression

$$\max_k J_k(r_0) \rightarrow \min_{r_0 \in G^k},$$

where $G^h = \{r \in G : r = (x, y, h)\}$.

Basically we need to determine the point r_0, for which the maximum of the functional values J_k is minimum. Since the area w is nonempty, it is clear that the point r_0 must belong to this area. Hence, if the dual equation and duality condition are used for the solution of this problem, then the search for the solution can only be confined to the area w that is generally much smaller than G^h. This permits a substantial reduction in the requisite computations.

Sequential decrease of the constant c may ensure that the region G would be composed of a single element, which is exactly the sought-for point r_0. This enables one to abandon exhaustion of the values of r_0 in the region w in favour of exhaustion of the constant c.

We shall now provide strict calculations. Suppose the area w is made up of a single element r_0. Then we have $J_k(r_0) \leq c$, $k = 1, 2, \ldots, m$, in which case $\max_k J_k = c$. For every r' different from r_0, we may explicitly select a number ℓ such that $J_\ell(r') > c$, and hence

$$\max_k J_k(r') > c = \max_k J_k(r_0).$$

From this it follows that $c = \min_r \max_k J_k(r)$.

On the strength of the above reasoning we may suggest that industrial enterprises can be sited in environmentally significant areas by conforming with pollution standards only if the sanitary standard is related to the solution of the minimum problem as follows: $c \geq \min_{r \in G_k} \max_k J_k(r)$.

2.4 Assessment of Emission from Operating Industrial Enterprises

Suppose that in a region there are n operating enterprises with harmful emission sources. The sources are located at the points $r_i \in G, i = 1, 2, \ldots, n$ and have the emission capacity $Q_i >= 0$. We are required to determine permissible emission limits for these sources so that the emissions in an environmentally significant area $G_0 \subset G$ conform with a sanitary standard c.

The pollutant transfer will be described by the equation

$$\frac{\partial q}{\partial t} + v_1 \frac{\partial q}{\partial y} + v_2 \frac{\partial q}{\partial z} + \sigma q = \frac{\partial}{\partial z} \nu \frac{\partial q}{\partial z} + \mu \Delta q + \sum_{i=1}^{n} Q_i \delta(r - r_i). \qquad (2.51)$$

Initial boundary conditions are taken to be

$$q = q_0 \text{ at } t = 0; \qquad (2.52)$$

$$q = 0 \text{ on } S; \qquad \frac{\partial q}{\partial z} = 0 \text{ with } z = H, \qquad (2.53)$$

$$\frac{\partial y}{\partial z} = \alpha q \text{ with } z = 0, \qquad q(T, r) = q(0, r).$$

The functional is expressed as

$$J = \int_0^T dt \int_{G_0} pq \, dG, \qquad (2.54)$$

$$p = \begin{cases} 1/T, & r \in G_0, \\ 0, & r \overline{\in} G_0. \end{cases}$$

We shall solve the problem by employing the dual equation and the dual representation of functional (2.54).

The dual of problem (2.51)–(2.53) is

$$-\frac{\partial q^*}{\partial t} - v_1 \frac{\partial q^*}{\partial x} - v_2 \frac{\partial q^*}{\partial y} - v_3 \frac{\partial q^*}{\partial z} + \sigma q^* =$$

$$= \frac{\partial}{\partial z} \nu \frac{\partial q^*}{\partial z} + \mu \Delta q^* + p, \qquad (2.55)$$

$$q^* = 0 \text{ at } t = T, \qquad q^* = 0 \text{ on } S;$$

$$\frac{\partial q^*}{\partial z} = \alpha q^* \text{ with } z = 0, \qquad \frac{\partial q^*}{\partial z} = 0 \text{ with } z = H, \qquad q^*(T, r) = q^*(0, r).$$

The functional for this problem is taken to be the dual representation of functional (2.54)

$$J = \int_0^T dt \int_G q^* \sum_{i=1}^{n} Q_i \delta(r - r_i) \, dG = \sum_{i=1}^{n} Q_i \int_0^T q^*(r_i, t) \, dt.$$

Denote $A_i = \int_0^T q^*(r_i, t)\, dt$. Condition $J \leq c$ then may be written as

$$\sum_{i=1}^n A_i Q_i \leq c. \tag{2.56}$$

The set of permissible emissions is thus described by inequality (2.56).

The emission values $\overline{Q}_1, \overline{Q}_2, \ldots, \overline{Q}_n$ are called maximum permissible if

$$\sum_{i=1}^n A_i \overline{Q}_i = c.$$

It is clear that the solution of this equation is not unique. Therefore, in order to calculate maximum permissible emission, we need to use additional optimality criteria. For example, if the criterion is taken to be the total costs incurred by enterprises to keep emissions within a sanitary standard c, then the problem of determining maximum permissible emissions may be formulated as

$$\sum_{i=1}^n H_i(\overline{Q}_i) \to \min,$$

$$\sum_{i=1}^n A_i \overline{Q}_i = c, \qquad i = 1, 2, \ldots, n,$$

where $H_i(\overline{Q}_i)$ are the costs incurred by enterprise i to maintain its emission at the level $\overline{Q}_i$.

In practice, assessment of maximum permissible emissions is often governed by several optimality criteria. In this case, decisions on setting maximum permissible limits for emissions are to be harmonized by a number of parties concerned which have their own optimality criteria. This calls for game-theoretic analysis of situations (see Chapter 3).

Suppose the region G has environmentally significant areas $G_1, G_2, \ldots, G_m$, for which the sanitary standards are respectively $c_1, c_2, \ldots, c_m$. Then we need to consider not the functional (2.54) for problem (2.51)–(2.53) but m functionals

$$J_k = \int_0^T dt \int_G p_k q\, dG, \qquad k = 1, 2, \ldots, m,$$

where

$$p_k = \begin{cases} \dfrac{1}{T}, & r \in G_k, \\[2mm] 0, & r \overline{\in} G_k. \end{cases} \tag{2.57}$$

To solve this problem, we need to examine m dual problems

$$-\frac{\partial q^*}{\partial t} - v_1 \frac{\partial q^*}{\partial x} - v_2 \frac{\partial q^*}{\partial y} - v_3 \frac{\partial q^*}{\partial z} + \sigma q^* = \frac{\partial}{\partial z} \nu \frac{\partial q^*}{\partial z} + \mu \Delta q^* + p_k$$

with functionals

$$J_k = \int\limits_0^T dt \sum_{i=1}^n Q_i \delta_i (r - r_i) q_k^* \, dG = \sum_{i=1}^n Q_i \int\limits_0^T q_k^*(r_i, t) \, dt,$$

where q_k^* is a solution of problem (2.55) with the relevant boundary conditions $k = 1, 2, \ldots, m$ and $p = p_k$.

The conditions to be satisfied by the functionals J_k for each $k = 1, 2, \ldots, m$ are

$$\sum_{i=1}^n Q_i \int\limits_0^T q_k^*(r_i, t) \, dt \le c_k.$$

Denote

$$A_{ki} = \int\limits_0^T q_k^*(r_i, t) \, dt.$$

Then the set of permissible emissions is described by the system of inequalities $\sum\limits_{i=1}^n A_{ki} Q_i \le c_k, \ k = 1, 2, \ldots, m.$

2.5 Assessment of Emissions from a Mobile Source

Let the source movements in the region G be described by the function $r = r(t)$ such that the emission intensity for this source at the time $t_i (0 \le t_1 \le t_2 \le \ldots \le t_n < T)$ is Q_i, $i = 1, 2, \ldots, n$. The region G has m environmentally significant areas G_k, $k = 1, 2, \ldots, m$, for which sanitary standards c_k are specified. We are required to determine maximum permissible emissions for each of the instants of time $t_i, i = 1, 2, \ldots, n$, at which the emission concentration in each area G_k conforms with a sanitary standard.

For pollutants emission from a mobile source, the equation with initial boundary conditions may be written as

$$\frac{\partial q}{\partial t} + v_1 \frac{\partial q}{\partial x} + v_2 \frac{\partial q}{\partial z} = \frac{\partial}{\partial z} \nu \frac{\partial q}{\partial z} +$$

$$+ \mu\Delta q + \sum_{i=1}^{n} Q_i\delta_i(r - r_i)\delta(t - t_i), \qquad (2.58)$$

where $r_i = r(t_i)$;

$$q = 0 \text{ at } t = 0, \qquad q = 0 \text{ on } S;$$

$$\frac{\partial q}{\partial z} = \alpha q \text{ with } z = 0, \qquad \frac{\partial q}{\partial z} = 0 \text{ with } z = H;$$

$$q(0,r) = q(T,r).$$

The functional for the primal problem is

$$J_k = \int_0^T dt \int_{G_k} p_k q \, dG,$$

where p_k is of the form (2.57).

Following the adopted procedure, for each of the functionals J_k we construct the dual of problem (2.58)

$$-\frac{\partial q_k^*}{\partial} - v_1\frac{\partial q_k^*}{\partial x} - v_2\frac{\partial q_k^*}{\partial y} - v_3\frac{\partial q_k^*}{\partial z} =$$

$$= \frac{\partial}{\partial z}\nu\frac{\partial q_k^*}{\partial z} + \mu\Delta q_k^* + p_k$$

with initial boundary conditions

$$q_k^* = 0 \text{ at } t = T; \ q_k^* = 0 \text{ on } S;$$

$$\frac{\partial q_k^*}{\partial z} = \alpha q_k^* \text{ with } z = 0; \ \frac{\partial q^*}{\partial z} = 0 \text{ with } z = H;$$

$$q_k^*(T,r) = q_k^*(0,r).$$

The dual functional is of the form

$$J_k = \int_0^T dt \int_{G_k} \sum_{i=1}^{n} Q_i q_k^*\delta(r - r_i)\delta(t - t_i) \, dG = \sum_{i=1}^{n} Q_i q_k^*(r_i, t_i). \qquad (2.59)$$

Thus, the constraints to be satisfied by the magnitudes Q_i become

$$\sum_{i=1}^{n} Q_i q_k^*(r_i, t_i) \le c_k, \qquad k = 1, 2, \ldots, m.$$

This problem provides a framework for examining the control problem given below.

Suppose the movements of a mobile pollution source are described by the system of differential equations

$$\dot{r} = f(r, u, t), \qquad r(0) = r_0, \tag{2.60}$$

where u is the control for source movements. The constraints which ensure the existence and uniqueness of a solution to equation (2.60) are imposed on the function f and control u.

We choose the optimality criterion to be

$$\max_k J_k \to \min.$$

In this case, an optimal control is taken to be such that the movements of the mobile source minimize the pollution concentration that is maximum over all environmentally significant areas. By (2.59), the optimality criterion may be written as

$$\max_k \sum_{i=1}^n Q_i q_k^*(r_i, t_i) \to \min.$$

In this manner we may formalize the siting problem for urban highways, main roads in recreation areas, woods, etc.

In this chapter we attempted to outline some of the conservation problems and familiarize the reader with possible approaches to their solutions. The most interesting among these methods is that of siting industrial enterprises with due regard for pollution in environmentally significant areas, because this involves application of dual diffusion equations.

The potential of this method has been illustrated most clearly by specific examples. The reader who wishes to take a closer look at the division of mathematical ecology dealing with environmental pollution problems may refer to [22, 25, 26].

Chapter 3

GAME-THEORETIC MODELS FOR ENVIRONMENTAL CONTROL

In environmental management, allocation problems accounting for users interests arise where resources are in short supply. Mathematically, such problems can be formalized as follows [13].

Let us suppose that n users may use (accumulate) some resource whose volume is bounded by the magnitude of $A > 0$. Denote by x_i the resource volume to be used (accumulated) by the i-th user. The users receive a payoff depending on the vector values $x = (x_1, x_2, \ldots, x_n)$. The payoff is evaluated for the i-th user by the function $h_i(x_1, x_2, \ldots, x_n)$ if the total volume of the utilized (accumulated) resource does not exceed a specified positive $\Theta > 0$, i.e.

$$\sum_{i=1}^{n} x_i \leq \Theta, \qquad x_i \geq 0.$$

If the inverse inequality is true, then the payoff to the i-th user is computed by the function $g_i(x_1, x_2, \ldots, x_n)$. It is assumed that the resource has a sharp decrease in utility if $\sum_{i=1}^{n} \geq \Theta$, i.e. in this case

$$g_i(x_1, x_2, \ldots, x_n) < h_i(x_1, x_2, \ldots, x_n).$$

We shall consider a nonzero-sum game in normal form

$$\Gamma = \langle I, \{X_i\}_{i \in I}, \{N_i\}_{i \in I} \rangle.$$

where the players' payoff functions are defined by

$$H_i(x_1, x_2, \ldots, x_n) = \begin{cases} h_i(x_1, x_2, \ldots, x_n), & \sum_{i=1}^{n} x_i \leq \Theta, \\ g_i(x_1, x_2, \ldots, x_n), & \sum_{i=1}^{n} x_i > \Theta, \end{cases}$$

$$X_i = [0, a_i], \qquad 0 \leq a_i \leq A, \qquad \sum_{i=1}^{n} a_i = A, \qquad I = \{1, 2, \ldots, n\}.$$

The players in the game are resource users. This formalization enables one to obtain a variety of ways of allocating resources by applying optimality principles that are known in the theory of games as Nash equilibrium, strong equilibrium, etc. In sections 1 and 5 we will demonstrate the potential of this approach with examples of static and dynamic problems for emission assessment.

In practice, a sharp decrease does not necessarily occur in the resource utility if the total volume of the resource utilized (accumulated) by the users exceeds a specified quantity Θ. The utility decrease, however, may be justified from the environmental point of view, and penalties may be introduced for resource "overutilization". This brings about the problem of determining penalty sizes. It is common practice to determine penalty sizes in terms of resource renewal costs. In many cases penalties are charged either too high, which substantially complicates their collection, or too low so that the users prefer to pay a penalty rather than to conform with resource utilization standards.

It seems wise to adopt a method such that the penalty would exceed the amount of "payoff" to the user allowing for resource "overutilization". We shall use a static model for emission assessment to illustrate this method.

Solution of environmental problems requires substantial expenditures, which brings about the problem of efficient use of funds. In industrial areas various departments may cooperate to put into effect air and water pollution control measures, to utilize waste, etc. Such cooperation must take into account the interests of departments and enterprises in a given area. The situation can be analyzed in terms of a game theoretic approach. In section 6 we will provide a mathematical model for cooperation in effecting pollution control measures.

3.1 Static Model for Emission Assessment. Existence and Uniqueness of Nash Equilibrium

Let us suppose that in an industrial area there are n enterprises each of which has one emission source. In this area there is an environmentally significant zone Ω, where emissions must not exceed maximum permissible concentration. As indicated in Chapter 2 (see sec. 2.3), the emission concentration averaged over time and zone Ω for n sources can be approximately calculated by the formula

$$q = \sum_{i=1}^{n} c_i x_i, \qquad i = 1, 2, \ldots, n, \qquad 0 \le x_i \le a_i, \tag{3.1}$$

where $c_i > 0$ are the solution integrals for the dual turbulent diffusion problem that are governed by parameters of atmospheric transfer, location and technical characteristics of emission sources. Let $\Theta < \sum_{i=1}^{n} c_i a_i$ be the value of maximum permissible concentration of dangerous pollutants.

We consider enterprises to be players and construct the game modeling a conflict situation for air pollution. Suppose each enterprise i may cut down its operating costs by increasing emissions x_i. However, a penalty $s_i > 0$ may be imposed on enterprises if the pollution in zone Ω exceeds maximum permissible concentration.

Suppose player (enterprise) i has an opportunity to select values x_i from the set $X_i = [0, a_i]$. The players' (enterprises') payoff functions are of the form

$$H_i(x_1, \ldots, x_n) = \begin{cases} h_i(x_1, x_2, \ldots, x_n), & q \le \Theta, \\ h_i(x_1, x_2, \ldots, x_n) - s_i, & q > \Theta, \end{cases} \tag{3.2}$$

where $h_i(x_1, x_2, \ldots, x_n)$ are functions that are continuous and increasing in argument x_i.

The optimality principle in this game is taken to be a Nash equilibrium. By monotonicity of each payoff function $h_i(x)$ in argument x_i, equilibria are on a hyperplane $\sum_{i=1}^{n} c_i x_i = \Theta$. Indeed, suppose the situation $x^0 = (x_1^0, x_2^0, \ldots, x_n^0)$ is equilibrium and such that $\sum_{i=1}^{n} c_i x_i^0 < \Theta$. Then there is $j \in I$ such that $x_j^0 < a_j$ $x_j' \in (x_j^0, a_j]$, in which case $\sum_{i=1, i \ne j}^{n} c_i x_i + x_j' c_j \le \Theta$. By monotonicity of function h_j we have $h_j(x^0) < h_j(x^0 \| x_j')$, or

$$H_j(x^0) = h_j(x^0) < h_j(x^0 \| x_j') = H_j(x^0 \| x_j').$$

If, however, $\sum_{i=1}^{n} c_i x_i^0 > \Theta$ and there is $j \in I$, such that $x_j^0 < a_j$ then apparently $h_j(x^0\|a_j) > h_j(x^0)$, or

$$H_j(x^0\|a_j) = h_j(x^0\|a_j) - s_j > h_j(x^0) - s_j > H_j(x^0).$$

Hence, x^0 is not an equilibrium.

In what follows, dealing with the existence of equilibria we shall mean equilibria in pure strategies without regard for the existence of equilibria in mixed strategies [5].

The equilibrium x is called admissible if $\sum_{i=1}^{n} c_i x_i \leq \Theta$, while the set of admissible equilibria is called an optimal solution in the game Γ.

We assume that an optimal solution exists and $x^* = (x_1^*, x_2^*, \ldots, x_n^*)$ is an admissible equilibrium. Let us select the value of x_i^* as a maximum permissible emission from enterprise i. The values of x_i^* have two important properties: first, if the emissions from enterprises do not exceed the values of x_i^*, then the pollution in zone Ω does not exceed maximum permissible concentration; second, if the emissions are above the maximum permissible concentration, this places enterprises at a disadvantage reducing their payoffs.

Following are examinations of games in which the existence and uniqueness conditions are provided for equilibria in pure strategies and optimal solutions are indicated.

1.Let us consider a noncooperative game

$$\Gamma_1 = \langle I, \{X_i\}_{i \in I}, \{H_i\}_{i \in I} \rangle,$$

in which the payoff functions are given by

$$H_i(x_1, \ldots, x_n) = \begin{cases} h_i(q), & q \leq \Theta, \\ h_i(q) - s_i, & q > \Theta, \end{cases} \qquad (3.3)$$

$$q = \sum_{i=1}^{n} c_i x_i,$$

where $h_i(q)$ are continuous and increasing. The function H_i is plotted in Fig.3.

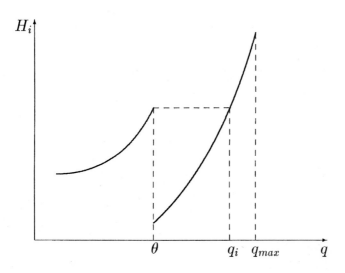

Fig. 3.

Let $q_{\max} = \sum\limits_{i \in I} c_i a_i$ and let $K \subseteq I$ be the set of players for which there exist $q_j \in (\Theta, \Theta + c_j a_j)$, $j \in K$, such that $h_j(\Theta) = h_j(q_j) - s_j$, $j \in K$.

Theorem 1. The set of solutions of the system

$$\sum_{i=1}^{n} c_i x_i = \Theta, \qquad 0 \leq x_i \leq a_i,$$

$$q_j - \sum_{i \in I, i \neq j} c_i x_i \geq c_j a_j, \qquad j \in K, \qquad c_j > 0, \tag{3.4}$$

coincides with the set of admissible equilibria in the game Γ_1.

P r o o f. Suppose the set K is nonempty. For some solution of (3.4) let there be $j \in K$ and values $x'_j \in [0, a_j]$, such that $H_j(x \| x'_j) > H_j(x)$. Assume that $x'_j < x_j$. Then

$$\sum_{i \in I, i \neq j} c_i x_i + c_j x'_j < \Theta,$$

and hence

$$H_j(x \| x'_j) = h_j \Big(\sum_{i \in I, i \neq j} c_i x_i + c_j x'_j \Big),$$

but since the function $h_j(q)$ is increasing and $H_j(x) = h_j(\Theta)$, there must be $H_j(x\|x'_j) < H_j(x)$. Now let $x'_j > x_j$. Then

$$\sum_{i \in I, i \neq j} c_i x_i + c_j x'_j > \Theta,$$

$$H_j(x\|x'_j) = h_j\Big(\sum_{i \in I, i \neq j} c_i x_i + c_j x'_j \Big) - s_j.$$

From conditions (3.4) we have

$$q_j \geq \sum_{i \in I, i \neq j} c_i x_i + c_j a_j \geq \sum_{i \in I, i \neq j} c_i x_i + c_j x'_j,$$

hence

$$h_j(q_j) \geq h_j\Big(\sum_{i \in I, i \neq j} c_i x_i + c_j x'_j \Big).$$

Thus we obtain

$$H_j(x\|x'_j) = h_j\Big(\sum_{i \in I, i \neq j} c_i x_i + c_j x'_j \Big) - s_j \leq h_j(q_j) - s_j = h_j(\Theta) = H_j(x),$$

or

$$H_j(x\|x_j) \leq H_j(x).$$

Therefore, for all $j \in K$ and $x'_j \in [0, a_j]$ there is $H_j(x\|x'_j) \leq H_j(x)$.

For any player $p \in I \setminus K$ $h_p(\Theta) > h_p(q) - s_j$ for any values $q \in [\Theta, \Theta + c_p a_p]$ and $h_p(\Theta) \geq h_p(q)$ for $q \in [0, \Theta]$. Hence, $H_j(x\|x'_p) \leq H_p(x)$ for any $x'_p \in [0, a_p]$.

We shall now show that any admissible equilibrium is a solution of system (3.4). Indeed, suppose an admissible equilibrium x is not a solution of system (3.4); then for some $j \in K$

$$q_j - \sum_{i \in I, i \neq j} c_i x_i < c_j a_j.$$

Hence, by monotonicity of function h_j,

$$H_j(x\|a_j) = h_j\Big(\sum_{i \in I, i \neq j} c_i x_i + c_j a_j \Big) - s_j > h_j(q_j) = H_j(x),$$

i.e. x is not an equilibrium. The resulting contradiction completes the proof of the theorem.

System (3.4) may be written as

$$\sum_{i \in I} c_i x_i = \Theta, \qquad 0 \leq x_i \leq a_i,$$

$$q_j \geq \sum_{i=1}^{n} c_i x_i - c_j x_j + c_j a_j, \qquad j \in K,$$

or

$$\sum_{i \in I} c_i x_i = \Theta, \qquad x_j \geq a_j - \frac{1}{c_j}(q_j - \Theta), \qquad (3.5)$$

$$j \in K, \qquad 0 \leq x_i \leq a_i, \qquad i \in I.$$

Clearly system (3.5) does not always have a solution. The following lemma gives the necessary and sufficient condition for existence of solutions to this system.

L e m m a 1. If $\sum_{j \in K} c_j a_j \geq \Theta$, then for system (3.5) to have a solution, it is necessary and sufficient that the following condition be satisfied

$$\sum_{j \in K}(q_j - c_j a_j) \geq \Theta(|K| - 1). \qquad (3.6)$$

P r o o f. N e c e s s i t y. Let $x = (x_1, \ldots, x_n)$ be a solution to system (3.5); then

$$x_j \geq a_j - \frac{1}{c_j}(q_j - \Theta), \qquad j \in K.$$

Considering that $\sum_{j \in K} c_j x_j \leq \Theta$, we obtain

$$\Theta \geq \sum_{j \in K}(c_j a_j - q_j) + |K|\Theta.$$

We finally have $\sum_{j \in K}(q_j - c_j a_j) \geq \Theta(|K| - 1)$.

S u f f i c i e n c y . Inequality (3.6) may be written as follows

$$\Theta \geq \sum_{j \in K}(c_j a_j - q_j) + |K|\Theta.$$

We seek a solution of system (3.5) in the form

$$x_j = a_j - (q_j - \Theta)/c_j + \varepsilon_j, \qquad j \in K, \qquad x_j = 0, \qquad j \in I \setminus K, \qquad (3.7)$$

where ε_j satisfies inequalities $0 \leq \varepsilon_j \leq (q_j - \Theta)/c_j, \qquad j \in K$.

Let us select ε_j as follows

$$\varepsilon_j = \frac{q_j - \Theta}{c_j} \cdot \frac{\sum\limits_{j \in K}(q_j - c_j a_j) - \Theta(|K| - 1)}{\sum\limits_{j \in K}(q_j - \Theta)}.$$

By (3.6) and $q_j > \Theta$, both cofactors are nonnegative, and hence $\varepsilon_j \geq 0$. Show that $\varepsilon_j \leq (q_j - \Theta)/c_j$. This inequality can be derived from condition $\Theta \leq \sum\limits_{j \in K} c_j a_j$. Indeed,

$$\Theta \leq \sum_{j \in K} c_j a_j + \sum_{j \in K} q_j - |K|\Theta - \sum_{j \in K} q_j + |K|\Theta,$$

or

$$\sum_{j \in K} (q_j - c_j a_j) - \Theta(|K| - 1) \leq \sum_{j \in K} (q_j - \Theta).$$

It follows that

$$\frac{\sum\limits_{j \in K} (q_j - c_j a_j) - \Theta(|K| - 1)}{\sum\limits_{j \in K} (q_j - \Theta)} \leq 1$$

and hence

$$\varepsilon_j \leq (q_j - \Theta)/c_j.$$

Thus

$$x_j \geq a_j - (q_j - \Theta)/c_j.$$

It remains now to see whether the solution constructed from (3.7) satisfies condition $\sum\limits_{i \in I} c_i x_i = \Theta$. Indeed,

$$\sum_{i \in I} c_i x_i = \sum_{j \in K} c_j a_j - \sum_{j \in K} (q_j - \Theta) + \sum_{j \in K} c_j \varepsilon_j =$$

$$= \sum_{j \in K} (c_j a_j - q_j) + |K|\Theta + \sum_{j \in K} (q_j - \Theta) \frac{\sum\limits_{j \in K} (q_j - c_j a_j) - \Theta(|K| - 1)}{\sum\limits_{j \in K} (q_j - \Theta)} = \Theta.$$

R e m a r k. In the case $\sum\limits_{j \in K} c_j a_j < \Theta$ the solution of system (3.5) exists always. For example, vector x with components

$$x_j = a_j, \qquad j \in K, \qquad x_i = a_i \frac{\Theta - \sum\limits_{j \in K} c_j a_j}{\sum\limits_{p \in I \setminus K} c_p a_p} \qquad i \in I \setminus K$$

.

is a solution of system (3.5).

Based on Theorem 1 and the lemma proved above is the following assertion.

Theorem 2. Let $K \neq \emptyset$ and $\sum\limits_{j \in K} c_j a_j \geq \Theta$, $c_j > 0$. Then for the game Γ_1 to have an admissible Nash equilibrium it is necessary and sufficient that

$$\Theta(|K| - 1) \leq \sum_{j \in K} (q_j - c_j a_j). \tag{3.8}$$

It is of interest to consider the case where an optimal solution is unique.

Theorem 3. An admissible equilibrium in the game Γ_1 is unique if the following conditions are satisfied:

1) $\sum\limits_{j \in K} q_j = (|K| - 1)\Theta + \sum\limits_{j \in K} c_j a_j$,

2) $\sum\limits_{j \in K} c_j a_j \geq \Theta$.

P r o o f. Let us show that condition $\Theta < q_j \Theta + c_j a_j$, $j \in K$, and conditions 1) and 2) are consistent. Set $q_j = \Theta + c_j a_j - \eta_j$, $j \in K$. Condition 1) then may be written as $\sum\limits_{j \in K} = \Theta$. Since $\sum\limits_{j \in K} c_j a_j \geq \Theta$, there always exist the values η_j, satisfying condition 1). For example, it is possible to select η_j as $\eta_j = c_j a_j \Theta / \sum\limits_{j \in K} c_j a_j$.

Indeed, $0 < \Theta / \sum\limits_{j \in K} c_j a_j \leq 1$, therefore $0 \leq \eta_j \leq c_j a_j$ and the sum of all η_j is equal to Θ.

Let q_j satisfy condition 1). Take x to be

$$x_i = 0, \quad i \in I \setminus K, \quad x_j = a_j - (q_j - \Theta)/c_j, \quad j \in K,$$

and consider the sum

$$\sum_{i \in I} c_i x_i = \sum_{j \in K} c_j a_j - \sum_{j \in K} q_j + |K|\Theta.$$

Making use of condition 1), we obtain

$$\sum_{i \in I} c_i x_i = \sum_{j \in K} c_j a_j - \sum_{j \in K} c_j a_j - (|K| - 1)\Theta + |K|\Theta = \Theta.$$

Clearly the x_j satisfy the inequality

$$x_j \geq a_j - (q_j - \Theta)/c_j, \quad j \in K.$$

It remains to find out whether this admissible equilibrium is unique. Suppose the vector x' is something other than x and is an admissible equilibrium. Then x' satisfies the system of inequalities:

$$\sum_{i \in I} c_i x_i' = \Theta, \quad x_j' \geq a_j - (q_j - \Theta)/c_j, \quad j \in K.$$

Since x' is different from x, the equalities

$$\sum_{j \in K} c_j x_j = \sum_{i \in I} c_i x_i = \sum_{i \in I} c_i x_i'$$

imply that there is a player $j_0 \in K$ such that $x_{j_0}' < x_{j_0}$, and hence $x_{j_0}' < a_{j_0} - (q_{j_0} - \Theta)/c_{j_0}$, which contradicts to the fact that x' is a solution of system (3.5).

2. The problem will now be stated somewhat differently. We assume that the losses sustained by enterprise i comprise waste treatment costs and pollution tax. Let $f_i(a_i - x_i)$ be a continuous decreasing function which defines waste treatment cost, where x_i is emission from the i-th enterprise ($0 \leq x_i \leq a_i$), while $a_i > 0$ are maximum possible emissions from the i-th enterprise. The pollution tax is defined as $k_i \sum_{i=1}^{n} c_i x_i$, where $k_i > 0$. The quantity $k_i > 0$ is called the pollution price for enterprise i. Suppose that the condition

$$f_i(a_i - x_i') - f_i(a_i - x_i'') > k_i c_i (x_i'' - x_i')$$

holds for any i and for any x_i' and x_i'' such that $0 \leq x_i' < x_i'' \leq a_i$. This means that, with increasing emission, the waste treatment cost for the enterprise decreases at a higher rate than the pollution tax grows.

Denote

$$h_i(x_i) = -f_i(a_i - x_i),$$

$$H_i(x_1, \ldots, x_n) = \begin{cases} h_i(x_i) - k_i \sum_{i=1}^{n} c_i x_i, & q \leq \Theta, \\ h_i(x_i) - k_i \sum_{i=1}^{n} c_i x_i - s_i, & q > \Theta, \end{cases} \qquad (3.9)$$

$$q = \sum_{i \in I} c_i x_i, \qquad c_i > 0, \qquad s_i > 0.$$

Consider a noncooperative n-person game $\Gamma_2 = \langle I, \{X_i\}_{i \in I}, \{H_i\}_{i \in I} \rangle$, where $H_i(x_1, \ldots, x_n)$ are of the form (3.9), $X_i = [0, a_i]$. Denote by N the set of players for whom there is $h_j(0) > h_j(a_j) - k_j c_j a_j - s_j$, $j \in N$.

Theorem 4. The set of solutions of the system

$$\sum_{i=1}^{n} c_i x_i = \Theta, \qquad 0 \leq x_i \leq a_i,$$

$$h_j(x_j) - k_j c_j x_j \geq h_j(a_j) - k_j c_j a_j - s_j, \qquad j \in N, \qquad (3.10)$$

coincides with the set of admissible equilibria in the game Γ_2.

P r o o f. Suppose that $x = (x_1, x_2, \ldots, x_n)$ is a solution of system (3.10). For some $j \in N$ let there be a value $x'_j \in X_j$, such that

$$H_j(x \| x'_j) > H_j(x). \qquad (3.11)$$

Since $h_j(x_j) - k_j \sum_{i \in I} c_i x_i$ increases, $x'_j > x_j$ and hence

$$\Theta = \sum_{i \in I} c_i x_i < \sum_{i \in I, i \neq j} c_i x_i + c_j x'_j.$$

It follows that

$$H_j(x \| x'_j) = h_j(x'_j) - k_j \Big(\sum_{i \in I, i \neq j} c_i x_i + c_j x'_j \Big) - s_j,$$

therefore inequality (3.11) can be written as

$$h_j(x_j) - k_j c_j x_j < h_j(x'_j) - k_j c_j x'_j - s_j.$$

Considering that $h_j(x'_j) - k_j c_j x'_j < h_j(a_j) - k_j c_j a_j$, we obtain

$$h_j(x_j) - k_j c_j x_j < h_j(a_j) - k_j c_j a_j - s_j.$$

Since x is a solution of system (3.10), the last inequality may not hold for $j \in N$. Moreover, this inequality may not hold for $j \in I \setminus N$ because

$$h_j(x_j) - k_j c_j x_j > h_j(0) \geq h_j(a_j) - k_j c_j a_j - s_j, \qquad j \in I \setminus N.$$

We shall now show that any admissible equilibrium x^* is a solution of system (3.10). Suppose x^* is not a solution of (3.10). Then it is possible to select $j \in N$ such that $h_j(x^*_j) - k_j c_j x^*_j < h_j(a_j) - k_j c_j a_j - s_j$, and hence

$$H_j(x^*) = h_j(x^*_j) - \sum_{i=1}^{n} k_i c_i x^*_i < H_j(x^* \| a_j),$$

but this seems contrary to the fact that x^* is an equilibrium. This completes the proof of the theorem.

Denote by $x^0_j \in [0, a_j]$ $(j \in N)$ the value of x_j for which $h_j(x^0_j) - k_j c_j x^0_j = h_j(a_j) - k_j c_j a_j - s_j$. By the property of functions h_j, the value x^0_j is uniquely determined for each $j \in N$.

To find out whether there exists an optimal solution in the game Γ_2, we shall use the theorem given below.

Theorem 5. In order for the game Γ_2 to have an admissible equilibrium, it is necessary and sufficient that

$$\sum_{j \in N} c_j x_j^0 \leq \Theta. \tag{3.12}$$

P r o o f. N e c e s s i t y. Let $x = (x_1, x_2, \ldots, x_n)$ be an admissible equilibrium in the game Γ_2. Then for $j \in N$ there is

$$h_j(x_j) - k_j c_j x_j \geq h_j(a_j) - k_j c_j a_j - s_j = h_j(x_j^0) - k_j c_j x_j^0.$$

It follows that $x_j \geq x_j^0$ for $j \in N$. Since $\sum\limits_{j \in N} c_j x_j^0 \leq \sum\limits_{j \in I} c_j x_j \leq \Theta$, we have $\sum\limits_{j \in N} c_j x_j^0 \leq \Theta$.

S u f f i c i e n c y. Suppose inequality (3.12) is true. Consider two cases.
C a s e 1: $\sum\limits_{j \in N} c_j a_j \geq \Theta$. The solution of system (3.10) may be written as

$$x_j = x_j^0 + \varepsilon_j, \qquad j \in N, \qquad x_j = 0, \qquad j \in I \setminus N,$$

where

$$\varepsilon_j = (a_j - x_j^0) \frac{\Theta - \sum\limits_{j \in N} c_j x_j^0}{\sum\limits_{j \in N} (c_j a_j - c_j x_j^0)}.$$

Ensure that the previously constructed vector $x = (x_1, \ldots, x_n)$ is a solution of system (3.10). Since $\sum\limits_{j \in N} c_j x_j^0 \leq \Theta \leq \sum\limits_{j \in N} c_j a_j$, we have

$$0 \leq \frac{\Theta - \sum\limits_{j \in N} c_j x_j^0}{\sum\limits_{j \in N} (c_j a_j - c_j x_j^0)} \leq 1$$

and hence $x_j = x_j^0 + \varepsilon_j \leq a_j$, $j \in N$. Now $x_j^0 \leq x_j$ for $j \in N$; therefore

$$h_j(x_j) - k_j c_j x_j \geq h_j(x_j^0) - k_j c_j x_j^0 = h_j(a_j) - k_j c_j a_j - s_j.$$

It remains to verify $\sum\limits_{j \in N} c_j x_j = \Theta$.
Indeed,

$$\sum_{j \in N} c_j x_j = \sum_{j \in N} c_j x_j^0 + \sum_{j \in N} c_j \varepsilon_j = \sum_{j \in N} c_j x_j^0 +$$

$$+ \sum_{j \in N} (c_j a_j - c_j x_j^0) \frac{\Theta - \sum\limits_{j \in N} c_j x_j^0}{\sum\limits_{j \in N} (c_j a_j - c_j x_j^0)} = \Theta.$$

C a s e 2: $\sum\limits_{j\in N} c_j a_j < \Theta$. In this case, one of the solutions of system (3.10) is taken to be vector x, whose components are

$$x_j = a_j, \qquad j \in N, \qquad x_i = a_i \frac{\Theta - \sum\limits_{j\in N} c_j a_j}{\sum\limits_{i\in I\setminus N} c_i a_i}, \qquad i \in I \setminus N.$$

We have thus completed the proof of the theorem.

Uniqueness conditions for an admissible equilibrium in the game Γ_2 can be expressed in terms of the theorem below.

Theorem 6. Let $\sum\limits_{j\in N} c_j a_j \geq \Theta$. In order for an admissible equilibrium in the game Γ_2 to be unique, it is necessary and sufficient that

$$\sum\limits_{j\in N} c_j x_j^0 = \Theta. \tag{3.13}$$

P r o o f. N e c e s s i t y. Let $x = (x_1, x_2, \ldots, x_n)$ be a unique solution of system (3.10). Suppose that equality (3.13) is not true, i.e. $\sum\limits_{j\in N} c_j x_j^0 < \Theta$. In this case, if $\sum\limits_{j\in N} c_j a_j < \Theta$, then the optimal solution apparently is nonunique, for there exists the whole set of solutions x such that $x_j = a_j$, $j \in N$, while x_i, $i \in I \setminus N$, are determined from the condition $\sum\limits_{i\in I\setminus N} c_i x_i = \Theta - \sum\limits_{j\in N} a_j$. Therefore, we need to assume $\sum\limits_{j\in N} c_j a_j \geq \Theta$. Then there are always two players $j_1 \in I \setminus N$ and $j_2 \in N$ such that

$$0 < x_{j_1} \leq a_{j_1}, \tag{3.14}$$

$$x_{j_2}^0 \leq x_{j_2} < a_{j_2}. \tag{3.15}$$

Then the solution to system (3.10) is also provided by any vector x', whose components coincide with those of vector x, other than components x'_{j_1} and x'_{j_2}, which satisfy conditions (3.14), (3.15) and

$$c_{j_1} x'_{j_1} + c_{j_2} x'_{j_2} = c_{j_1} x_{j_1} + c_{j_2} x_{j_2}.$$

The resulting contradiction proves that $\sum\limits_{j\in N} c_j x_j^0 = \Theta$.

S u f f i c i e n c y . Suppose that equality (3.13) is true; then the unique solution of system (3.10) is vector x such that $x_j = x_j^0$, $j \in N$, $x_i = 0$, $i \in I \setminus N$.

Let x' be a solution of system (3.10) differing from x . Then it is possible to select a player $j \in N$, for whom $x'_j < x_j$. In this case, however,

$$h_j(x'_j) - k_j c_j x'_j < h_j(x^0_j) - k_j c_j x^0_j = h_j(a_j) - k_j c_j a_j - s_j,$$

which seems contrary to the fact that x' is a solution of system (3.10). This proves the theorem.

3.2   On Existence of Strong Equilibria

In section 3.1 we have defined an equilibrium as the set of n tuples of strategies under which no player can benefit from a unilateral change of his strategy. The previously obtained solutions, however, cease to be satisfactory if the possibility of players' cooperation is taken into account.

We shall define a strong equilibrium as the n tuple of strategies (which, as the occasion requires, may be selected jointly) such that there is no coalition $S \subseteq N$, which can increase the payoffs to its members by unilaterally changing their strategies if the other players do not change their strategies. The situation x^* in the game Γ is strong equilibrium if there are no $S \subseteq I$ and $x_S = \{x_j\}_{j \in S}$ such that $0 \geq x_j \geq a_j$ and $H_j(x^*\|x_S) \geq H_j(x^*)$ for all $j \in S$.

As before, the equilibrium is called admissible if $\sum\limits_{i=1}^{n} c_i x_i \leq \Theta$. An optimal solution is called the set of admissible strong equilibria.

We shall consider the existence of admissible strong equilibria in the game Γ_1. Note that the set of admissible strong equilibria is contained in the set of admissible Nash equilibria; therefore for any strong equilibrium $x = (x_1, x_2, \ldots, x_n)$ there is

$$\sum_{i \in I} c_i x_i = \Theta.$$

Recall that the payoff functions in the game Γ_1 are

$$H_i(x) = \begin{cases} h_i(q), & q \leq \Theta, \\ h_i(q) - s_i, & q > \Theta, \end{cases}$$

where $q = \sum\limits_{i \in I} c_i x_i$. Define the set $K \subseteq I$ to be the set of players for whom there exist values $q_j \in (\Theta, \sum\limits_{i \in I} c_i a_i)$ such that $h_j(q_j) - s_j = h_j(\Theta), j \in K$.

We shall consider auxiliary games Γ_S $(S \subseteq K)$. The set of players in the game Γ_S is made up of players who are not members of S, and coalition S acting as one player j_S. The strategy set of player j_S is defined as follows :

$$X_{j_S} = \{x_{j_S} : 0 \leq x_{j_S} \leq a_{j_S}\},$$

where $a_{j_S} = \sum\limits_{k \in S} c_k a_k$.

Denote $q_{j_S} = \max\limits_{k \in S} q_k$. Let $k_S \in S$ be a player for whom the value q_{k_S} is the largest of all q_j for $j \in S$. The payoff function of player j_S is

$$H_{j_S}(x) = H_{k_S}(x) = \begin{cases} h_{k_S}(q), & q \leq \Theta, \\ h_{k_S}(q) - s_{k_S}, & q > \Theta, \end{cases}$$

where $q = \sum\limits_{j \in I \setminus S} c_j x_j + x_{j_S}$. The payoff functions of the other players are defined as in the game Γ_1.

Denote by X^S the set of admissible equilibria in the game Γ_S, and by X_{Γ_1} the set of admissible strong equilibria in the game Γ_1.

Any admissible strong equilibrium $x^* \in X_{\Gamma_1}$ belongs to X^S for any $S \subseteq K$. Indeed, if x^* is an admissible strong equilibrium in the game Γ_1, then no coalition $S \subseteq I$ can increase the payoff to all its members by unilaterally changing their strategies. Hence, no player in the game Γ_S (including player j_S) would be able to change his strategy so as to increase his payoff. Thus, for any coalition $S \subseteq I$ there is an inclusion $X_{\Gamma_1} \subseteq X^S$, or $X_{\Gamma_1} \subseteq \bigcap\limits_{S \subseteq K} X^S$.

On the other hand, if $\bigcap\limits_{S \subseteq K} X^S \neq \emptyset$ and $x^0 \in \bigcap\limits_{S \subseteq K} X^S$, then for any coalition $S \subseteq K$ $H_{j_S}(x^0 \| x_S) \leq H_{j_S}(x^0)$. This means that no coalition $S \subseteq K$ in equilibrium x^0 would be able to increase simultaneously the payoff to all its players in the game Γ_1 by unilaterally changing their strategies. Any coalition $R \subseteq I$ $(R \neq \emptyset)$, such that $R \cap K \neq R$, has at least one player j, who is not a member of coalition K. For such a player $h_j(\Theta) \geq h_j(q) - s_j$ for any $q \in [0, \sum\limits_{i \in I} c_i a_i]$. Hence, coalition R would not be able to increase in equilibrium x^0 the payoff to this player. Thus, since in equilibrium x^0 no coalition $S \subseteq I$ can increase in the game Γ_1 the payoff to its players, $\bigcap\limits_{S \subseteq K} X^S \subseteq X_{\Gamma_1}$.

We finally obtain $X_{\Gamma_1} = \bigcap\limits_{S \subseteq K} X^S$.

By Theorem 1 the set of admissible equilibria in the game Γ_S coincides with the set of solutions to the system of equations and inequalities

$$\sum\limits_{i \in I \setminus S} c_i x_i + x_{j_S} = \Theta,$$

$$0 \leq x_i \leq a_i, \qquad 0 \leq x_{js} \leq a_{js}, \qquad x_j \geq a_j - (q_j - \Theta)/c_j,$$

$$j \in K_S, \qquad x_{js} \geq a_{js} - q_{js} + \Theta,$$

if $q_{js} < a_{js} + \Theta$, and the system

$$\sum_{i \in I \setminus S} c_i x_i + x_{js} = \Theta,$$

$$0 \leq x_i \leq a_i, \qquad 0 \leq x_{js} \leq a_{js}, \qquad x_j \geq a_j - (q_j - \Theta)/c_j,$$

$$j \in K_S \setminus S,$$

if $q_{js} \geq a_{js} + \Theta$. Here $K_S = \{j : j \in K \setminus S, q_j < \Theta + c_j a_j\}$.

The set of strong equilibria in the game Γ_1 coincides with the intersection of sets X^S over all $S \subseteq K$ and hence is defined by the system of equations and inequalities

$$\sum_{i=1}^{n} c_i x_i = \Theta, \qquad 0 \leq x_i \leq a_i, \qquad i = 1, 2, \ldots, n,$$

$$\sum_{j \in S} c_j x_j \geq \sum_{j \in S} c_j a_j - q_{js} + \Theta,$$

$$S \subseteq K. \tag{3.16}$$

If $q_{js} < \Theta + a_{js}$, then the necessary and sufficient condition for existence of an admissible equilibrium in the game Γ_S can be written according to Theorem 2.

$$\sum_{j \in K_S} (q_j - c_j a_j) + q_{js} - a_{js} \geq \Theta(|K_S| - 1). \tag{3.17}$$

If $q_{js} \geq \Theta + a_{js}$, then condition (3.17) becomes

$$\sum_{j \in K_S} (q_j - c_j a_j) \geq \Theta(|K_S| - 1).$$

Let us formulate the necessary and sufficient condition for existence of an admissible strong equilibrium in the game Γ_1.

Theorem 7. If $q_{js} < \Theta + a_{js}$ for all $S \subseteq K$, then in order that an admissible strong equilibrium exist in the game Γ_1 it is necessary and sufficient that

$$q_{jK} - \sum_{i \in K} c_i a_i \geq 0. \tag{3.18}$$

P r o o f. N e c e s s i t y. Let us consider the game Γ_K and write out for it the necessary and sufficient condition for existence of an admissible equilibrium (3.17). Since $K_K = \emptyset$, we get $q_{jK} - \sum_{i \in K} c_i a_i \geq 0$.

S u f f i c i e n c y. Suppose inequality (3.18) is true. Then inequality (3.17) is true for any $S \subseteq K$. Take $j \in K$ and see that inequality (3.17) is true for $S = K \setminus \{j\}$. Indeed, since

$$q_{jK} = \begin{cases} q_{jK \setminus \{j\}}, & \text{if } q_j \neq \max_{i \in K} q_i, \\ q_j, & \text{if } q_j = \max_{j \in K} q_i, \end{cases}$$

we have

$$q_{jK} \leq q_{jK \setminus \{j\}} + q_j - \Theta. \tag{3.19}$$

In fact, if $q_{jK} = q_{jK \setminus \{j\}}$, then assuming $q_j > \Theta$, we may write $q_{jK} \leq q_{jK \setminus \{j\}} + q_j - \Theta$. Hence (3.19) is true for this case. If, however, $q_{jK} = q_j$, then since $q_{jK \setminus \{j\}} > \Theta$, we get $q_j \leq q_j + q_{jK \setminus \{j\}} - \Theta$. Therefore, (3.19) is also true for this case. Inequality (3.17) may be written as $q_{jK} - a_{jK \setminus \{j\}} - c_j a_j \geq 0$. Using inequality (3.19), we obtain

$$q_{jK \setminus \{j\}} + q_j - \Theta - a_{jK \setminus \{j\}} - c_j a_j \geq 0,$$

or

$$q_j - c_j a_j \geq \Theta + a_{jK \setminus \{j\}} - q_{jK \setminus \{j\}}.$$

Suppose (3.17) is true for $S \subseteq K$. Show that it is also true for $S \setminus \{j\}$ $(j \in S)$. It can be readily shown that the inequality $q_{jS} \leq q_{jS \setminus \{j\}} + q_j - \Theta$ is true.

Inequality (3.17) may be rearranged to give

$$\sum_{i \in K_S} (q_i - c_i a_i) + q_{jS \setminus \{j\}} + q_j - \Theta - a_{jS \setminus \{j\}} - c_j a_j \geq \Theta(|K_s| - 1).$$

Finally we have

$$\sum_{j \in K_{S \setminus \{j\}}} (q_j - c_j a_j) + q_{jS \setminus \{j\}} - a_{jS \setminus \{j\}} \geq \Theta(|K_S| - 1).$$

Considering that $|K_S| - 1 = |K_{S \setminus \{j\}}|$, we have that the inequality (3.17) is true for coalition $S \setminus \{j\}$.

We shall now consider two cases:

C a s e 1: $\sum_{j \in K} c_j a_j \leq \Theta$. Since inequality (3.17) is here fulfilled, the solution of system (3.16) must exist. It is possible to point out, e.g., the following solution:

$$x_j = a_j, \qquad j \in K, \qquad x_i = a_i \frac{\Theta - \sum\limits_{j \in K} c_j a_j}{\sum\limits_{j \in I \setminus K} c_j a_j}, \qquad i \in I \setminus K.$$

It can be readily seen that $\sum\limits_{j \in I} c_j x_j = \Theta$ and for any $S \subseteq K$

$$\sum_{j \in K} c_j a_j \geq \sum_{j \in K} c_j a_j + \Theta - q_{js}.$$

C a s e 2: $\sum\limits_{j \subset K} c_j a_j > \Theta$. We seek a solution of the form

$$x_j = a_j - \frac{1}{c_j}\varepsilon_j, \qquad j \in K, \qquad x_i = 0, i \in I \setminus K.$$

Inequality (3.16) must hold for any $S \subseteq K$. Hence

$$\sum_{j \in S} c_j x_j = \sum_{j \in S} c_j a_j - \sum_{j \in S} \varepsilon_j \geq \sum_{j \in S} c_j a_j - q_{js} + \Theta,$$

or

$$\sum_{j \in S} \varepsilon_j \leq q_{js} - \Theta.$$

On the other hand, for $S = \{j\}$ $c_j x_j \geq c_j a_j - q_j + \Theta$, and hence $0 \leq \varepsilon_j \leq q_j - \Theta$.

Let us arrange q_j $(j \in K)$ in ascending order: $q_{j_1} \leq q_{j_2} \leq \ldots \leq q_{j_{|K|}}$. Select ε_{j_r} such that $\varepsilon_{j_1} \leq q_{j_1} - \Theta$, $\varepsilon_{j_r} \leq q_{j_r} - q_{j_{r-1}}$. If $l = \max\limits_{j_r \in S} r$, then $q_{j_l} = q_{js}$. Since $\sum\limits_{j \in S} \varepsilon_j \leq \sum\limits_{r=1}^{l} \varepsilon_{j_r}$, it is apparent that $\sum\limits_{j \in S} \varepsilon_j \leq q_{js} - \Theta$.

The above conditions are satisfied, say, by the following values ε_{j_r}:

$$\varepsilon_{j_r} = (q_{j_r} - q_{j_{r-1}})\frac{\sum\limits_{j \in K} c_j a_j - \Theta}{q_{j_K} - \Theta}, \qquad r = 2, 3, \ldots, |K|,$$

$$\varepsilon_{j_1} = (q_{j_1} - \Theta)\frac{\sum\limits_{j \in K} c_j a_j - \Theta}{q_{j_K} - \Theta}.$$

It is easy to verify that $\sum\limits_{i \in I} c_i x_i = \Theta$. Indeed,

$$\sum_{i \in I} c_i x_i = \sum_{j \in K} c_j a_j - \sum_{j \in K} \varepsilon_j = \sum_{j \in K} c_j a_j - \sum_{r=1}^{|K|} \varepsilon_{j_r} =$$

$$= \sum_{j \in K} c_j a_j - \sum_{j \in K} c_j a_j + \Theta = \Theta.$$

Thus the theorem is proved.

In the game Γ_2, the set of admissible strong equilibria coincides with the set of admissible Nash equilibria. In fact, any admissible Nash equilibrium x is an admissible strong equilibrium, for no effort by any one of the coalitions $S \subset I$ can give rise to an equilibrium x' so that $H_j(x) < H_j(x \| x')$ for all $j \in S$. This follows from the inequality

$$h_j(x_j) - k_j c_j x_j \geq h_j(a_j) - c_j k_j a_j - s_j$$

for any $j \in N$ and especially for $j \in I \setminus N$.

Conversely, any admissible strong equilibrium is an admissible Nash equilibrium.

Thus, in order to find admissible strong equilibria in the game Γ_2, we may use theorems from the preceding section.

3.3 Optimization of Selecting Pollution Penalty Sizes

In selecting penalty sizes, we shall be guided by the following principle: if the set of admissible or strong equilibria in the game Γ is not empty for the selected penalty system $\{s_i\}_{i=1}^n$, this penalty system and penalty sizes are thought of as being optimal.

Let us consider a simple example. Suppose an enterprise incurs waste treatment costs that are proportional to the waste volume and are evaluated by $m(a - x)$. In this case, the size of the penalty imposed on the enterprise for discharge $x > x^0$ is s. The losses sustained by the enterprise can be represented as

$$f(x) = \begin{cases} m(a - x), & x \leq x^0, \\ m(a - x) + s, & x > x^0, \end{cases}$$

where $m > 0$, $0 \leq x \leq a$, $s > 0$.

We assume that the enterprise seeks to minimize its losses. The minimum losses are

$$\min f(x) = \begin{cases} m(a - x), & x \leq x^0, \\ m(a - x) + s, & x > x^0, \end{cases}$$

or

$$\min_{x \in [0,a]} f(x) = \begin{cases} f(x^0), & m(a - x^0) \leq s, \\ f(a), & m(a - x^0) > s, \end{cases}$$

as the penalty size may be. Thus, if the penalty is not large, e.g., $s < m(a - x^0)$, the enterprise finds it more advantageous to pay a penalty than to process wastes.

Selection of pollution penalty sizes becomes more complicated as enterprises increase in number. We shall examine the possibilities of selecting penalty sizes by referring for the games Γ_1 and Γ_2.

1. Let us consider the game Γ_1. The payoff functions in this game are defined by

$$H_i(x_1, x_2, \ldots, x_n) = \begin{cases} h_i(q), & q \leq \Theta, \\ h_i(q) - s_i, & q > \Theta, \end{cases}$$

where $q = \sum_{i \in I} c_i x_i$ $(c_i > 0)$, while the functions $h_j(q)$ are continuous and increasing. In section 3.1 we have determined the quantities $q_j (j \in K)$ from the condition

$$h_j(\Theta) = h_j(q_j) - s_j, \qquad q_j \in (\Theta, \Theta + c_j a_j).$$

By monotonicity of functions h_j, penalties s_j can be uniquely expressed via q_j:

$$s_j = h_j(q_j) - h_j(\Theta), \qquad j \in K. \tag{3.20}$$

Let us consider the system of inequalities

$$\sum_{j \in I}(\alpha_j - c_j a_j) \geq \Theta(n - 1), \qquad \Theta < \alpha_j \leq \Theta + c_j a_j. \tag{3.21}$$

Let $\alpha^0 = (\alpha_1^0, \alpha_2^0, \ldots, \alpha_n^0)$ be a solution of this system. Set $q_j = \alpha_j^0$, $j \in I$ and choose penalties for players

$$s_j = h_j(\alpha_j^0) - h_j(\Theta), \qquad j \in I. \tag{3.22}$$

With such a choice of penalties, the set K coincides with I. Since α^0 is the solution of (3.21), there is $q_j = \alpha_j^0$, and hence the condition of Theorem 2 for existence of the admissible equilibrium is satisfied. Therefore, if the players' penalties are calculated from (3.22), then admissible equilibria necessarily exist.

Let us consider the system of inequalities

$$\sum_{j \in I}(\alpha_j - c_j a_j) \geq \Theta(n - 1), \qquad \Theta < \alpha_j \leq \Theta + c_j a_j, \qquad j = 1, 2, \ldots, n.$$

Let $\alpha^* = (\alpha_1^*, \alpha_2^*, \ldots, \alpha_n^*)$ be a solution of this system. Set penalties s_j as follows

$$s_j = h_j(\alpha_j^*) - h_j(\Theta), \qquad j = 1, 2, \ldots, n. \tag{3.23}$$

The quantities $q_j = \alpha_j^*$ here satisfy the conditions of Theorem 3, and hence an admissible equilibrium is unique.

For example, α^* can be chosen as follows:

$$\alpha_j = \Theta + \lambda \frac{c_j a_j}{\sum\limits_{j \in I} c_j a_j}, \qquad j = 1, 2, \ldots, n,$$

where $\lambda = \sum\limits_{j \in I} c_j a_j - \Theta$ is the difference between the maximum possible and the maximum permissible pollution level. Thus, choosing penalties s_j by (3.22) and (3.23), we ensure in one case the existence and in the other the uniqueness of an optimal solution.

2. Let us consider the game Γ_2. The payoff functions in this game are defined by

$$H_i(x_1, \ldots, x_n) = \begin{cases} h_i(x_i) - k_i \sum\limits_{i=1}^{n} c_i x_i, & q \leq \Theta, \\ h_i(x_i) - k_i \sum\limits_{i=1}^{n} c_i x_i - s_i, & q > \Theta \end{cases}$$

By hypothesis, the difference $h_i(x_i) - k_i \sum\limits_{i=1}^{n} c_i x_i$ is the function which is increasing in x_i. Therefore, the quantities x_j^0 (see sec. 1) are uniquely expressed via s_j, and conversely

$$s_j = h_j(a_j) - h_j(x_j^0) - k_j c_j(a_j - x_j^0), \qquad j \in K.$$

Set for $i = 1, 2, \ldots, n$

$$s_i = h_i(a_i) - h_i\left(\frac{a_i \Theta}{\sum\limits_{r \in I} c_r a_r}\right) - k_i c_i\left(a_i - \frac{a_i \Theta}{\sum\limits_{r \in I} c_r a_r}\right). \tag{3.24}$$

With such a choice of s_i, the set K coincides with I and $x_i^0 = a_i \Theta / \sum\limits_{r \in I} c_r a_r$. The vector x^0 satisfies the conditions for existence and uniqueness of an admissible equilibrium (3.12) and (3.13), since

$$\sum\limits_{i \in I} c_i x_i^0 = \sum\limits_{i \in I} c_i a_i \frac{\Theta}{\sum\limits_{i \in I} c_i a_i} = \Theta.$$

Thus the choice of penalties by (3.24) ensures existence and uniqueness of an admissible equilibrium.

We shall now discuss some examples.

E x a m p l e 1. Let $I = \{1,2\}$, $q = x_1 + x_2$, $0 \leq x_1 \leq 4$, $0 \leq x_2 \leq 5$, $\Theta = 6$. The player's payoff functions are of the form

$$H_1(x_1, x_2) = \begin{cases} x_1 + x_2, & q \leq 6, \\ x_1 + x_2 - s_1, & q > 6; \end{cases}$$

$$H_2(x_1, x_2) = \begin{cases} 3(x_1 + x_2), & q \leq 6, \\ 3(x_1 + x_2) - s_2, & q > 6. \end{cases}$$

Suppose the penalties are initially selected as follows: $s_1 = 2$, $s_2 = 1.5$. Using Theorem 2, we shall verify whether an equilibrium exists in this game. To do this, we define the values q_1 and q_2: $q_1 = \Theta + s_1 = 8$, $q_2 = \Theta + s_2/3 = 6.5$. In our example $K = \{1, 2\}$, therefore the condition for existence of an admissible equilibrium becomes $\sum_{i=1}^{2}(q_i - a_i) \geq \Theta$. Let us substitute the values q_i, a_i and Θ:

$\sum_{i=1}^{2}(q_i - a_i) = 5.5 < \Theta = 6$. Hence, the admissible equilibrium does not exist. We shall modify penalties in such a way that $\Theta + s_1 - a_1 + \Theta + s_2/3 - a_2 \geq \Theta$. This inequality can also be written as $s_1 + s_2/3 \geq a_1 + a_2 - \Theta = 3$. Select $s_1 = 4/3$, $s_2 = 5$. Recalculating the values q_j then yields $q_1 = 7\frac{1}{3}$, $q_2 = 7\frac{2}{3}$.

An optimal solution can be determined from (3.7):

$$x_i = a_i - \frac{1}{c_i}(q_i - \Theta) + \varepsilon_i,$$

where

$$\varepsilon_i = \frac{q_i - \Theta}{c_i} \cdot \frac{\sum_{i=1}^{2}(q_i - c_i a_i) - \Theta}{\sum_{i=1}^{2}(q_i - \Theta)}.$$

It follows that $\varepsilon_1 = 0$, $\varepsilon_2 = 0$, and the unique admissible equilibrium is

$$x_1 = 4 - \frac{4}{3} = 2\frac{2}{3}, \qquad x_2 = 5 - \frac{5}{3} = 3\frac{1}{3}.$$

Having selected penalties $s_1 = \frac{4}{3}$ and $s_2 = 5$, we can now determine maximum permissible emission for enterprise 1 as $2\frac{2}{3}$, and for enterprise 2 as $3\frac{1}{3}$. In this situation, no enterprise can benefit from exceeding MPE.

E x a m p l e 2. Suppose the game Γ_1 is played by three players $I = \{1, 2, 3\}$. The average pollutants concentration in zone Ω is calculated from the formula $q = x_1 + 2x_2 + 3x_3$; $a_1 = 2, a_2 = 1, a_3 = 2, \Theta = 7$.

The player's payoff functions are

$$H_1(x_1, x_2, x_3) = \begin{cases} 3(x_1 + 2x_2 + 3x_3), & q \leq \Theta, \\ 3(x_1 + 2x_2 + 3x_3) - 3, & q > \Theta; \end{cases}$$

$$H_2(x_1, x_2, x_3) = \begin{cases} 2(x_1 + 2x_2 + 3x_3), & q \leq \Theta, \\ 2(x_1 + 2x_2 + 3x_3) - 6, & q > \Theta; \end{cases}$$

$$H_3(x_1, x_2, x_3) = \begin{cases} x_1 + 2x_2 + 3x_3, & q \leq \Theta, \\ x_1 + 2x_2 + 3x_3 - 1, & q > \Theta. \end{cases}$$

We are required to find an admissible strong equilibrium in this game.

Let us calculate the values of q_j:

$$q_1 = (3\Theta + s_1)/3 = 8, \qquad q_2 = (2\Theta + s_2)/2 = 10, \qquad q_3 = \Theta + s_3 = 8.$$

The set K is composed of two players: $K = \{1, 3\}$. We may take q_{j_K} to be either q_1 or q_2. Let $q_{j_K} = q_1$. Inequality (3.18) holds for this case. Therefore the admissible strong equilibrium exists. As in the proof of Theorem 6, an optimal solution can be written as

$$x_j = a_j - \varepsilon_j/c_j, \qquad j = 1, 3, \qquad x_2 = 0,$$

where ε_j are

$$\varepsilon_1 = (q_1 - q_3)\frac{a_1 + 3a_2 - \Theta}{q_1 - \Theta} = 0,$$

$$\varepsilon_3 = (q_3 - \Theta)\frac{a_1 + 3a_2 - \Theta}{q_1 - \Theta} = 1.$$

Thus, one of the admissible strong equilibria in the game Γ_1 is the vector $x = \left(2, 0, 1\frac{2}{3}\right)$.

E x a m p l e 3. Let us consider the game Γ_2, in which $I = \{1, 2, 3\}$; $q = 2x_1 + 3x_2 + 4x_3$; $a_1 = 2$, $a_2 = 3$; $\Theta = 10$; the player's payoff functions are defined by

$$H_1(x_1, x_2, x_3) = \begin{cases} 3x_1 - k_1(2x_1 + 3x_2 + 4x_3), & q \leq \Theta, \\ 3x_1 - k_1(2x_1 + 3x_2 + 4x_3) - s_1, & q > \Theta; \end{cases}$$

$$H_2(x_1, x_2, x_3) = \begin{cases} 4x_2 - k_2(2x_1 + 3x_2 + 4x_3), & q \leq \Theta, \\ 4x_2 - k_2(2x_1 + 3x_2 + 4x_3) - s_2, & q > \Theta; \end{cases}$$

$$H_3(x_1, x_2, x_3) = \begin{cases} 5x_3 - k_3(2x_1 + 3x_2 + 4x_3), & q \leq \Theta, \\ 5x_3 - k_3(2x_1 + 3x_2 + 4x_3) - s_3, & q > \Theta. \end{cases}$$

Suppose the pollution price for each of the players is fixed and $k_i = 1$, $i = 1, 2, 3$. Select penalties s_i so that there will exist an admissible Nash equilibrium. We make use of the conditions

$$s_1 = 3a_1 - 3x_1^0 - 2(a_1 - x_1^0),$$

$$s_2 = 4a_2 - 4x_2^0 - 3(a_2 - x_2^0),$$

$$s_3 = 5a_3 - 5x_3^0 - 4(a_3 - x_3^0)$$

and express x_i^0 via s_i:

$$x_1^0 = a_1 - s_1, \qquad x_2^0 = a_2 - s_2, \qquad x_3^0 = a_3 - s_3.$$

Penalties are selected subject to $\sum\limits_{i \in I} c_i x_i^0 \leq \Theta$. Obtain

$$\sum_{i=1}^{3} c_i s_i \geq \sum_{i=1}^{3} c_i a_i - \Theta = 1, \qquad 2s_1 + 3s_2 + 4s_3 \geq 9.$$

Take $s_1 = 1.5$, $s_2 = 1$, $s_3 = 1.5$. Now find x_j^0:

$$x_1^0 = a_1 - s_1 = 0.5, \qquad x_2^0 = a_2 - s_2 = 2, \qquad x_3^0 = a_3 - s_3 = 0.5.$$

An optimal solution is determined from the formula $x_i = x_i^0 + \varepsilon_i$, $i = 1, 2, 3$, where

$$\varepsilon_i = (a_i - x_i^0) \frac{\Theta - \sum\limits_{i \in N} c_i x_i^0}{\sum\limits_{i \in N} c_i(a_i - x_i^0)}.$$

Substituting the values a_i, c_i, x_i^0, yields $\varepsilon_1 = 1/8, \varepsilon_2 = 1/12, \varepsilon_3 = 1/8$. It follows that the situation $x = \left(\frac{5}{8}, 2\frac{1}{12}, \frac{5}{8}\right)$ is an admissible Nash equilibrium.

Given the penalties $s_1 = s_2 = s_3 = 1$, it is necessary to establish a pollution price k_i for each enterprise so that $k_1 + k_2 + k_3 = 3$ and an admissible equilibrium exists. The quantities x_i^0 and s_i are related by the equations

$$x_1^0 = \frac{3a_1 - 2k_1a_1 - s_1}{3 - 2k_1} = a_1 - \frac{s_1}{3 - 2k_1},$$

$$x_2^0 = \frac{4a_2 - 3k_2a_2 - s_2}{4 - 3k_2} = a_2 - \frac{s_2}{4 - 3k_2},$$

$$x_3^0 = \frac{5a_3 - 4k_3a_3 - s_3}{5 - 4k_3} = a_3 - \frac{s_3}{5 - 4k_3}.$$

Hence, for an admissible equilibrium to exist, it is sufficient that

$$\frac{s_1}{3 - 2k_1} + \frac{s_2}{4 - 3k_2} + \frac{s_3}{5 - 4k_3} \geq \sum_{i=1}^{3} c_i a_i - \Theta,$$

or

$$\frac{1}{3 - 2k_1} + \frac{1}{4 - 3k_2} + \frac{1}{5 - 4k_3} \geq 11.$$

In addition, the following conditions are imposed on k_i

$$k_1 < \frac{3}{2}, \qquad k_2 < \frac{4}{3}, \qquad k_3 < \frac{5}{4}, \qquad k_1 + k_2 + k_3 = 3.$$

Take $k_1 = \frac{7}{8}$, $k_2 = 1$, $k_3 = \frac{9}{8}$. Compute x_i^0: $x_1^0 = 1.2$, $x_2^0 = 2$, $x_3^0 = 0$. In this case, the set N contains two players: 1, 2. Since $c_1 a_1 + c_2 a_2 > \Theta$, we seek a solution of the form $x_j = x_j^0 + \varepsilon_j$, $j \in N$, $x_3 = 0$, where

$$\varepsilon_j = \left(a_j - x_j^0\right) \frac{\Theta - \sum\limits_{j \in N} c_j x_j^0}{\sum\limits_{j \in N} c_i\left(a_j - x_j^0\right)}.$$

Obtain $\varepsilon_1 = 32/115, \varepsilon_3 = 8/23$. This results in the optimal solution $x = (170/115, 54/23, 0)$.

3.4 Assessment of Emissions with Regard for Market Influence

In the preceding sections the players' payoff functions were dependent on the amount of emissions from pollution contributors. The methods developed for such games, however, may also be applied to the games in which the players are agents of some market. In this case their income depends on the parameters of market and natural environment. This approach permits harmonization of players' interests both in production and environmental pollution.

We assume that n players (market agents) are producing and selling identical products. Player i's output of products per period $[0, T]$ is designated $y_i, 0 \leq y_i \leq b_i$. Following traditions of mathematical economics, player i's production costs are expressed by a convex function $f_i(y_i)$ that is continuous and satisfies the condition

$$\frac{df_i(y_i)}{dy_i} > 0.$$

If the market price for products is equal to π, then the income from sales with regard for production costs is expressed for player i as follows

$$P_i(y_i) = \pi y_i - f_i(y_i).$$

Production is assumed profitable for all players, i.e. there exists $y_i > 0$ for which $P_i(y_i) > 0$. Referring to [62, 63], we have that the emissions x_i from the player i's enterprise can be expressed in terms of output y_i by a convex nonnegative function $\varphi_i(y_i)$ that is continuous and such that

$$\frac{d\varphi_i(y_i)}{dy_i} > 0.$$

Then the pollution level in the area with a specified production output is evaluated by

$$Q(y) = \sum_{i=1}^{n} c_i \varphi_i(y_i), \qquad y = (y_1, \ldots, y_n).$$

Denote by $a_i = \arg\max\{\pi y_i - f_i(y_i)\}$. Notice that the function $P_i(y_i)$ is increasing on the interval $[0, a_i]$. Suppose the penalties imposed on players are $s_1, s_2, \ldots, s_n$, if the air pollution concentration $Q(y)$ exceeds a maximum permissible limit Q. The players' payoff functions then become

$$H_i(y_1, \ldots, y_n) = \begin{cases} \pi y_i - f_i(y_i), & \sum_{i=1}^{n} c_i \varphi_i(y_i) \leq \Theta, \\ \pi y_i - f_i(y_i) - s_i, & \sum_{i=1}^{n} c_i \varphi_i(y_i) > \Theta, \end{cases}$$

$$y_i \in [0, a_i], \quad i = 1, \ldots, n.$$

It is easy to see that we have the game in which the players' payoff functions have the properties that are similar to those discussed in the preceding sections. Therefore, the results obtained in those sections can be readily extended to this case.

Indeed, suppose

$$\sum_{i=1}^{n} c_i \varphi_i(a_i) > \Theta.$$

Let y_i^0 be a solution of the equation

$$\pi y_i - f_i(y_i) = \pi a_i - f_i(a_i) - s_i, \; y_i \in [0, a_i],$$

and let N be the set of players for whom the solution exists. In order for an (admissible) Nash equilibrium to exist in this game, it is necessary and sufficient that

$$\sum_{j \in N} c_j \varphi_j(y_j^0) \leq \Theta.$$

In a similar manner, we obtain the uniqueness condition for a Nash equilibrium

$$\sum_{j \in N} c_j \varphi_j(y_j^0) = \Theta.$$

It is clear that the above conditions make possible the method of selecting penalty sizes which ensure the existence and, if necessary, the uniqueness of Nash equilibrium.

The method of environmental monitoring based on selection of penalties for excessive pollution is not unique in this field.

Another method has been the focus of much discussion in literatures dealing with environmental monitoring problems [61]. Suppose each player pays an individual tax that is proportional to a pollution level and is assumed as

$$s_i = k_i \sum_{j=1}^{n} c_j \varphi_j(y_j), \qquad i = 1, 2, \ldots, n.$$

Player i's payoff function now takes the form

$$H_i(y_1, \ldots, y_n) = \pi y_i - f_i(y_i) - k_i \sum_{j=1}^{n} c_j \varphi_j(y_j).$$

In order that the production output y_i^* securing maximum income to the player should meet environmental quality requirements, it is sufficient that

$$\sum_{i=1}^{n} c_i \varphi_i(y_i) = \Theta.$$

The equation for finding an optimal value y_i^* is

$$\frac{\partial H_i(y_1, \ldots, y_n)}{\partial y_i} = \pi - f_i'(y_i) - k_i c_i \varphi_i'(y_i) = 0.$$

Hence the y_i^* can be expressed in terms of k_i

$$y_i^* = g_i(k_i).$$

Then we obtain the condition for selecting individual taxes for the players

$$s_i^* = k_i^* \sum_{j=1}^{n} c_j \varphi_j(y_j), \qquad i = 1, 2, \ldots, n,$$

where $k_i^*, \ldots, k_n^*$ is a solution of the equation

$$\sum_{i=1}^{n} c_i \varphi_i(g_i(k_i)) = 0.$$

3.5 Principle of Fair Distribution of Environmental Damages

We suppose that enterprises cause an environmental damage measured by an economic damage and are forced to pay a penalty equal to this damage. We shall consider the question of how the penalty is to be distributed among such enterprises if the damage caused is equal to C.

Suppose we are not in a position to determine which of the coalitions $S \subseteq I$ is damaging, i.e. causes a damage. However, we assume that the probability distribution for formation of a damaging coalition $p(S)$ has been specified.

Let $W(S)$ be a maximal damage that a coalition S is capable of doing if no damage is caused by the players who are not members of this coalition S.

The function $W(S)$ is said to possess the property that $W(S) \geq W(T)$ for any coalitions S and T such that $T \subseteq S$.

The penalty distribution $W(S)$ is determined for each coalition $S \subseteq I$ from the formula

$$\psi_i^S = \frac{W(S) - W(S \setminus i)}{\sum\limits_{i \in S} (W(S) - W(S \setminus i))} W(S), \qquad i \in S.$$

If $W(S) = W(S \setminus i)$, set $\psi_i^S = 0$. The quantity ψ_i^S can be interpreted to mean a maximal penalty for player i in coalition S.

The maximal coalition-average penalty for the player is determined as follows:

$$\overline{\psi}_i = \sum_{S \subseteq I} p(S) \psi_i^S = \sum_{S \subseteq I : S \ni i} p(S) \psi_i^S.$$

In a similar manner we determine the maximal coalition-average damage $\overline{W} = \sum\limits_{S \subseteq I} p(S) W(S)$.

The penalty distribution G is said to be equitable if the player incurs a penalty that is proportional to the quantity

$$\xi_i = \overline{\psi}_i / \overline{W}.$$

Show that $\sum\limits_{i \in I} \xi_i = 1$. Indeed,

$$\sum_{i \in I} \xi_i = \sum_{i \in I} \frac{\overline{\psi}_i}{\overline{W}} = \sum_{i \in I} \frac{\sum\limits_{S \subseteq I} p(S) \psi_i^S}{\sum\limits_{S \subseteq I} p(S) W(S)} =$$

$$= \frac{\sum\limits_{i \in I} \sum\limits_{S \subseteq I} p(S) \psi_i^S}{\sum\limits_{S \subseteq I} p(S) W(S)} = \frac{\sum\limits_{S \subseteq I} p(S) \sum\limits_{i \in I} \psi_i^S}{\sum\limits_{S \subseteq I} p(S) W(S)} =$$

$$= \frac{\sum\limits_{S \subseteq I} p(S) W(S)}{\sum\limits_{S \subseteq I} p(S) W(S)} = 1.$$

Principle of fair distribution. Distribution of charges is said to be fair if each player's share in damages is determined by

$$\xi_i = \overline{\psi}_i / \overline{W}.$$

In this case, if formation of any coalition is equiprobable, the ξ_i can be computed from the formula

$$\xi_i = \sum_{S \subseteq I} \psi_i^S \Big/ \sum_{S \subseteq I} W(S).$$

We will look closely at the case where formation of any coalition is equiprobable.

Let us introduce the notions of weak and strong damageabilities for coalition S. Weak damageability for coalition S is taken to mean a damage that is averaged over all coalitions R containing at least one player from S: $\frac{1}{2^n} \sum\limits_{R \subseteq I : R \cap S \neq \emptyset} W(R)$. Strong damageability for coalition S is taken to mean a damage that is averaged over all coalitions appearing in S: $\frac{1}{2^n} \sum\limits_{R \subseteq S} W(R)$.

It is apparent that for the coalition containing all players these two values coincide and are equal $\frac{1}{2^n}\sum\limits_{R\subseteq I} W(R)$. Consider the functions

$$\bar{v}_C(S) = \frac{\sum\limits_{R\subseteq I:R\cap S\neq\emptyset} W(R)}{\sum\limits_{R\subseteq I} W(R)} - C, \qquad \underline{v}_C(S) = \frac{\sum\limits_{R\subseteq S} W(R)}{\sum\limits_{R\subseteq I} W(R)} - C.$$

Show that the $\bar{v}_C$ is concave, i.e. $\bar{v}_C(S\bigcup T) \leq \bar{v}_C(S) + \bar{v}_C(T) - \bar{v}_C(S\bigcap T)$, $S \subseteq I$, $T \subseteq I$. Indeed,

$$\sum\limits_{R\subseteq I:R\cap(S\bigcup T)\neq\emptyset} W(R) \leq \sum\limits_{R\subseteq I:R\cap S\neq\emptyset} W(R) +$$

$$+ \sum\limits_{S\subseteq I:R\cap T\neq\emptyset} W(R) - \sum\limits_{R\subseteq I:R\cap(S\cap T)\neq\emptyset} W(R),$$

which proves the required concavity of the function $\bar{v}_C$. In a similar manner we may show that the function $\underline{v}_C$ is convex.

Take $\underline{v}_C$ to be the characteristic function of the game. Define the core of this game as a set of imputations $x = (x_1, x_2, \ldots, x_n)$, such that $x_i(S) \geq 0$, $x(S) = \sum\limits_{i\in S} x_i \leq \bar{v}_C(S)$, $S \subset I$. By the concavity of the characteristic function, the core is nonempty. Show that the imputation defined by the principle of fair distribution belongs to the core of cooperative game $\bar{v}_C$. Indeed,

$$x(S) = \sum\limits_{i\in S}\xi_i C = \frac{\sum\limits_{i\in S}\sum\limits_{R\subseteq I}\psi_i^R}{\sum\limits_{R\subseteq I} W(R)} C =$$

$$= \frac{\sum\limits_{R\subseteq S} W(R) + \sum\limits_{i\in S}\sum\limits_{R\subseteq S}\psi_i^R}{\sum\limits_{R\subseteq I} W(R)} C \leq \frac{\sum\limits_{R\subseteq S} W(R) + \sum\limits_{R\subseteq S:R\cap S\neq\emptyset} W(R)}{\sum\limits_{R\subseteq I} W(R)} C =$$

$$= \frac{\sum\limits_{R\subseteq I:R\cap S\neq\emptyset} W(R)}{\sum\limits_{R\subseteq I} W(R)} C = \bar{v}_C(S).$$

It can easily be shown that the inequality $\sum\limits_{i\in S}\xi_i C \geq \underline{v}_C(S)$ is also true.

Thus the imputation ξC satisfies the condition: $\underline{v}_C(S) \leq \sum\limits_{i\in S}\xi_i C \leq \bar{v}_C(S)$. Note that $\underline{v}_C(I) = \sum\limits_{i\in I}\xi_i C = \bar{v}_C(I) = C$.

We shall now show that if one of the inequalities is violated for coalition S, then the second inequality is violated for coalition $I \setminus S$, and conversely. Indeed, let $x(S) = \sum_{i \in S} \xi_i C < \underline{v}_C(S)$, then

$$x(I \setminus S) = \sum_{i \in I \setminus S} \xi_i C = (1 - \sum_{i \in S} \xi_i)C > C - \underline{v}_C(S) =$$

$$= \left(1 - \frac{\sum_{R \subseteq S} W(R)}{\sum_{R \subseteq I} W(R)}\right)C = \frac{\sum_{R \subseteq I : R \bigcap (I \setminus S) \neq \emptyset} W(R)}{\sum_{R \subseteq I} W(R)} C = \bar{v}_C(I \setminus S).$$

Thus we get the following properties:

1. $\bar{v}_C(S \bigcup T) + \bar{v}_C(S \bigcap T) \leq \bar{v}_C(S) + \bar{v}_C(T)$, $S \subseteq I, I \supseteq T$.
2. $\underline{v}_C(S \bigcup T) + \underline{v}_C(S \bigcap T) \geq \underline{v}_C(S) + \underline{v}_C(T)$, $S \subseteq I, T \subseteq I$.
3. $\{x : x_i \geq 0, \sum_{i \in I} x_i = C, \sum_{i \in S} x_i \geq \underline{v}_C(S), S \subseteq I\} =$
   $= \{x : x_i \geq 0, \sum_{i \in I} x_i = C, \sum_{i \in S} x_i \leq \bar{v}_C(S), S \subseteq I\}$.
4. $\underline{v}_C(S) \leq \sum_{i \in S} \xi_i C \leq \bar{v}_C(S)$, $S \subseteq I$.
5. If $W(S) = W(S \bigcup i)$ for any coalition $S \subseteq I$, then $\xi_i = 0$.
6. For any real number $k \xi^W = \xi^{kW}$.

3.6 Dynamic Model for Air Pollution Control

In the preceding sections we have discussed static models in which the intensities of harmful emissions were taken to be constants. Now it seems appropriate to examine models in which the emission intensities are functions of time. In setting maximum permissible limits, this will allow the use of the techniques of differential games and the notion of dynamic stability of solutions.

We assume that the intensity of maximum permissible emission from enterprise i at the time t is described by a nonnegative intergrable function $\gamma_i(t)$. Denote by $u_i(t)$ the intensity of emissions from enterprise i at the time t. Suppose that some expenditures enable the enterprise to completely separate the released aerosol from pollutants, and $u_i(t)$ satisfies the constraints

$$0 \leq u_i(t) \leq \gamma_i(t), \qquad i = 1, 2, \ldots, n, \qquad (3.25)$$

at each time $t \in [t_0, T]$.

In order to describe variations in average concentrations of emissions from several sources, we will use the turbulent diffusion equation (see sec. 1, ch. 2)

$$\frac{\partial q}{\partial t} + v_1 \frac{\partial q}{\partial x} + v_2 \frac{\partial q}{\partial y} + v_3 \frac{\partial q}{\partial z} - pq =$$

$$= \frac{\partial}{\partial z} \nu \frac{\partial q}{\partial z} + \mu(\frac{\partial^2 q}{\partial x^2} + \frac{\partial^2 q}{\partial y^2}) + \sum_{i=1}^{n} u_i(t) \omega_i(x, y, z). \qquad (3.26)$$

Here the x and y axes are lying in a horizontal plane, while the z axis is vertical; v_1, v_2, v_3 are the average velocity components for pollutants movements along the respective x, y, z axes satisfying the equation of continuity

$$\frac{\partial v_1}{\partial x} + \frac{\partial v_2}{\partial y} + \frac{\partial v_3}{\partial z} = 0.$$

The coefficient p describes variations in concentration caused by transmutation of pollutants. Coefficients ν, μ are selected in terms of the theory of statistic turbulence. The function $\omega_i(x, y, z) = \delta(r - r_i)$ specifies the location of source i, where $r = (x, y, z)$, $r_i = (x_i, y_i, z_i)$.

Equation (3.26) is given in domain $D \times \Xi$, where $D \subset R^3$ is a cylindrical region bounded by planes and piecewise smooth lateral surface G, and the set Ξ is of the form $\Xi = [t_0, T]$. Boundary conditions for equation (3.26) may be written as

$$a \frac{\partial q}{\partial z} + bq = 0 \text{ for } z = 0,$$

$$\frac{\partial q}{\partial z} = 0 \text{ for } z = z_H, \qquad q = 0 \text{ on } G. \qquad (3.27)$$

Here a and b are the given constants or the functions of x, y. Suppose that the concentration distribution is given at the initial time $t = t_0$ and is taken to be the initial condition for (3.26):

$$q(t_0, x, y, z) = q_0(x, y, z) \geq 0. \qquad (3.28)$$

The set U_i of measurable functions satisfying (3.25) is called the set of admissible controls for player i, and $U = U_1 \times U_2 \times \ldots \times U_n$ is the set of admissible controls in the game.

We assume that some conditions hold for the coefficients of (3.26) and boundary conditions (3.27). These conditions ensure the existence and uniqueness in space $H_2(D, \Xi)$ of the solution of (3.26) with initial boundary conditions (3.27), (3.28) for any $q_0 \in H_2(D)$ and $u \in U$, where $H_2(D, \Xi)$ is the Sobolev second-order space in the region $D \times \Xi$ of square summable functions such that for all variables there exist total derivatives up to second order inclusive [24].

The solution $q(t, x, y, z, t_0, q_0, u_1, u_2, \ldots, u_n)$ of equation (3.26) with initial boundary conditions (3.27),(3.28) specifies the pollutants concentration distribution at the time t resulting from the release $u_i(\tau)$, $0 \le \tau < t$.

Let I denote the set of players (enterprises) as before. The player's payoff is defined as the enterprise expenditures reversed in sign. The enterprise draws income depending on whether it has an opportunity to discharge pollutants or is forced to allocate funds for their treatment. Integral income that the enterprise draws at the time t may be written as $\int_{t_0}^{t} h_i(u_i(\tau)) \, d\tau$, where $h_i(u_i(\tau))$ is a nonnegative integrable function such that at any fixed time τ_0 the function $h_i(u_i)$ is monotone increasing in u_i, $0 \le u_i \le \gamma_i(\tau_0)$. Suppose the enterprise pays a pollution "tax" depending on the air pollutants concentration in a region which is evaluated by the pollutants concentration averaged over time and area Ω. Define the pollution "tax" for enterprise i as follows

$$\int\limits_{t_0}^{t} \int\limits_{\Omega} c_i(x, y, z) q(\tau, x, y, z) \, d\Omega \, d\tau, \qquad \Omega \in D,$$

where $c_i(x, y, z)$ is the nonnegative integrable function which permits specification of tax values for each of the players. Finally, we assume that the enterprise may incur a penalty if the air pollutants concentration exceeds the maximum permissible limit. Let the penalty be given by the function

$$s_i = \begin{cases} H_i(\int\limits_{t_0}^{T} \int_{\Omega} q(\tau, x, y, z) \, d\Omega \, d\tau), & \frac{1}{T - t_0} \int\limits_{t_0}^{T} \int_{\Omega} q(\tau, x, y, z) \, d\Omega \, d\tau > \Theta, \\ 0, & \frac{1}{T - t_0} \int\limits_{t_0}^{T} \int_{\Omega} q(\tau, x, y, z) \, d\Omega \, d\tau \le \Theta, \end{cases}$$

where Θ is the average maximum permissible concentration of pollutants. Now we may define the payoffs to players as follows:

$$K^i(q(t, x, y, z), u_i(t)) = \int\limits_{t_0}^{T} h_i(u_i(\tau)) \, d\tau -$$

$$- \int\limits_{t_0}^{T} \int\limits_{\Omega} c_i(x, y, z) q(\tau, x, y, z) \, d\tau \, d\Omega - s_i.$$

Admissible strategies for players are taken to be piecewise open-loop [36]. Denote by $U_i([t_1, t_2])$ the set of all restrictions of player i's admissible controls onto the interval $[t_1, t_2)$, $t_0 < t_2 \leq T$. Let $\Delta_i = \{t_0 = t_0^i < t_1^i < \ldots < t_{m_i}^i = T\}$ be partitions of the interval $[t_0, T]$, $i = 1, 2, \ldots, n$.

D e f i n i t i o n 1. The pair $u_i(\cdot) = \{\Delta_i, a_i\}$, $a_i = (a_i^0, a_i^1, \ldots, a_i^{m_i-1})$, where $a_i^{k_j}$ is the mapping which places the time $t_{k_j}^i$ and the state $q(t_{k_j}^i, x, y, z)$ in correspondence with an open-loop control $u(t_i^{k_j}) \in U([t_{k_j}^i, t_{k_j+1}^i))$, is called player i's piecewise open-loop strategy.

Denote by $X_i = \{u_i(\cdot)\}$ the set of piecewise open-loop strategies for player i, and by $u = (u_1(\cdot), \ldots, u_n(\cdot))$ a situation in the game. The set of all situations in the game is designated $X = X_1 \times X_2 \times X_3 \ldots \times X_n$.

We shall show that each situation $(u_1(\cdot), u_2(\cdot), \ldots, u_n(\cdot))$ determines a trajectory that is unique in the space $H_2(\Xi, D)$. Suppose that at the initial time in the state $q_0(x, y, z) \in H_2(D)$ the players choose their piecewise open-loop strategies $u_1 = (\Delta_1, a_1)$, $u_2 = (\Delta_2, a_2), \ldots, u_n = (\Delta_n, a_n)$. Arrange the numbers $t_{k_j}^i$ in ascending order. Then we get a sequence $t_0 < t_1 \leq \ldots \leq t_m = T$, $m = m_1 + m_2 + \ldots + m_n$. At the initial time the players choose according to a_i^0 their controls

$$u_i^0(t) = a_i(t_0, a_0) \in U_i([t_0, t_1^i)), \qquad t \in [t_0, t_1^i)$$

and keep them unchanged until the time t_1^i. Denote by $I_1 \subset I$ the set of players for which $t_1 = t_1^i$, $i \in I_1$.

Denote by $u_i([\tau_1, \tau_2))$ player i's control on the interval $[\tau_1, \tau_2)$. The players from I_1 choose at the time t_i new controls $u_i([t_1, t_2))i \in I_1$. In this case,

$$u_i^1([t_1, t_2^i)) = a_1(t_1, x, y, z, t_0, q_0, u_1(\tau), \ldots, u_n(\tau)),$$

where $q(t_1, x, y, z, t_0, q_0, u_1(\tau), \ldots, u_n(\tau)) \in H_2(D)$ is the solution of (3.26) with initial boundary conditions (3.27), (3.28) at the time t_1 under admissible controls $u_i(\tau) = u_i([t_0, t_1^i))$. Suppose the set I_1 consists of l players. Then $t_1 = t_2 = \ldots = t_l < t_{l+1}$. Denote $I_{21} = \{i \in I; t_{l+1} = t_1^i\}$, $I_{22} = \{i \in I, t_{l+1} = t_2^i\}$. Note that $I_{21} \bigcap I_{22} = \emptyset$.

The players from I_{21} choose at the time t_{l+1} the control

$$u_i^1([t_{l+1}, t_2^i)) = a_i(t_{l+1}, q(t_{l+1}, x, y, z, t_0, q_0, u_1(\tau), \ldots, u_n(\tau))),$$

where $i \in I_{21}$, $q(t_{l+1}, x, y, z, t_0, q_0, u_1(\tau), \ldots, u_n(\tau)) \in H_2(D)$ is the solution of (3.26) at the time t_{l+1} with initial boundary conditions (3.27), (3.28). The players from I_{22} choose the controls

$$u_i^0([t_{l+1}, t_3^i)) = a_i(t_{l+1}, q(t_{l+1}, x, y, z, t_0, q_0, u_1(\tau), \ldots, u_n(\tau))),$$

in which case the controls $u_i(\tau)$ for $\tau \in [t_1, t_{l+1})$ become

$$u_i(\tau) = \begin{cases} u_i^0([t_1, t_{l+1})), & i \in I \setminus I_1, \\ u_i^1([t_1, t_{l+1})), & i \in I_1. \end{cases}$$

Following this route, we obtain a unique set of controls $u = (u_1(t), \ldots, u_n(t))$, generated by strategies $u_1(\cdot), \ldots, u_n(\cdot)$. Since the resulting control $u \in U(\Xi) \subset H_2(\Xi)$, it determines the solution $q(t, x, y, z, t_0, q_0, u_1(t), u_2(t), \ldots, u_n(t))$ that is unique in the space $H_2(D, \Xi)$. Therefore, each situation $u(\cdot) = (u_1(\cdot), \ldots, u_n(\cdot)) \in X$ determines a trajectory that is unique in $H_2(D, \Xi)$. Since, $u(t) \subset U$ and $q(t, x, y, z, t_0, q_0, u_1(t), \ldots, u_n(t)) \in H_2$, the functional $K^i(q(t, x, y, z)), u_i(t))$ is uniquely determined, and hence player i's payoff function is defined on the set of situations X

$$K_{t_0 q_0}^i(u_1(\cdot), \ldots, u_n(\cdot)) = K_i(t_0, q_0, u_1, u_2, \ldots, u_n) =$$

$$= K^i(q(t, x, y, z), u_i(t)).$$

We have thus defined an n-person differential game in normal form with prescribed duration $T - t_0$, whose dynamics is given by (3.26) with initial boundary conditions (3.27), (3.28):

$$\Gamma(t_0, q_0) = \langle X_i, K_{t_0, q_0}^i, i \in I \rangle.$$

Once the problem has been formalized to be an n-person differential game, the choice of an optimality principle becomes crucial. The payoffs are considered to be transferable, i.e. each player may transfer part of his payoff to other players. This allows the players to form coalitions in order to increase their total payoff and distribute it in accordance with the chosen principle of optimality. To examine the possibilities of such behavior, we shall construct a dynamic cooperative game.

We suppose that coalition S has been formed. Then the set of players from this coalition is recognized as one player with the set of strategies

$$X_S = \prod_{i \in S} X_i = \{u_S(\cdot) = (u_{i_1}(\cdot), \ldots, (u_{i_{|S|}}(\cdot)), i_k \in S\}$$

and the payoff

$$K_S(t_0, q_0, u_S, u_{I \setminus S}) = \sum_{i \in S} K_i(t_0, q_0, u_1, u_2, \ldots, u_n).$$

Define the characteristic function of the game $\Gamma(t_0, q_0)$ as follows :

$$v(\emptyset) = 0, \quad v(I) = \sup_{u \in U} \sum_{i \in I} K_i(t_0, q_0, u_1, u_2, \ldots, u_n).$$

For every coalition $S \subset I(\emptyset \neq S \neq I)$

$$v(S) = \text{val } \Gamma_{S/I\setminus S}(t_0, q_0),$$

where $\Gamma_{S/I\setminus S}(t_0, q_0)$ is a differential zero-sum game for two persons: the set S acting as the maximizing player and the set $I \setminus S$ acting as the minimizing player. The set of strategies for players S and $I\setminus S$ are respectively $X_S = \prod_{i \in S} X_i$ and $X_{I\setminus S} = \coprod_{i \in I\setminus S} X_i$. In the game $\Gamma_{S/I\setminus S}(t_0, q_0)$, the payoff in each situation $(u_S, u_{I\setminus S})$ is defined for coalition S as

$$K_S(t_0, q_0, u_S, u_{I\setminus S}) = \sum_{i \in S} K_i(t_0, q_0, u_S, u_{I\setminus S}).$$

Under certain conditions the value of the antagonistic game $\Gamma_{S/I\setminus S}(t_0, q_0)$ may not exist. In this case the characteristic function can be defined as follows:

$$v(S) = \sup_{u_S \in X_S} \inf_{u_{I\setminus S} \in X_{I\setminus S}} K_S(t_0, q_0, u_S, u_{I\setminus S}).$$

D e f i n i t i o n 2. The solution $\overline{q}(t, x, y, z)$ of (3.26) with initial boundary conditions (3.27),(3.28) and its associated open-loop control $\overline{u}(t) = (\overline{u}_1(t), \overline{u}_2(t), \ldots, \overline{u}_n(t)$ are called an optimal trajectory and an optimal control in the game $\Gamma(t_0, q_0)$ if

$$\sum_{i \in I} K_i(t_0, q_0, \overline{u}_1, \ldots, \overline{u}_n) = \sup_{u \in U} \sum_{i \in I} K_i(t_0, q_0, u_1, \ldots, u_n) \qquad (3.29)$$

subject to

$$\frac{1}{T - t_0} \int_{t_0}^{T} \int_{\Omega} \overline{q}(t, x, y, z, t_0, q_0, \overline{u}_1, \ldots, \overline{u}_n) \, d\Omega \, dt \leq \Theta. \qquad (3.30)$$

Note that an optimal trajectory and an optimal control do not always exist.

If condition (3.30) is violated when (3.29) is satisfied, the trajectory $q(t, x, y, z)$ may not be thought of as being environmentally admissible. In this case, enterprises (players) are interested in maximizing their payoffs, and so their interests come into conflict with environmental quality requirements. Therefore, we have to ensure the fulfillment of condition (3.30) by increasing penalties.

We assume that an optimal trajectory and an optimal control exist. Consider a differential game in the form of characteristic function $v(S, t_0, q_0)$. The notation $E(t_0, q_0) = \{\xi = (\xi_1, \xi_2, \dots, \xi_n) \colon \xi_i \geq v(\{i\}, t_0, q_0)$ for all $i \in I$, $\sum_{i \in I} \xi_i = v(I, t_0, q_0)\}$ denotes the set of all imputations that are realizable in the game $\Gamma(t_0, q_0)$. By the solution of cooperative game is meant same fixed subset $M(t_0, q_0)$ of the set $E(t_0, q_0)$ whose definition is depends from the chosen principle of optimality.

Suppose the players have agreed to realize some imputation in terms of the characteristic function v, and payments to the players are made continuously. This raises the question of determining a "stationary" share (the player is to receive by the time t) such that the player would respect the agreement during the game.

Suppose $\bar{q}(t, x, y, z)$ is an optimal trajectory in the game $\Gamma(t_0, q_0)$, while $\Gamma(t, \bar{q}(t, x, y, z))$, $t_0 \leq t < T$, is the current game with a solution

$$M(t, \bar{q}(t, x, y, z)) \subset E(t, \bar{q}(t, x, y, z)),$$

where

$$E(t, \bar{q}(t, x, y, z)) = \{\xi = (\xi_1, \xi_2, \dots, x i_n) \colon \xi_i \geq v(\{i\}, t, \bar{q}(t, x, y, z))$$

for all $i \in I$, $\sum_{i \in I} \xi_i = v(I, t, \bar{q}(t, x, y, z))\}$.

Here $v(I, t, \bar{q}(t, x, y, z))$ denotes the characteristic function of the current game $\Gamma(t, \bar{q}(t, x, y, z))$. We assume $M(t, \bar{q}(t, x, y, z)) \neq \emptyset$ for all $t \in [t_0, T]$.

De f i n i t i o n 3. The imputation $\xi \in M(t_0, q_0)$ is called dynamically stable (time-consistent) along the trajectory $\bar{q}(t, x, y, z)$, if for every $t \in [t_0, T]$ it is possible to select a nonempty subset $M'(t, \bar{q}(t, x, y, z))$ of the set $M(t, \bar{q}(t, x, y, z))$ such that

$$\xi \in \{\alpha(t) + M'(t, \bar{q}(t, x, y, z))\} \subseteq M(t_0, q_0),$$

where $\alpha(t)$ is the vector of payoffs due to the players at the time t; $\alpha(t) + M'(t, \bar{q}(t, x, y, z))$ is the set of all vectors of the form $\alpha(t) + y$, where $y \in M'(t, \bar{q}(t, x, y, z))$.

The solution of cooperative game is called dynamically stable if all the imputations contained therein are dynamically stable.

The notion of dynamic stability employed in differential nonzero sum games was initially introduced in [34,36]. Dynamic stability of the solution of cooperative differential game implies that at any time interval $[t_0, t]$ each player is to receive a payoff $\alpha(t)$ such that the remaining part of imputation $\xi - \alpha(t)$

is an optimal imputation in the current game $\Gamma(t, q(t, x, y, z))$. Dynamically stable solutions have the important property that the agreement made by the players at the initial time on the choice of a imputation prevails during the game if the players do not depart from the chosen principle of optimality. In what follows, it is assumed that the players would not depart during the game from the chosen principle of optimality.

The accrued payoffs due to the players by the time t in the interval $[t_0, t]$ may be represented as

$$\alpha_i(t) = \int_{t_0}^{t} h_i(\overline{u_i}(\tau))\, d\tau - \beta_i(t) \sum_{i \in I} \int_{t_0}^{t} \int_{\Omega} c_i(x, y, z)\bar{q}(\tau, x, y, z)\, d\Omega\, d\tau \qquad (3.31)$$

where the functions $\beta_i(t)$ for all $t \in [t_0, T]$ satisfy the conditions

$$0 \leq \beta_i(t) \leq 1, \qquad i \in I, \qquad \sum_{i \in I} \beta_i(t) = 1.$$

The choice of functions $\beta_i(t)$ is of great importance, because it permits adjustment of payoffs due to the players at the time t, and hence serves to maintain dynamic stability of solutions. In what follows, we shall show which of the conditions are to be satisfied by the functions $\beta_i(t)$ so that the solutions are dynamically stable.

We shall examine dynamic stability of solutions to cooperative game $v(t_0, q_0)$ using the core as an example.

D e f i n i t i o n 4. The core of the current game $\Gamma(t, \bar{q}(t, x, y, z))$ is called the set of imputations

$$C(t, \bar{q}(t, x, y, z)) = \{\xi^t = (\xi_1^t, \ldots, \xi_n^t) \in E(t, \bar{q}(t, x, y, z)) :$$

$$\sum_{i \in S} \xi_i^t \geq v(S, t, \bar{q}(t, x, y, z), S \in I)\}.$$

Suppose the payoffs $\alpha_i(t)$ due to the players at the time t are determined according to (3.31). We shall establish the conditions to be satisfied by the functions $\beta_i(t)$, so that the core of the game $\Gamma(t_0, q_0)$ would be dynamically stable. Let us adjust the vector $\beta(t)$ in such a way that $\xi - \alpha(t) \in C(t, \bar{q}(t, x, y, z))$. This means that

$$\sum_{i \in S} \xi_i - \sum_{i \in S} \alpha_i(t) \geq v(S, t, \bar{q}(t, x, \dot{y}, z)), \qquad S \subset I;$$

$$\sum_{i \in I} \xi_i - \sum_{i \in I} \alpha_i(t) = v(I, t, \bar{q}(t, x, y, z)).$$

Since

$$\sum_{i \in I} \xi_i = v(I, t_0, q_0), \qquad \sum_{i \in I \setminus S} \xi_i \geq v(I \setminus S, t_0, q_0),$$

we get

$$\sum_{i \in S} \alpha_i(t) \leq v(I, t_0, q_0) - v(I \setminus S, t_0, q_0) - v(S, t, \bar{q}(t, x, y, z)),$$

or

$$\sum_{i \in S} \beta_i(t) \sum_{j \in I} \int_{t_0}^{t} \int_{\Omega} c_j(x, y, z) \bar{q}(t, x, y, z)) \, d\Omega \, d\tau \leq$$

$$\leq v(I, t_0, q_0) - v(I \setminus S, t_0, q_0) - v(S, t, \bar{q}(t, x, y, z)) -$$

$$- \sum_{i \in S} \int_{t_0}^{t} h_i(\overline{u_i}(\tau)) \, d\tau.$$

Finally, we rewrite the inequality in the form

$$\sum_{i \in S} \beta_i(t) \geq (v(I \setminus S, t_0, q_0) - v(S, t, \bar{q}(t, x, y, z))) - v(I, t_0, q_0) +$$

$$+ \sum_{i \in S} \int_{t_0}^{t} h_i(\overline{u_i}(\tau)) \, d\tau \Big/ \sum_{i \in I} \int_{t_0}^{t} \int_{\Omega} c_i(x, y, z) \bar{q}(\tau, x, y, z) \, d\Omega \, d\tau.$$

Note that at each time

$$\sum_{i \in I} \alpha_i(t) = v(I, t_0, q_0) - v(I, t, \bar{q}(t, x, y, z)) =$$

$$= - \sum_{i \in I} \int_{t_0}^{t} \int_{\Omega} c_i(x, y, z) \bar{q}(t, x, y, z) \, d\Omega \, d\tau +$$

$$+ \sum_{i \in I} \int_{t_0}^{t} h_i(\overline{u_i}(\tau)) \, d\tau,$$

and hence (see (3.31)) $\sum_{i \in I} \beta_i(t) = 1$.

Thus the theorem below is true.

Theorem 8. In order for the core $C(t_0, q_0)$ to be dynamically stable in the game $\Gamma(t_0, q_0)$ with the characteristic function $v(S, t_0, q_0)$, it is necessary that for every imputation $\xi \in C(t_0, q_0)$ there exist a vector function $\beta(t)$ such that

$$\xi_i = \int_{t_0}^{T} h_i(\overline{u_i}(\tau)) \, d\tau -$$

$$- \beta_i(T) \sum_{j \in I} \int_{t_0}^{T} \int_{\Omega} c_j(x,y,z) \bar{q}(\tau,x,y,z)\, d\Omega\, d\tau, \qquad i \in I$$

and for any $t \in (t_0, T]$ the following conditions hold:

1) for all $\subset I$

$$\sum_{i \in S} \beta_i(t) \geq (v(I \setminus S, t_0, q_0) - v(I, t_0, q_0,) + v(S, t, \bar{q}(t,x,y,z)) +$$

$$+ \sum_{i \in S} \int_{t_0}^{t} h_i(\overline{u_i}(\tau))\, d\tau \Big/ \sum_{i \in I} \int_{t_0}^{t} \int_{\Omega} c_i(x,y,\bar{z}) q(\tau,x,y,z))\, d\Omega\, d\tau;$$

2) $\sum_{i \in I} \beta_i(t) = 1,\ 0 \leq \beta_i(t) \leq 1$.

Theorem 8 gives the necessary conditions for dynamic stability of the core in the game of interest.

Suppose there exists a vector function $\beta(t)$ such that for all $S \subset I, t \in [t_0, T]$

$$\sum_{i \in S} \beta_i(t) \geq (v(S, t, \bar{q}(t,x,y,z)) - v(S, t_0, q_0) +$$

$$+ \sum_{i \in S} \int_{t_0}^{t} h_i(\overline{u_i}(\tau))\, d\tau \Big/ \sum_{i \in I} \int_{t_0}^{t} \int_{\Omega} c_i(x,y,z) \bar{q}(\tau,x,y,z)\, d\Omega\, d\tau,$$

$$\sum_{i \in I} \beta_i(t) = 1.$$

Then

$$\sum_{i \in S} \alpha_i(t) \leq v(S, t_0, q_0) - v(S, t, \bar{q}(t,x,y,z)).$$

Since $\xi = (\xi_1, \xi_2, \ldots, \xi_n)$ belongs to the core of the game $\Gamma(t_0, q_0)$, i.e. $\sum_{i \in S} \xi_i \geq v(S, t_0, q_0)$, $S \subset I$, we have the inequality

$$\sum_{i \in S} \xi_i - \sum_{i \in S} \alpha_i(t) \geq v(S, t, \bar{q}(t,x,y,z))$$

Hence, $\xi - \alpha(t) \in C(t, \bar{q}(t,x,y,z))$.

Theorem 9. If for every $\xi \in C(t_0, q_0)$ there exists a vector function $\beta(t)$ such that

$$\xi_i = \int_{t_0}^{T} h_i(\overline{u_i}(\tau))\, d\tau - \beta_i(T) \sum_{j \in I} \int_{t_0}^{T} \int_{\Omega} c_j(x,y,z) \bar{q}(\tau,x,y,z)\, d\Omega\, d\tau,$$

and for any $t \in (t_0, T)$ there are

$$\sum_{i \in S} \beta_i(t) \geq (v(S, t, \dot{\bar{q}}(t, x, y, z)) - v(s, t_0, q_0) +$$

$$+ \sum_{i \in S} \int_{t_0}^{t} h_i(\overline{u_i}(\tau)) \, d\tau \Big) \Big/ \sum_{i \in I} \int_{t_0}^{t} \int_{\Omega} c_i(x, y, z) \bar{q}(\tau, x, y, z) \, d\Omega \, d\tau, \qquad S \subset I;$$

$$\sum_{i \in I} \beta_i(t) = 1, \qquad 0 \leq \beta_i(t) \leq 1,$$

the core is dynamically stable in the game $\Gamma(t_0, q_0)$ with the characteristic function $v(S, t_0, q_0)$.

3.7 Dynamic Model for Environmental Cooperation

Let us assume that the amount of investments allocated by enterprises for implementation of an environmental control project during a planned period $[0, T]$ is defined by a vector $w = (w_1, w_2, \ldots, w_n)$, where w_i is the amount of investments allocated by enterprise i. It is known that in the year l ($l = 1, 2, \ldots, T$) this amount accounts for $w_{il} \geq 0$. Obviously, $\sum_{l=1}^{T} w_{il} = w_i$. Each enterprise is proposed to reduce emissions during a period $[0, T]$ by a quantity Δx_i. The emission reduction task and the allocated amount of investments are related by $w_i = \Delta x_i / \gamma_i$, $\gamma_i > 0$, $i = 1, 2, \ldots, n$.

Emission reduction tasks follow from the necessity to reduce pollutants concentration in environmentally significant areas $\Omega_1, \Omega_2, \ldots, \Omega_m$, located in a given region. For each of these areas such a reduction is specified by the quantity $\{\Delta q_j\}$. The quantities $\{\Delta q_j\}$ and $\{\Delta x_j\}$ are related by

$$\Delta q_j = \sum_{i=1}^{n} c_{ji} \Delta x_i, \qquad c_{ji} > 0, \qquad j = 1, \ldots, m.$$

Enterprises are presented with a possibility to pool their resources in order to carry out pollution control measures in the areas Ω_j at lower costs. In this case, cooperation may release some funds that are distributed among the enterprises concerned in the form of a premium.

Suppose a group of enterprises S has an opportunity to implement a package of pollution control measures designated as R^S; $a_k^S > 0$ is the amount of investments required for the group S to carry out a measure $k \in R^S$ at the cost of investments $w(S) = \sum_{i \in S} w_i$; $\mu_{ik}^S > 0$ is the coefficient defining a reduction in emissions from enterprise $i \in S$ per unit of investments in carrying out a measure from S (emission reduction is taken to be directly proportional to the amount of investments allocated to emission control measures).

Suppose for any $Q \subset I$ and $F \subset I$ such that $Q \cap F = \emptyset$, we have

$$R^Q \bigcap R^F = \emptyset, \tag{3.32}$$

for S and S' such that $S \subseteq S' \subseteq I$

$$R^S \subseteq R^{S'}, \tag{3.33}$$

$$a_k^{S'} \leq a_k^S, \qquad k \in R^S, \tag{3.34}$$

$$\mu_{ik}^S a_k^S \leq \mu_k^{S'} a_k^{S'}, \qquad k \in R^S, \qquad i \in S, \tag{3.35}$$

and for any $i \in I$

$$\gamma_i = \max_{k \in R^{(i)}} \mu_{ik}^{\{i\}}. \tag{3.36}$$

Condition (3.33) implies that a larger coalition has more opportunities to carry out joint measures. Condition (3.34) implies that if a measure k is carried out by a larger coalition, this requires a smaller amount of investments. It would appear natural that a larger coalition would use investments more efficiently at the cost of its internal organizational reserves. This fact is well represented by condition (3.35).

The implication of condition (3.36) is that, operating individually, each enterprise chooses a pollution control measure which requires minimal costs.

Let us suppose that $\Delta q_j^S = \sum_{i \in S} c_{ji} \Delta x_i$ is a contribution made by the group of enterprises S to pollution control in the area Ω_j, while $\Delta q^S = (\Delta q_1^S, \Delta q_2^S, \ldots, \Delta q_m^S)$ is the vector characterizing the planned contribution of this group to pollution abatement in all environmentally significant areas. We introduce the function

$$\bar{v}(S) = \min_y \sum_{k \in R^S} a_k^S y_k \tag{3.37}$$

subject to

$$\sum_{k \in R^S} \sum_{i \in S} c_{ji} \mu_{ik}^S a_k^S y_k \geq \Delta q_j^S, \qquad j = 1, 2, \ldots, m; \tag{3.38}$$

$$\sum_{k \in R^S} a_k^S y_k \leq \sum_{i \in S} w_i,$$

where y_k takes values 0 or 1. The allocated investments are taken to be such that there at least one permissible solution to problem (3.38). The function $\bar{v}(S)$ defines minimal costs incurred by the group of enterprises S in order to effect the target pollution abatement Δq^S and has the following property:

$$\bar{v}(Q + F) \leq \bar{v}(Q) + \bar{v}(F), \qquad Q \bigcap F = \emptyset. \tag{3.39}$$

Indeed, let us take any disjoint groups of enterprises $Q \subset I, F \subset I$. Suppose y^Q and y^F are the solutions to the problem for S equal to Q and F, respectively. Denote by P_Q the package of measures to be implemented by the group of enterprises Q in order to effect the target pollution abatement Δq^Q at minimal costs, i.e. $P^Q = \{k \in R^Q : y_k^Q = 1\}$. Similarly, $P_F = \{k \in R^F : y_k^F = 1\}$. By (3.34), we have

$$\sum_{k \in P^Q} a_k^Q \geq \sum_{k \in P^Q} a_k^{Q \cup F}, \qquad \sum_{k \in P^F} a_k^F \geq \sum_{k \in P^F} a_k^{Q \cup F}.$$

By (3.32), we then get

$$\sum_{k \in P^Q} a_k^Q + \sum_{k \in P^F} a_k^F \geq \sum_{k \in P^Q \cup P^F} a_k^{Q \cup F}. \tag{3.40}$$

Making use of properties (3.32) and (3.35), we obtain

$$\sum_{k \in P^Q} \sum_{i \in Q} c_{ji} \mu_{ik}^Q a_k^Q + \sum_{k \in P^F} \sum_{i \in F} c_{ji} \mu_k^F a_k^F \leq$$

$$\leq \sum_{k \in P^Q} \sum_{i \in Q} c_{ji} \mu_{ik}^{Q \cup F} a_k^{Q \cup F} + \sum_{k \in P^F} \sum_{i \in F} c_{ji} \mu_k^{Q \cup F} a_k^{Q \cup F} \leq$$

$$\leq \sum_{k \in P^Q} \sum_{i \in Q} c_{ji} \mu_{ik}^{Q \cup F} a_k^{Q \cup F} + \sum_{k \in P^F} \sum_{i \in Q} c_{ji} \mu_{ik}^{Q \cup F} a_k^{Q \cup F} +$$

$$+ \sum_{k \in P^F} \sum_{i \in F} c_{ji} \mu_{ik}^{Q \cup F} a_k^{Q \cup F} + \sum_{k \in P^Q} \sum_{i \in F} c_{ji} \mu_{ik}^{Q \cup F} a_k^{Q \cup F} =$$

$$= \sum_{k \in P^F \cup P^Q} \sum_{i \in Q \cup F} c_{ji} \mu_{ik}^{Q \cup F} a_k^{Q \cup F}.$$

Thus

$$\sum_{k \in P^Q} \sum_{i \in Q} c_{ji} \mu_{ik}^Q a_k^Q + \sum_{k \in P^F} \sum_{i \in F} c_{ji} \mu_k^F a_k^F \leq$$

$$\leq \sum_{k \in P^F \cup P^Q} \sum_{i \in Q \cup F} c_{ji} \mu_{ik}^{Q \cup F} a_k^{Q \cup F}, \qquad j = 1, 2, \ldots, m.$$

Let $y^{Q \cup F}$ be a solution of problem (3.37)–(3.38) for $S = Q \bigcup F$. Since

$$\sum_{k \in P^Q} \sum_{i \in Q} c_{ji} \mu_{ik}^{Q} a_k^{Q} \geq \Delta q_j^{Q},$$

$$\sum_{k \in P^F} \sum_{i \in F} c_{ji} \mu_{ik}^{F} a_k^{F} \geq \Delta q_i^{F},$$

$$\Delta q_j^{Q \cup F} = \Delta q_j^{Q} + \Delta q_j^{F}, \qquad j = 1, 2, \ldots, m,$$

by (3.40), we have

$$\sum_{k \in P^Q \cup P^F} \sum_{i \in Q \cup F} c_{ji} \mu_{ik}^{Q \cup F} a_k^{Q \cup F} \geq \Delta q_j^{Q \cup F}, \qquad j = 1, 2, \ldots, m$$

Hence, by $P^Q \bigcup P^F \subset R^{Q \cup F}$, we obtain

$$\sum_{k \in R^{Q \cup F}} a_k^{Q \cup F} y_k^{Q \cup F} \leq \sum_{k \in P^Q \cup P^F} a_k^{Q \cup F} y_k^{Q \cup F},$$

and finally

$$\bar{v}(Q) + \bar{v}(F) = \sum_{k \in P^Q} a_k^{Q} + \sum_{k \in P^F} a_k^{F} \geq$$

$$\geq \sum_{k \in P^{Q \cup F}} a_k^{Q \cup F} y_k^{Q \cup F} = \bar{v}(Q \cup F).$$

We have thus proved (3.39). Since $\gamma_i = \max_{k \in R^{\{i\}}} \mu_{ik}^{\{i\}}$, we have $w_i = \bar{v}(\{i\})$. From (3.39) it follows that

$$\bar{v}(S) \leq \bar{v}(S \setminus \{i\}) + \bar{v}(\{i\}) \leq \ldots \leq \sum_{i \in S} \bar{v}(\{i\}) = \sum_{i \in S} w_i.$$

Hence we conclude that (3.38) is also true.

Suppose all enterprises have united for purposes of implementing a package of measures $P^I \subseteq R^I$ that ensure under cooperation conditions the target pollution abatement Δq_j $(j = 1, 2, \ldots, m)$ at lower costs. The amount of investments allocated to carry out a measure $k \in P^I$ comes to a_k^I. The result of allocation in the l-th year of a_{kl}^I roubles for purposes of carrying out a measure $k \in P^I$ is that the pollution concentration in the area Ω_j is reduced at the end of that year at the cost of enterprises S by the quantity

$$\Delta q_{ji}^{S} = \sum_{i \in S} c_{ji} \sum_{k \in P^I} \mu_{ik}^{I} \sum_{r=1}^{l} a_{kr}^{I}.$$

Define the function $\bar{v}(S, l)$ as follows:

$$\bar{v}(S, l) = \min_{y} \sum_{k \in P_S^l} a_k^{S,l} y_k$$

subject to

$$\sum_{k \in R_l^S} a_k^{S,l} y_k \leq \sum_{r=l+1}^{T} \sum_{i \in S} w_{ir},$$

$$\sum_{k \in R_l^S} \sum_{j \in S} c_{ji} \mu_{ik}^{S,l} a_k^{S,l} \geq \Delta q_j^S - \Delta q_{jl}^S, \qquad j = 1, 2, \ldots, m,$$

where R_l^S is the package of measures to be implemented by the group of enterprises S in a period $[l+1, T]$; $\mu_{ik}^{S,l}$ is the coefficient defining reduction of emissions from enterprise $i \in S$ when a unit amount is invested in a measure $k \in R_l^S$ by cooperative enterprises from S during a period $[l+1, T]$; $a_k^{S,l}$ is the amount of investments to be allocated to the group of enterprises S for purposes of carrying out a measure $k \in R_l^S$ during a period $[l+1, T]$.

Suppose that for any $l = 1, 2, \ldots, T$ there are conditions similar to (3.34), (3.35). Then obviously

$$\bar{v}(Q, l) + \bar{v}(F, l) \geq \bar{v}(Q \bigcup F, l), \qquad Q \bigcap F = \emptyset.$$

D e f i n i t i o n 5. The annual capital distribution plan $\{a_{kl}^I\}_{k \in P^I}$, ($l = 1, 2, \ldots, T$) is called feasible if

$$\sum_{k \in P^I} a_{kl}^I \leq \sum_{i \in I} w_{il}, \qquad l = 1, 2, \ldots, T;$$

$$\sum_{r=1}^{T} a_{kr}^I = a_k^I, \qquad k \in P^I.$$

Suppose a feasible investment plan is $\{a_{kl}^I\}_{k \in P^I}$, $l = 1, 2, \ldots, T$.

The unemployed part of capital to be distributed among enterprises as a premium is equal to $\sum_{i \in I} w_i - \sum_{k \in P^I} a_k^I$.

To define the principle of awarding a premium, we construct a game theoretic model in which enterprises are considered as players. The characteristic function of a suitable n-person cooperative game may be written as $v(S) = \sum_{i \in S} w_i - \bar{v}(S)$, $S \subseteq I$. Since $\bar{v}(I) = \sum_{k \in P^I} a_k^I$, we have

$$v(I) = \sum_{i \in I} w_i - \sum_{k \in P^I} a_k^I.$$

Now the total amount of unemployed investments in the cooperative game is to be divided. The premium accumulated by the end of the year l amounts to $\sum_{r=1}^{l}(\sum_{i \in S} w_{ir} - \sum_{k \in P^I} a_{kr}^l)$. Suppose the entire annual premium is to be divided. This raises the question of how the premium is to be distributed over the entire interval $[t_0, T]$ so that the players would agree on participation in a general coalition I and form no subcoalitions. Moreover, we must find the answer to the question of how the premium is to be distributed from year to year so that the players would not cancel the agreement on cooperation.

The premium distribution is taken to be good, e.g. where the imputation belongs to the core of the game defined on the interval $[0, T]$.

We consider the core as a solution of the game. Let $\xi = (\xi_1, \ldots, \xi_n)$ be some imputation from the core. This imputation must satisfy the inequalities

$$\xi_i \geq 0, \qquad \sum_{i \in S} \xi_i \geq v(S),$$

$$\sum_{i \in I} \xi_i = v(I) = \sum_{i \in I} w_i - \sum_{k \in P_I} a_k^l,$$

where ξ_i is the premium due to enterprises for the entire period $[0, T]$.

Now, in order to determine the annual premium amount which may guarantee stability of the agreement on cooperation, the premium must be divided each year in such a way that its remainder would belong to the core of the current game. For this reason, we suppose the core to be nonempty along the chosen plan $\{a_{kl}^l\}$ and examine it for dynamic stability.

The characteristic function of the current game may written as

$$v(S, l) = \sum_{r=l+1}^{T} \sum_{i \in S} w_{ir} - \bar{v}(S, l).$$

Since $\bar{v}(I, l) = \sum_{r=l+1}^{T} \sum_{i \in S} a_{kr}^l$, we have

$$v(I, l) = \sum_{r=l+1}^{T} \left(\sum_{i \in I} w_{ir} - \sum_{k \in P^I} a_{kr}^l \right).$$

Hence, the part of the premium for the period $[l+1, T]$ is to be divided in the current game.

Note that $v(S, 0) = v(S)$. Denote by $\alpha_i(l)$ the accumulated payoff due to a player at the end of the year l. Suppose $\alpha_i(l)$ is determined from the formula

$$\alpha_i(l) = \beta_i(l) \sum_{r=1}^{T} \left(\sum_{i \in I} w_{ir} - \sum_{k \in P^I} a_{kr}^l \right), \qquad (3.41)$$

where

$$\sum_{i \in I} \beta_i(l) = 1, \qquad l = 1, 2, \ldots, T,$$

$$0 \leq \beta_i(l) \leq 1, \qquad i = 1, 2, \ldots, n. \tag{3.42}$$

The imputation is a dynamically stable element of the core if for any l the imputation $\xi_l = (\xi_1 - \alpha_1(l), \ldots, \xi_n - \alpha_n(l))$ belongs to the core of the current game $v(S, l)$, i.e. the following conditions are satisfied:

$$\xi_i - \alpha_i(l) \geq 0, \tag{3.43}$$

$$\sum_{i \in S} (\xi_i - \alpha_i(l)) \geq v(S, l), \qquad S \subset I, \tag{3.44}$$

$$\sum_{i \in I} (\xi_i - \alpha_i(l)) = v(I, l) = \sum_{r=l+1}^{T} \left(\sum_{i \in I} w_{ir} - \sum_{k \in P^I} a_{kr}^I \right). \tag{3.45}$$

Due to (3.41) and (3.42) condition (3.45) holds. Substitute $\alpha_i(l)$ from (3.41) into (3.44), than condition for $\beta_i(l)$ will be as:

$$\sum_{i \in S} \beta_i(l) \leq \frac{\sum_{i \in S} \xi_i - v(S, l)}{\sum_{r=1}^{l} \left(\sum_{i \in I} w_{ir} - \sum_{k \in P^I} a_{kr}^I \right)}. \tag{3.46}$$

Now, if we succeed in selecting for each imputation from the core a vector function $\beta(l)$ satisfying the conditions (3.41) and (3.42), then the core is dynamically stable in the cooperative game with characteristic function v.

Dynamic stability of the solution of the game implies the possibility of awarding a premium to enterprises such that they would be interested in implementation of the outlined plan of cooperation during the entire period

Chapter 4

HIERARCHICAL DEVELOPMENT CONTROL SYSTEMS

4.1 Major and Minor Components of Closed Ecosystem Development

In constructing dynamic development models for comparatively small ecologically closed regions, we need to take into account complex relationships between the model components that bring substantial influence to bear on alternatives of development and the achievement of specified objectives. Intercomponent relations can be described by a finite graph $\Gamma = (Z, \Gamma)$ (see [3]), whose nodes are components of the model. In the intercomponent relation graph Γ, we may distinguish major components of the development model that can be externally controlled by allocating resources and capital investments, and minor components whose states are uniquely determined by the states of major components. In modeling such a complex system, we must keep in mind that development of major components can be guided by relatively independent parties pursuing their own objectives that do not necessarily coincide with general objectives of regional development. This generates a need for examination of a hierarchical graph Γ of intercomponent relations defining the constraints that the system components impose upon one another, and formulating the general development objectives for each of the major components. Mathematical models for the functioning of hierarchical control systems taking into account distinct interests of system components are hierarchical games.

We shall clarify the above assertions by taking the development of an Alpine village Oberhull (Austria) as an example. This village is located at a height of 2000 m above see level and attracts a constantly increasing flow of tourists both in summer and winter. Environmental consequences of rapid development of construction of hotels and elevators, an increasing number of people and traffic flows in the village and its environs have become obvious by the early 1970s. It seems plausible that tourists will cease to visit the village if it loses its attractions.

The lack of avalanche-safe areas and construction areas for new hotels is a limiting factor in development of tourism. On the initiative of the National MAB Committee (Austria), Oberhull was selected to be an object to intensive studies. Close cooperation of various scientists - botanists, zoologists, microbiologists, meteorologists, geographers, economists, sociologists and even anthropologists - resulted in dynamic development models for Oberhull. No detailed description will be provided here for these models, because they employ simple mathematics. Instead, we shall focus on the graph of major component relations which should be incorporated in the balanced development planning.

Referring to [49], we have such a graph and a qualitative analysis of unexpected effects that a change in one of the graph components may exert on the other components. At the same time, [49] fails to subdivide them into major and minor components.

Let us suppose that a general finite graph (Z, Γ) defines the relationship between components of a closed ecological system [3]. The nodes $z \in Z$ are components and the mapping of Γ defines the relationship between components.

We assume that the set Z is partitioned into two subsets $X, Y(X \cup Y = Z, X \cap Y = \emptyset)$ of externally controlled major (X) and minor (Y) components. Let us designate components of the set X by indices $i = 1, \ldots, m$, and components of the set Y by indices $j = 1, \ldots, n$. The quantitative state of component $i \in X$ is defined by vector $x^i \in R^n$ and that of component $j \in Y$ by vector $y^j \in R^n$.

We introduce the following notation:

$$x^{\Gamma^{-1}(j)} = \{x^k : k \in \Gamma^{-1}(j)\}, \qquad y^{\Gamma^{-1}(j)} = \{y^k : k \in \Gamma^{-1}(j)\},$$

i.e. $x^{\Gamma^{-1}(j)}$, $y^{\Gamma^{-1}(j)}$ are vectors whose coordinates represent quantitative states of components from the sets $\Gamma^{-1}(j) \cap X$ and $\Gamma^{-1}(j) \cap Y$, respectively.

The designations $h_j[x^{\Gamma^{-1}(j)}, y^{\Gamma^{-1}(j)}]$, $f_i[x^{\Gamma^{-1}(i)}, y^{\Gamma^{-1}(i)}]$, $u_i[x^{\Gamma^{-1}(i)}, y^{\Gamma^{-1}(i)}]$ will be used to express dependencies of the relevant functions on the quantitative states of components from the sets $\Gamma^{-1}(i), \Gamma^{-1}(j)$. We may define the balance relationships as follows:

$$y^{(j)} = h_j[x^{\Gamma^{-1}(j)}, y^{\Gamma^{-1}(j)}], \quad j \in Y; \qquad x^i = f_i\{[x^{\Gamma^{-1}(i)}, y^{\Gamma^{-1}(i)}], u_i\}, \quad i \in X,$$

where h_j, f_i are real-valued n-dimensional vector functions; u_i is a control from the set

$$U_i[x^{\Gamma^{-1}(i)}, y^{\Gamma^{-1}(i)}] \subset R^l,$$

whose structure is defined by the quantitative states of components affecting variations in component x^i. With each component $i \in X$ we associate a payoff to the party which is interested in development of this component and has an opportunity to affect the process of development by a proper choice of control $u_i \subset U_i[x^{\Gamma^{-1}(i)}, y^{\Gamma^{-1}(i)}]$. This payoff is generally determined not only by the quantitative state of component i, but also by that of the other components. Denote it by $H_i(x, y)$, where the vector sets $x = \{x^i, i \in X\}, y = \{y^j, j \in Y\}$ determine the quantitative states of the entire system. Since the states x, y are dependent on the choice of control $u_i, i \in X$ made by all parties interested in development of components $i \in X$, it is possible to determine a new payoff for M_i from the formula

$$M_i(u_1, \ldots, u_m) = H_i(x, y), \qquad i \in X, \tag{4.1}$$

where x, y are the quantitative states realized in the choice of control $u_i \in U_i[x^{\Gamma^{-1}(i)}, y^{\Gamma^{-1}(i)}]$.

Now we have a hierarchical m-person game (parties interested in development of major components $i \in X, i = 1, \ldots, m$) with the sets of strategies

$$\{u_i\} = U_i[x^{\Gamma^{-1}(i)}, y^{\Gamma^{-1}(i)}]$$

and the payoff functions determined from (4.1).

This game is different from classical noncooperative games in normal form as defined in the preceding chapters. Its special feature is that the player's sets of strategies $U_i[x^{\Gamma^{-1}(i)}, y^{\Gamma^{-1}(i)}]$ are dependent on the quantitative states of components affecting component i, and hence on the choices made by other players, $i' \in X, i' \neq i$, and affecting variations in the states of components from the set $\Gamma^{-1}(i)$. Therefore, the players may not choose strategies simultaneously and independently, because such a choice can yield a contradiction. Indeed, in order to choose his strategy u_i, player i must be informed about the set $U_i[x^{\Gamma^{-1}(i)}, y^{\Gamma^{-1}(i)}]$, and hence the quantitative states $x^{\Gamma^{-1}(i)}, y^{\Gamma^{-1}(i)}$, determined by strategies of the respective players. This becomes possible in specifying an information structure for major components of hierarchical system which is determined by a priority order in which the players select their strategies. Analyses of specific hierarchical games will provide a detailed treatment of this problem.

Optimal behavior in hierarchical games poses a sufficiently serious problem and may become the subject of special studies. In the subsequent sections of this chapter, we shall focus on some of the simplest hierarchical games — tree-like games and versions of games with diamond-shaped structure - in order to illustrate the possible ways of constructing the optimal behavior principles in hierarchical system (see [53, 55]).

It should be noted that when controls $u_i \in U_i[x^{\Gamma^{-1}(i)}, y^{\Gamma^{-1}(i)}]$ for all $i \in X$ can be selected by one control center we have a multicriteria optimization problem with a vector criterion $M = \{M_1, \ldots, M_m\}$. This problem will be discussed in the next chapter.

4.2 Hierarchical Tree-like Games

The games examined in this chapter provide models for conflict-controlled systems with a hierarchical structure, i.e. the systems with a complex structure representing a sequence of control levels following one another in a certain priority order.

The paper [28] seems to be the first to provide systematic treatment of mathematical models for hierarchical control structures and an analysis of benefits derived from a variety of applications of the hierarchical approach. The necessity to allow for the distinct interests of components in the controlled system, the presence of unidentified factors and availability of various amounts of information at different levels has been recognized by investigators in similar problems laying particular emphasis on the information theory of hierarchical systems. The essentials of this theory were given by N. N. Moiseev in the mid-sixties [6, 28-30]. Hierarchical decision models in various applications have recently become the focus of much research [6,8,52].

Mathematically, it is convenient to classify hierarchical systems according to the number of levels and the nature of vertical relations. The simplest of these is a two-level system (Fig.4).

Control (coordination) center A_0, which is at the top level of hierarchy, selects a vector $u = (u_1, \ldots, u_n)$ from a specified control set U; u_i is the control action of the center on its subordinate division B_i which is placed at the second level of hierarchy. Now, B_i, $i = 1, \ldots, n$ select controls $v_i \in U_i(u)$, where $U_i(u)$ is the set of controls for divisions B_i specified by control center A_0. The control center has the right to the first move and can restrict opportunities available to its subordinate divisions by channelling their actions as may be desired. Center A_0 wishes to maximize some functional $h_0(u, v_1, \ldots, v_n)$, while divisions B_i have their own objectives:

$$h_i(u_i, v_i) \to \max_{v_i}, \quad i = 1, \ldots, n.$$

An example of two-level systems is provided by the allocation problem in which the administrative center of an environmentally closed region allocates resources among its subordinate manufacturing divisions. It is clear that the production conditions for each division are generally different. Moreover, for each division and for the administrative center the payoffs associated with the output of final products are also different. The problem is that of constructing a rather optimal production program for manufacturing divisions and an optimal plan for allocation of resources by the administrative center.

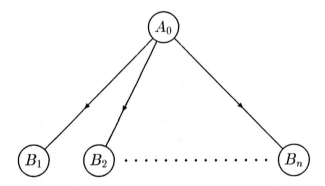

Fig. 4.

Let us formalize the problem as a noncooperative game for $n + 1$ person, the administrative center A_0, and the manufacturing divisions $B_1, \ldots, B_n$.

Player A_0 selects a system of n vectors $u = (u_1, \ldots, u_n)$, $u_i \geq 0$, $u_i \in R^l$, $i = 1, \ldots, n$, $\sum_{i=1}^{n} u_i \leq b$, $b \geq 0$. The vector u_i will be interpreted to mean the set of l different resources allocated by center A_0 to the i-th manufacturing division. Each of the players B_i is informed about the choice made by A_0 and selects a vector $v_i \in R^m$ from the set of vectors constrained by

$$v_i A_i \leq u_i + \alpha_i, \qquad v_i \geq 0, \tag{4.2}$$

The vector v_i is interpreted as a production program of the i-th manufacturing division for different products; A_i is a production or technological matrix for the i-th manufacturing division $(A_i \geq 0)$; α_i is the vector of available resources for the i-th manufacturing division $(\alpha_i \geq 0)$.

Let us define payoffs. For player A_0 the payoff is set equal to

$$J_0(u, v_1(u), \ldots, v_n(u)) = \sum_{i=1}^{n} (a_i v_i(u)), \quad a_i \geq 0, \quad a_i \in R^m, \quad i = 1, \ldots, n,$$

where $u = (u_1, \ldots, u_n)$ is the strategy of player A_0; $v_i(u_i)$ is the strategy for player B_i satisfying condition (4.2) (the production program of B_i is dependent on the resource u_i allocated thereto by the center A_0; therefore its strategy is a function of parameter u_i or, in the general case, a function of u); a_i is the vector of payoffs to center A_0 from the products manufactured by the i-th division; $(a_i v_i(u_i))$ is the scalar product of vector a_i and $v_i(u_i)$.

The payoff function for players
B_i $(i = 1, \ldots, n)$ is set equal to $J_i(u, v_1, \ldots, v_n(u)) = (c_i v_i(u)), c_i \geq 0, c_i \in R^m$,
where c_i is the vector of payoffs to B_i from its different products.

Each of the players wishes to maximize his payoff. Note that players B_i $(i = 1, \ldots, n)$ select their production programs depending on the strategy of player A_0.

This game is the game with perfect information; therefore according to the Zermelo theorem [24] it has an equilibrium in pure strategies. Let us find an equilibrium in this game. Suppose $v_i^*(u)$ is a solution of the parametric programming problem (here the parameter is taken to be the vector u)

$$\max_{v_i}(c_i v_i),$$

$$v_i A_i \leq u_i + \alpha_i, \qquad u_i \geq 0, \qquad \alpha_i \geq 0, \qquad v_i \geq 0,$$

while $u^* = (u_1^*, \ldots, u_n^*)$ is a solution of the problem *

$$\max_{u} \sum_{i=1}^{n} (a_i v_i^*(u)),$$

$$\sum_{i=1}^{n} u_i \leq b, \qquad u_i \geq 0, \qquad i = 1, \ldots, n. \tag{4.3}$$

Problem (4.3) is a nonlinear programming problem with an essentially discontinuous objective function (maximization is over u, while $v_i^*(u)$ is generally a discontinuous function of the parameter u).

We shall show that the point $(u^*, v_1^*(u), \ldots, v_n^*(u))$ is an equilibrium in our game. Indeed,

$$J_0(u^*, v_1^*(u), \ldots, v_n^*(u)) = \sum_{i=1}^{n} (a_i v_i^*(u^*)) \geq$$

$$\geq \sum_{i=1}^{n} (a_i v_i^*(u)) = J_0(u, v_1^*(u), \ldots, v_n^*(u)),$$

for all $i = 1, \ldots, n$

$$J_i(u^*, v_1^*(u), \ldots, v_n^*(u)) = c_i v_i^*(u^*) \geq c_i v_i(u^*) =$$

$$= J_i(u^*, v_1^*(u), \ldots, v_{i-1}^*(u), v_i(u), v_{i+1}^*(u), \ldots, v_n^*(u)).$$

Thus, no player A_0, B_1, $\ldots$, B_n can benefit by unilaterally deviating from the point $(u^*, v_1^*(u), \ldots, v_n^*(u))$, i.e. it is equilibrium. This point is also stable against deviations therefrom the coalition of players $S \subset \{B_1, \ldots, B_n\}$ may perform. Indeed, let $S = \{B_{i_1}, \ldots, B_{i_q}\}$ be an arbitrary group of players (without center A_0). For each $B_{i_k} \in S$ and any strategy $v_{i_k}(u), k = 1, \ldots, q$, we have

$$J_{i_k}(u^*, v_1^*, \ldots, v_n^*(u)) = (c_{i_k} v_{i_k}^*(u^*)) \geq (c_{i_k} v_{i_k}(u^*)) =$$

$$J_{i_k}(u^*, v_1^*(u), \ldots, v_{i_{k-1}}^*(u), v_{i_k}(u), v_{i_{k+1}}^*(u), \ldots, v_n^*(u)) =$$

$$J_{i_k}(u^*, v_1^*(u), \ldots, v_{i_{k-1}}^*(u), v_{i_1}(u), \ldots, v_{i_k}(u), \ldots, v_{i_q}(u),$$

$$v_{i_{q+1}}^*(u), \ldots, v_n^*(u)),$$

and hence group deviation from an equilibrium would provide no benefit to any one of the players $B_1, \ldots, B_{i_q}$.

Let us consider a cooperative variant of the previous problem. Proceeding from the conceptual meaning of the problem and making use of the strategies forming a Nash equilibrium, we shall define for each coalition S its guaranteed income:

$$v(S) = \begin{cases} 0, & \text{if } S = \{A_0\}, \\ \sum_{i \in S} c_i v_i^*(0), & \text{if } S \subset \{B_1, \ldots, B_n\}, \\ \max_u \sum_{i:B_i \in S} (a_i + c_i) v_i^*(u), & \text{if } S \supset \{A_0\}, \\ u \in \{u : \sum_{i:B_i \in S} u_i \leq b; \ u_i \geq 0, \ i \in S\}, \end{cases} \quad (4.4)$$

where $v_i^*(u)(i = 1, \ldots, n)$ is a solution of the parametric programming problem

$$\max_{v_i}(c_i v_i),$$

$$v_i A_i \leq u_i + \alpha_i, \qquad u_i \geq 0, \qquad \alpha_i \geq 0, \qquad i = 1, \ldots, n.$$

Equality (4.4) is true, because: coalition $\{B_1, \ldots, B_n\}$ can ensure a zero payoff to player A_0 by selecting all $v_i = 0$, $i = 1, \ldots, n$; the player can always guarantee for S the payoff of at most $\sum_{i \in S} c_i v_i^*(0)$ by allocating a zero resource to each $i \in S$; coalition S incorporating A_0 can always ensure allocation of the entire resource b to its members only.

Let $\bar{u}^S = (\bar{u}_1^S, \ldots, \bar{u}_n^S)$ be a solution of the nonlinear programming problem (1.1) for $i : B_i \bar{\in} S$, $\bar{u}_i^S \equiv 0$).

For $S = \{A_0, B_1, \ldots, B_n\}$, the allocation u^S is designated $\bar{u}$.

Let $S \subset K$, $b_i \geq 0$, then

$$\sum_{i \in K} b_i v_i^*(\bar{u}^K) \geq \sum_{i \in K} b_i v_i^*(\bar{u}^S), \qquad (b_i = a_i + c_i),$$

i.e. the allocation of resources (according to (4.4)) to a larger number of enterprises is more beneficial.

Let S, $Q \subset \{A_0, B_1, \ldots, B_n\}$ and $S \cap Q = \emptyset$. Then $A_0 \in S$ implies $A_0 \bar{\in} Q$. Under our assumption and condition $a_i \geq 0$, $c_i \geq 0$, $v_i \geq 0$, $i = 1, \ldots, n$, we have

$$V(S \cup Q) = \sum_{i: B_i \in S \cup Q} (a_i + c_i) v_i^*(\bar{u}^{S \cup Q}) \geq$$

$$\geq \sum_{i: B_i \in S \cup Q} (a_i + c_i) v_i^*(\bar{u}^S) = \sum_{i: B_i \in S} (a_i + c_i) v_i^*(\bar{u}^S) +$$

$$+ \sum_{i: B_i \in Q} (a_i + c_i) v_i^*(0) =$$

$$= V(S) + V(Q) + \sum_{i \in Q} a_i v_i^*(0) \geq V(S) + V(Q),$$

where $\sum_{i \in Q} a_i v_i^*(0) \geq 0$ is the profit due to the center A_0 from "nonfinaced" enterprises. Having defined a super-additive function V, we can consider a cooperative game $\langle \{A_0, B_1, \ldots, B_n\}, V \rangle$ in the form of characteristic function V.

Let us consider an $(n + 1)$ vector

$$\xi = \left(\sum_{i=1}^{n} a_i v_i^*(\bar{u}), c_1 v_1^*(\bar{u}), \ldots, c_n v_n^*(\bar{u}) \right). \tag{4.5}$$

Since

1) $\sum_{k=0}^{n} \xi_k = \sum_{i=1}^{n} a_i v_i^*(\bar{u}) = \sum_{i=1}^{n} (a_i + c_i) v_i^*(\bar{u}) = V(\{A_0, B_1, \ldots, B_n\}),$

2) $\xi_0 = \sum_{i=1}^{n} a_i v_i^*(\bar{u}) \geq 0 = V(\{A_0\}),$

$\xi_i = c_i v_i^*(\bar{u}) \geq c_i v_i^*(0) = V(\{B_i\}), \qquad i = 1, \ldots, n$

the vector $\xi = (\xi_0, \xi_1, \ldots, \xi_n)$ given by (4.5) is an imputation. Recall the condition for membership of an imputation in the core. According to definition of the core, the necessary condition is that the inequality

$$\sum_{i \in S} \xi_i \geq V(S) \tag{4.5a}$$

holds for all coalitions $S \subset \{A_0, B_1, \ldots, B_n\}$.

Let us introduce the condition under which the sharing ξ belongs to the core. When $S = \{A_0\}$ and $S \subset \{B_1, \ldots, B_n\}$, condition (4.5a) is satisfied, since

$$\xi_0 = \sum_{i=1}^{n} a_i v_i^* \geq 0 = V(\{A_0\}),$$

$$\sum_{i=1}^{n} \xi_i = \sum_{i:B_i \in S} c_i v_i^*(\bar{u}) \geq \sum_{i:B_i \in S} c_i v_i^*(0) - V(S).$$

When $S \supset \{A_0\}$, condition (4.5a) can be rewritten as

$$\sum_{i=1}^{n} a_i v_i^*(\bar{u}) + \sum_{i:B_i \in S} c_i v_i^*(\bar{u}) =$$

$$= \sum_{i:B_i \in S} a_i v_i^*(\bar{u}) + \sum_{i:B_i \in S} c_i v_i^*(\bar{u}) + \sum_{i:B_i \bar{\in} S} a_i v_i^*(\bar{u}) \geq$$

$$\geq \sum_{i:B_i \in S} (a_i + c_i) v_i^*(\bar{u}^S).$$

Hence, the condition for an imputation (4.5) to belong to the core is of the form

$$\sum_{i:B_i \bar{\in} S} a_i v_i^*(\bar{u}) \geq \sum_{i:B_i \in S} (a_i + c_i)[v_i^*(\bar{u}^S) - v_i^*(\bar{u})].$$

The implication of the above inequality is as follows. The administrative center A_0 receives a larger payoff by enlisting the cooperation of new enterprises than in the case where only the set S is used even though all of the profits from allocation of additional resources are immediately given by the enterprises of group S to player A_0. Note that we have defined here the characteristic function of the game in terms of the payoff in the Nash equilibrium. The quantity $\quad V(N) = \max\limits_{u} \sum\limits_{i=1}^{n}(a_i+c_i)\, v_i^*(u) \quad$ is generally less than the maximum total payoff to all players

$$\max_{\substack{u \in U = \\ =\{u: u_k \geq 0, \sum\limits_{k=1}^{n} u_k \leq b\}}} \quad \max_{\substack{v_k \in B_k(u_k)= \\ =\{v_k : v_k A_k \leq u_k + \alpha_k\}}} \left\{ \sum_{k=1}^{n}(a_k + c_k)v_k \right\}$$

(as distinct from the adopted definition of characteristic function).

4.3   Diamond-shaped Control Systems

Hierarchical systems with dual-subordinate divisions are referred to as diamond-shaped. A simple diamond-shaped system is shown schematically in Fig.5. The choice of control for a dual-subordinate division C is dependent on both the control of division B_1 and that of division B_2. We can visualize a situation in which the center B_1 represents the interests of an industry, while B_2 represents regional interests, including environmental issues.

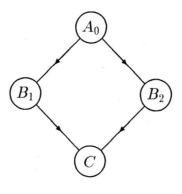

Fig. 5.

A simple diamond-shaped control system provides an example of the hierarchical system with three levels of decision-making. The administrative center placed at the top level commands material and labor resources. By using its resources and authority, this center can bring some influence to bear upon the functioning of its two subordinate centers placed at the next level below. The decisions made by the last two centers largely determine the output of products for the enterprise placed at the bottom level of this hierarchical system.

We shall consider the decision-making process as a four-person game Γ. The challenge now is to construct a rather optimal operation plan for the manufacturing division C and an optimal plan for the administrative centers A_0, B_1, B_2. In the game setting, it is assumed that player A_0 chooses at the first step an element (a strategy) $u = (u_1, u_2)$ from the set A which is called the set of strategies for player A_0. The element $u \in A$ imposes restrictions on the choices to be made by players B_1 and B_2 at the next step. In other words, the set of alternatives for player B_1 is found to be a function of the parameter u_1 and, similarly, the set of alternatives for B_2 is a function of u_2. Denote this sets by $B_1(u_1)$, $B_2(u_2)$ correspondingly. Denote by $w_1 \in B_1(u_1)$ and $w_2 \in B_2(u_2)$ the elements of the sets of alternatives for players B_1 and B_2, respectively.

The parameters w_1 and w_2 selected by players B_1 and B_2 impose restrictions on the set of alternatives (production programs) to be selected by player C at the third step of the game. This set of alternatives will be function of parameters, w_1 and w_2. Denote this set by $C(w_1, w_2)$, and its elements (production programs) by v.

Now the strategies of player A_0 are the elements $u = (u_1, u_2) \in A$; the strategies of players B_1, B_2 and C are the functions $w_1(u_1, u_2)$, $w_2(u_1, u_2)$, $v(w_1, w_2)$ with their values in the respective sets $B_1(u_1)$, $B_2(u_2)$, $C(w_1, w_2)$, setting up a correspondence between the choices made by higher-level players and the alternative selected by this player.

The payoffs to all players are only dependent on the production program v selected by player C and are respectively $f_1(v), f_2(v), f_3(v), f_4(v)$. We assume that $f_i(v) \geq 0$, $i = 1, \ldots, 4$, and there exists $v_0 \in C(w_1, w_2)$ such that $f_i(v_0) = 0$ for any u, w_1, w_2.

We have thus defined a four-person noncooperative game in normal form: $\Gamma = \langle A_0, B_1, B_2, C, f_1, \ldots, f_4 \rangle$.

We shall find a Nash equilibrium in the game Γ. For each pair (w_1, w_2), $w_1 \in B_1$, $w_2 \in B_2$, player C solves the parametric programming problem

$$\max \ f_4(v) \tag{4.6}$$

subject to

$$v \in C(w_1, w_2), \qquad v \geq 0.$$

The solution of problem (4.6) $v^* = v^*(w_1, w_2)$, is found to be a function of the parameters w_1 and w_2.

Further, we need to consider an auxiliary parametric (with u_1, u_2 as parameters) game $\Gamma'(u_1, u_2) = \langle B_1(u_1), B_2(u_2), f_2, f_3 \rangle$ for two persons B_1 and B_2, where $f_2 = f_2(v^*(w_1, w_2))$ and $f_3 = f_3(v^*(w_1. w_2))$ are the payoff functions for B_1 B_2, respectively. Suppose the game $\Gamma'(u_1, u_2)$ has a Nash equilibrium $(w_1^*(u_1, u_2), w_2^*(u_1, u_2))$.

Let the pair (u_1^*, u_2^*) be a solution of the nonlinear optimization problem

$$\max f_1(v^*(w_1^*(u_1, u_2), w_2^*(u_1, u_2))) \tag{4.7}$$

subject to

$$u = (u_1, u_2) \in A.$$

L e m m a 1. The collection

$$(v^*, w_1^*, w_2^*, (u_1^*, u_2^*)), \tag{4.8}$$

where v^* is a solution of problem (4.6) with w_1, w_2 as parameters, (w_1^*, w_2^*) is an equilibrium in the game $\Gamma'(u_1^*, u_2^*)$; and (u_1^*, u_2^*), the solution of problem (4.7), is a Nash equilibrium in the game Γ.

P r o o f.

For convenience, we rename

$$J_{A_0}((u_1, u_2), w_1(u_1, u_2), w_2(u_1, u_2), v(w_1, w_2)) =$$
$$= f_1(v(w_1(u_1, u_2), w_2(u_1, u_2))),$$
$$J_{B_1}((u_1, u_2), w_1(u_1, u_2), w_2(u_1, u_2), v(w_1, w_2)) =$$
$$= f_2(v(w_1(u_1, u_2), w_2(u_1, u_2))),$$
$$J_{B_2}((u_1, u_2), w_1(u_1, u_2), w_2(u_1, u_2), v(w_1, w_2)) =$$
$$= f_3(v(w_1(u_1, u_2), w_2(u_1, u_2))),$$
$$J_C((u_1, u_2), w_1(u_1, u_2), w_2(u_1, u_2), v(w_1, w_2)) =$$
$$= f_4(v(w_1(u_1, u_2), w_2(u_1, u_2))),$$

By the definition of the solution of problem (4. 6) for all $(u_1, u_2) \in A$

$$J_{A_0}((u_1^*, u_2^*), w_1^*(u_1^*, u_2^*), w_2^*(u_1^*, u_2^*), v^*(w_1^*, w_2^*)) =$$
$$= \max_{(u_1, u_2) \in A} f_1(v^*(w_1^*(u_1, u_2), w_2^*(u_1, u_2))) =$$

$$= f_1(v^*(w_1^*(u_1^*, u_2^*), w_2^*(u_1^*, u_2^*))) \geq$$

$$\geq f_1(v^*(w_1^*(u_1, u_2), w_2^*(u_1, u_2))) =$$

$$= J_{A_0}((u_1, u_2), w_1^*(u_1, u_2), w_2^*(u_1, u_2), v^*(w_1, w_2)).$$

Since w_1^* and w_2^* form a Nash equilibrium in the auxiliary game Γ', we have

$$J_{B_1}((u_1^*, u_2^*), w_1^*(u_1, u_2), w_2^*(u_1, u_2), v^*(w_1, w_2)) =$$

$$= f_2(v^*(w_1^*, w_2^*)) \geq f_2(v^*(w_1, w_2^*)) =$$

$$= J_{B_1}((u_1^*, u_2^*), w_1(u_1, u_2), w_2^*(u_1, u_2), v^*(w_1, w_2))$$

for all $w_1 \in B_1(u_1^*)$. A similar reasoning applies to player B_2.

By the definition of the solution of problem (4. 6) for all $v \in C(w_1^*, w_2^*)$

$$J_C((u_1^*, u_2^*), w_1^*(u_1, u_2), w_2^*(u_1, u_2). v^*(w_1, w_2)) =$$

$$= \max_{v \in C(w_1^*, w_2^*)} f_4(v) = f_4(v^*(w_1^*, w_2^*)) \geq$$

$$\geq f_4(v(w_1^*, w_2^*)) = J_C((u_1^*, u_2^*), w_1^*(u_1, u_2), w_2^*(u_1, u_2), v(w_1^*, w_2^*)).$$

Hence, situation (4.8) is a Nash equilibrium in the four person game.

Consider now the cooperative approach and construct the characteristic function $V(S)$ (see [33]). Applying the minimax approach, for each coalition $S \subset \{A_0, B_1, B_2, C\}$ we define $V(S)$ as the largest quaranteed payoff to S in the zero-sum game between coalition S (the maximizing player) and coalition $S' = \{A_0, B_1, B_2, C\} \setminus S$.

We distinguish two forms of coalition:

1)$S : C \bar{\in} S$;

2)$S : C \in S$.

In the first case, $S \subset \{A_0, B_1, B_2\}$ and player C, a member of coalition S', can choose a strategy $v_0 : f_i(v_0) = 0$, $i = 1, 2, 3, 4$.

Therefore $V(S) = 0$. The second case breaks up into the following subcases:

a) $S = \{C\}$:

$$V(\{C\}) = \min_{u \in A} \{ \min_{w_1 \in B_1(u_1)} \min_{w_2 \in B_2(u_2)} [\max_{v \in C(w_1, w_2)} f_4(v)] \}$$

(in what follows, it is assumed that all max and min are attainable);

b) $S = \{A_0, C\}$:

$$V(\{A_0, C\}) =$$

$$= \max_{u \in A} \{ \min_{w_1 \in B_1(u_1)} \min_{w_2 \in B_2(u_2)} [\max_{v \in C(w_1, w_2)} [f_1(v) + f_4(v)] \};$$

c) $S = \{B_1, C\}$:
$$V(\{B_1, C\}) =$$
$$= \min_{u \in A}\{ \max_{w_1 \in B_1(u_1)} \min_{w_2 \in B_2(u_2)} [\max_{v \in C(w_1, w_2)} [f_2(v) + f_4(v)]]\};$$

d) $S = \{B_2, C\}$:
$$V(\{B_2, C\}) =$$
$$= \min_{u \in A}\{ \min_{w_1 \in B_1(u_1)} \max_{w_2 \in B_2(u_2)} [\max_{v \in C(w_1, w_2)} [f_3(v) + f_4(v)]]\}$$

e) $S = \{B_1, B_2, C\}$:
$$V(\{B_1, B_2, C\}) =$$
$$= \min_{u \in A}\{ \max_{w_1 \in B_1(u_1)} \max_{w_2 \in B_2(u_2)} [\max_{v \in C(w_1, w_2)} \sum_{i=2}^{4} f_i(v)]\};$$

f) $S = \{A_0, B_1, C\}$:
$$V(\{A_0, B_1, C\}) =$$
$$\max_{u \in A}\{ \max_{w_1 \in B_1(u_1)} \min_{w_2 \in B_2(u_2)} [\max_{v \in C(w_1, w_2)} \sum_{i=1,2,4} f_i(v)]\};$$

g) $S = \{A_0, B_2, C\}$:
$$V(\{A_0, B_2, C\}) =$$
$$= \max_{u \in A}\{ \max_{w_2 \in B_2(u_2)} \min_{w_1 \in B_1(u_1)} [\max_{v \in C(w_1, w_2)} \sum_{i=1,3,4} f_i(v)]\};$$

h) $S = \{A_0, B_1, B_2, C\}$:
$$V(\{A_0, B_1, B_2, C\}) =$$
$$= \max_{u \in A}\{ \max_{w_1 \in B_1(u_1)} \max_{w_2 \in B_2(u_2)} [\max_{v \in C(w_1, w_2)} \sum_{i=1}^{4} f_i(v)]\};$$

By this definition, the characteristic function shows superadditivity, i.e. for any $S, R \subset \{A_0, B_1, B_2, C\}$, $S \cap R = \emptyset$, $V(S \cup R) \geq V(S) + V(R)$.

We shall now construct the characteristic function by employing the previously obtained strategies and payoffs in a Nash equilibrium. Denote this function by V'.

1)$S \subset \{A_0, B_1, B_2\}$, $V'(S) = 0$;
2)$S : C \in S$;
a) $S = \{C\}$:
$$V'(\{C\}) = \min_{u \in A} \min_{w_1 \in B_1(u_1)} \min_{w_2 \in B_2(u_2)} f_4(v^*(w_1, w_2)) =$$

$$= \min_{w_1 \in B_1(\bar{u}_1)} \min_{w_2 \in B_2(\bar{u}_2)} f_4(v^*(w_1, w_2)) = f_4(v^*(\bar{w}_1, \bar{w}_2)),$$

where $(\bar{u}_1, \bar{u}_2), \bar{w}_1, \bar{w}_2$ are the points at which the relevant minima are attained, while $v^*(\bar{w}_1, \bar{w}_2)$ is the solution of problem (4.6) for parameters $\bar{w}_1$ and $\bar{w}_2$;

b) $S = \{A_0, C\}$:

$$V'(\{A_0, C\}) = \min_{w_1 \in B_1(u_1^*)} \min_{w_2 \in B_2(u_2^*)} [f_1(v^*(w_1, w_2)) + f_4(v^*(w_1, w_2))] =$$

$$= f_1(v^*(\bar{w}_1, \bar{w}_2)) + f_4(v^*(\bar{w}_1, \bar{w}_2)),$$

where $\bar{w}_1, \bar{w}_2$ are the points at which the relevant minima are attained, while v^* and (u_1^*, u_2^*) is the solution of (4.6) (4.7).

Further,

c) $S = \{B_1, C\}$:

$$V'(\{B_1, C\}) = \min_{u \in A} \min_{w_2 \in B_2(u_2)} [f_2(v^*(w_1^*(u_1), w_2)) + f_4(v^*(w_1^*(u_1), w_2))];$$

d) $S = \{B_2, C\}$:

$$V'(\{B_2, C\}) = \min_{u \in A} \min_{w_1 \in B_1(u_1)} [f_3(v^*(w_1, w_2^*(u_2))) + f_4(v^*(w_1, w_2^*(u_2)))];$$

e) $S = \{B_1, B_2, C\}$:

$$V'(\{B_1, B_2, C\}) = \min_{u \in A} [\sum_{i=2}^{4} f_i(v^*(w_1^*(u_1), w_2^*(u_2)))];$$

f) $S = \{A_0, B_1, C\}$:

$$V'(\{A_0, B_1, C\}) = \min_{w_2 \in B_2(u_2^*)} [\sum_{i=1,2,4} f_i(v^*(w_1^*(u_1^*), w_2(u_2^*)))];$$

g) $S = \{A_0, B_2, C\}$:

$$V'(\{A_0, B_2, C\}) = \min_{w_1 \in B_1(u_1^*)} [\sum_{i=1,3,4} f_i(v^*(w_1(u_1^*), w_2^*(u_2^*)))];$$

h) $S = \{A_0, B_1, B_2, C\}$:

$$V'(\{A_0, B_1, B_2, C\}) = \sum_{i=1}^{4} f_i(v^*(w_1^*(u_1^*), w_2^*(u_2^*))).$$

L e m m a 2. The function V' is super additive.

P r o o f . From the construction of the function V' it follows that for any $S \subset \{A_0, B_1, B_2, C\}$ and $i \in [\{A_0, B_1, B_2, C\} \setminus S]$ $V'(S \cup i) \geq V'(S)$ V', i.e. the function V' is monotonic. Let $K, R \subset \{A_0, B_1, B_2, C\}, K \cap R = \emptyset$. Since player C, ensuring the positiveness of $V'(S)$, can only become a member of one of the coalitions, K or R, and hence only one of the addendum, $V'(K)$ or $V'(R)$, can always be nonzero, the superadditivity merely follows from the monotonicity of V'.

Theorem 1.   The vector $\xi^* = \{f_i(v^*(w_1^*(u_1^*), w_2^*(u_2^*))), i = 1, \ldots, 4\}$, where $(u_1^*, u_2^*), w_1^*, w_2^*, v^*$ are the players' strategies from the equilibrium (4.13), is an imputation in the game $\Gamma_{V'}$ and belongs to its core.

P r o o f. Since

$$\sum_{i=1}^{4} \xi_i^* = V'(\{A_0, B_1, B_2, C\}),$$

$$V'(\{A_0\}) = V'(\{B_1\}) = V'(\{B_2\}) = 0,$$

$$f_i(v^*(w_1^*(u_1^*), w_2^*(u_2^*))) \geq 0, i = 1, 2, 3,$$

$$f_4(v^*(w_1^*(u_1^*), w_2^*(u_2^*))) \geq$$

$$\geq \min_{u \in A} \{ \min_{w_1 \in B_1(u_1)} \min_{w_2 \in B_2(u_2)} f_4(v^*(w_1(u_1), w_2(u_2)))\} = V'(\{C\}),$$

then ξ^* is an imputation.

We shall now show that for any $S \subset \{A_0, B_1, B_2, C\}$

$$\sum_{i \in S} f_i(v^*(w_1^*(u_1^*), w_2^*(u_2^*))) \geq V'(S). \tag{4.9}$$

i.e. the imputation ξ^* belongs to the core of the game $\Gamma_{V'}$.

For $S = \{A_0, B_1, B_2, C\}$ and single-element coalitions, this follows from the fact that ξ^* is an imputation. For all $S \in \{A_0, B_1, B_2, C\}$, condition (4.9) follows from the nonnegativity of functions $f_i(v)$, $i = 1, \ldots, 4$, since in this case $V'(S) = 0$. In all other cases, condition (4.9) follows from the fact that the sum on the left-hand side of (4.9) differs from $V'(S)$ in that the minimum is taken in $V'(S)$ over the variables which do not appear in S. For example, we may show this for the case $S = \{A_0, B_2, C\}$. We have

$$V'(\{A_0, B_2, C\}) = \min_{w_1 \in B_1(u_1^*)} [\sum_{i=1,3,4} f_i(v^*(w_1(u_1^*), w_2^*(u_2^*)))] \leq$$

$$\leq \sum_{i=1,3,4} f_i(v^*(w_1^*(u_1^*), w_2^*(u_2^*))).$$

This completes the proof of the theorem.

As is evident from the above examples, hierarchical control systems envisage the presence of several parties each of which pursues its own objective, i.e. it is a typical conflict-controlled system. Therefore a study of decision-making in such systems seems to be justified from the point of view of the theory of games with many players. Unlike the previously described games, in the games that are models of hierarchical systems one player chooses his strategies independently, whereas the other players' strategies are dependent on the choices made by one or more players. In this setting, parametric optimization problems naturally arise where the player's optimal strategies are to be determined. Of course, this involves additional complexities that are primarily technical in nature. For the solution of parametric problems, however, there are adequate computational algorithms, and hence this method of determining optimal strategies for players can be thought of as constructive.

It should be noted that the "economic" terms, such as production program, resources, and manufacturing divisions, are pure conventions used for convenience. In fact, we have discussed here special cases of the general graph (Z, Γ) for the intercomponent relations of section 1 in this chapter.

We shall now discuss a situation which may arise in a study of actual control systems. The administrative center A_0 commands certain resources to be allocated among several divisions C_1, C_2, B. In this case, the products manufactured by division B are used as raw materials in the manufacturing divisions C_1 and C_2. The latter, in turn, turn out final products using the resources supplied by A_0 and B. The relevant graph is shown in Fig.6.

We shall now construct a game theoretic model for this control system. Denote by b the vector of resources available to player A_0. At the first step, A_0 selects a system of three vectors from the set

$$ A = \{u = (u_1, u_2, u_3) : u_i \in R^l, \ i = 1, 2, 3, \ \sum_{i=1}^{3} u_i \le b, \ b \ge 0\}. $$

The vector u_i is interpreted as the set of l resources allocated by center A_0 to the i-th manufacturing division. In this case, $u_i, i = 1, 2$, are destined for $C_i, i = 1, 2$, while u_3 for B. At the second step, player B determines his production program $w = (w^1, w^2)$, allocating w^1 to player C_1 and w^2 to player C_2. The vector w is selected from the set

$$ B(u_3) = \{w = (w^1, w^2) : (w^1 + w^2)A_1 \le u_3, $$

$$ w^1, w^2 \ge 0, \ w^1, w^2 \in R^n, \ A_1 \ge 0\}, $$

where A_1 is a technological matrix for player B.

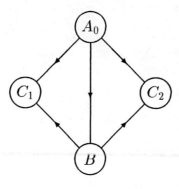

Fig. 6.

Players C_1 and C_2 make their moves at the third step. The choices of the players C_1 and C_2 are dependent on the initial allocation of resources by player A_0 and the resources w^1, w^2 allocated by player C_1. Player C_2 chooses some element from the set

$$C_1(w^1, w^2) = \{v_1 : v_1 A_2 \leq z_1, \ v_1 \geq 0, \ v_1 \in R^k, \ A_2 \geq 0\},$$

where A_2 is a technological matrix for player C_1. Components of the vector $z_1 = (u_1, w^1)$ are components of the vector of resources used by player C_1. Player C_2 selects some element from the set

$$C_2(u_2, w^2) = \{v_2 : v_2 A_2 \leq z_2, \ v_2 \geq 0, \ v_2 \in R^q, \ A_3 \geq 0\},$$

where A_3 is a technological matrix for player C_2. Components of the vector $z_2 = (u_2, w^2)$ are components of the vector of resources used by player C_2.

We shall now determine the payoffs to players. The payoff to player A_0 is only dependent on the output of products by B, C_1, C_2. The payoffs to B, C_1, C_2 are only dependent on their own output of products.

Let $((u_1, u_2, u_3), w(u_3), v_1(u_1, w^1), v_2(u_2, w^2))$ constitute a situation, i.e. $u = (u_1, u_2, u_3) \in A$, $w \in B$, $v_1 \in C_1$, $v_2 \in C_2$. The payoff to player A_0 is

$$J_{A_0}((u_1, u_2, u_3), w(u_3), v_1(u_1, w^1(u_3)), v_2(u_2, w^2(u_3))) =$$
$$= a_1 w(u_3) + a_2 v_1(u_1, w^1) + a_3 v_2(u_2, w^2),$$

where the vectors a_1, a_2, a_3 are unit payoffs to player A_0, when B, C_1 and C_2 select their production programs w, v_1, v_2.

The payoff to player B is

$$J_B((u_1, u_2, u_3), w(u_3), v_1(u_1, w^1(u_3)), v_2(u_2, w^2(u_3))) =$$

$$c_1 w^1(u_3) + c_2 w^2(u_3),$$

where the vectors $c_1, c_2 \geq 0$ are unit payoffs to player B from production $c_1, c_2 \in R^n$.

The payoff to player C_1 is

$$J_{C_1}((u_1, u_2, u_3), w(u_3), v_1(u_1, w^1(u_3)), v_2(u_2, w^2(u_3))) =$$

$$= c_3 v_1(u_1, w^1),$$

where $c_3 \geq 0$ is to be interpreted in much the same way as vectors c_1, c_2. The payoff to player C_2 is determined in a similar manner

$$J_{C_2}((u_1, u_2, u_3), w(u_3), v_1(u_1, w^1(u_3)), v_2(u_2, w^2(u_3))) = c_4 v_2(u_2, w^2), \quad c_4 \geq 0$$

We have thus defined a four-person game in normal form:

$$\Gamma = \langle A, B, B, C_1, C_2; J_{A_0}, J_B, J_{C_1}, J_{C_2} \rangle.$$

We shall construct a Nash equilibrium in this game. Optimal strategies for player C_1 and C_2 will be constructed as a solution to some of the linear programming problems.

Suppose player C_1 chooses a strategy $v_1^*(u_1, w^{(1)})$ from the condition

$$\max(c_3 v_1) = c_3 v_1^*(u_1, w^{(1)}) \tag{4.10}$$

subject to

$$v_1 A_2 \leq z_1 \ (z_1 = (u_1, w^{(1)})), v_1 \geq 0, A_2 \geq 0.$$

When the optimal strategy is used, his payoff is $c_3 v_1^*(u_1, w^{(1)})$.

Suppose player C_2 chooses a strategy $v_2^*(u_2, w^{(2)})$ from the condition

$$\max(c_4 v_2) = c_4 v_2^*(u_2, w^{(2)}) \tag{4.11}$$

subject to

$$v_2 A_3 \leq z_2 \ (z_2 = (u_2, w^{(2)})), v_2 \geq 0, A_3 \geq 0.$$

When the optimal strategy is used, his payoff is $c_4 v_2^*(u_2, w^{(2)})$.

The optimal strategy of player B will be constructed as a solution of the linear parametric programming problem below. Player B chooses his strategy $w^*(u_3) = (w^{(1)*}(u_3), w^{(2)*}(u_3))$ from the condition

$$\max[c_1 w^{(1)} + c_2 w^{(2)}] = c_1 w^{(1)*}(u_3) + c_2 w^{(2)*}(u_3) \tag{4.12}$$

subject to

$$(w^{(1)} + w^{(2)})A_1 \leq u_3, \quad w^{(1)} \geq 0, \quad w^{(2)} \geq 0, \quad A_1 \geq 0.$$

When the optimal strategy is used, his payoff is $c_1 w^{(1)*}(u_3) + c_2 w^{(2)*}(u_3)$. Introducing the vector $c = (c_1, c_2)$, $w = (w^{(1)}, w^{(2)})$, we may represent the payoff function as $c_1 w^{(1)} + c_2 w^{(2)} = cw$. The optimal strategy of player A_0 is determined from the solution of the nonlinear programming problem

$$\max[a_1 w^*(u_3) + a_2 v_1^*(u_1, w^{(1)*}(u_3)) + a_3 v_2^*(u_2, w^{(2)*}(u_3))] \tag{4.13}$$

subject to

$$u_1 + u_2 + u_3 \leq b, \quad u_1 \geq 0, \quad u_2 \geq 0, \quad u_3 \geq 0.$$

The objective function in this problem is essentially nonlinear, since the functions $w^*(u_3), v_1^*(u_1, w^{(1)*}), v_2^*(u_2, w^{(2)*})$ are also essentially nonlinear. Solving this problem yields the vectors u_1^*, u_2^*, u_3^* which determine resource allocation plans that are optimal from the point of view of player A_0.

L e m m a 3. The collection

$$((u_1^*, u_2^*, u_3^*), w^*, v_1^*, v_2^*) \tag{4.14}$$

where (u_1^*, u_2^*, u_3^*) is a solution of problem (4.13); $w^*(w^{(1)*}, w^{(2)*})$ is a solution of problem (4.12); v_1^*, v_2^* is a solution of problems (4.10) and (4.11), is an equilibrium in the game Γ.

P r o o f . For all $u \in A$

$$J_{A_0}(u^*, w^*(u_3), v_1^*(u_1, w^{(1)}(u_3)), v_2^*(u_2, w^{(2)}(u_3))) =$$

$$= a_1 w^*(u_3^*) + a_2 v_1^*(u_1^*, w^{(1)*}(u_3^*)) + a_3 v_2^*(u_2^*, w^{(2)*}(u_3^*)) \geq$$

$$\geq a_1 w^*(u_3) + a_2 v_1^*(u_1, w^{(1)*}(u_3)) + a_3 v_2^*(u_2, w^{(2)*}(u_3)) =$$

$$= J_{A_0}(u, w^*(u_3), v_1^*(u_1, w^{(1)}(u_3)), v_2^*(u_2, w^{(2)}(u_3))).$$

For all $w \in B(u_3)$, $(w = (w^{(1)}, w^{(2)}))$

$$J_B(u^*, w^*(u_3), v_1^*(u_1, w^{(1)}(u_3)), v_2^*(u_2, w^{(2)}(u_3))) =$$

$$= c_1 w^{(1)*}(u_3^*) + c_2 w^{(2)*}(u_3^*) \geq c_1 w^{(1)}(u_3^*) + c_2 w^{(2)}(u_3^*) =$$

$$= J_B(u^*, w(u_3), v_1^*(u_1, w^{(1)}(u_3)), v_2^*(u_2, w^{(2)}(u_3))).$$

For all $v_1 \in C_1(u_1, w^{(1)})$

$$J_{C_1}(u^*, w^*(u_3), v_1^*(u_1, w^{(1)}(u_3)), v_2^*(u_2, w^{(2)}(u_3))) =$$

$$= c_3 v_1^*(u_1^*, w^{(1)*}(u_3^*)) \geq c_3 v_1(u_1^*, w^{(1)*}(u_3^*)) =$$

$$= J_{C_1}(u^*, w^*(u_3), v_1(u_1, w^{(1)}(u_3)), v_2^*(u_2, w^{(2)}(u_3))).$$

Finally, for all $v_2 \in C_2(u_2, w^{(2)})$

$$J_{C_2}(u^*, w^*(u_3), v_1^*(u_1, w^{(1)}(u_3)), v_2^*(u_2, w^{(2)}(u_3))) =$$

$$= c_4 v_2^*(u_2^*, w^{(2)*}(u_3^*)) \geq c_4 v_2(u_2^*, w^{(2)*}(u_3^*)) =$$

$$= J_{C_2}(u^*, w^*(u_3), v_1^*(u_1, w^{(1)}(u_3)), v_2(u_2, w^{(2)}(u_3))).$$

All of the above inequalities follow from the definitions of max in the problems (4.10)- (4.13), i.e. the equilibrium (4.14) is actually a Nash equilibrium in the game four person Γ.

We shall construct a characteristic function. Note that players B, C_1 and C_2 have no resources except those they receive from A_0. Therefore, in the construction of characteristic function we distinguish two cases:

1) $S \subset \{B, C_1, C_2\}$, i.e. $A_0 \bar{\in} S$;

2) $S : A_0 \in S$.

1. We first use the minimax method. Since in case 1) player A_0 can always denude coalition $\{B, C_1, C_2\}$ and its any subcoalition of resources, thereby stopping production, we have $V(S) = 0$. Case 2) breaks up into the following subcases:

) $S = \{A_0\}$. The payoff to player A_0 is dependent on the output of products by players B, C_1 and C_2 which, having formed a coalition, can refuse to manufacture products, thereby assuring player A_0 of getting a zero payoff $V(\{A_0\}) = 0$.

b) $S = \{A_0, B\}$. Player A_0 allocates all the available resources to player B. Therefore the maximum profit the coalition $\{A_0, B\}$ guarantees itself is $\max_w((a_1 + c)w), c = (c_1, c_2)$ subject to

$$(w_{(1)} + w_{(2)})A_1 \leq b, \qquad w_{(1)} \geq 0, \qquad w_{(2)} \geq 0.$$

Denote by $\tilde{w}(b)$ the solution of this problem. Then $V(\{A_0, B\}) = (a_1 + c)\tilde{w}(b)$.

Note that, in general, $\tilde{w}(b) \neq w^*(b)$, where $w^*(b)$ is a solution of problem (4.12) for $u_3 = b$.

c) $S = \{A_0, C_1\}$. Player A_0 allocates all of his resources to player C_1, whereas B allocates a zero resource to player C_1. The profit to coalition $\{A_0, C_1\}$ is $\max_{v_1}((a_2 + c_3)v_1)$ subject to $v_1 A_2 \leq (b, 0)$, $v_1 \geq 0$.

Denote by $\tilde{v}_1(b, 0)$ the solution of this problem. In the general case, $\tilde{v}_1(b, 0) \neq v_1^*(b, 0)$, where $v_1^*(b, 0)$ is a solution of problem (4.15) for $u_1 = b$, $w^{(1)} = 0$. The required value is $V(\{A_0, C_1\}) = (a_2 + c_3)\tilde{v}_1(b, 0)$.

d) $S = \{A_0, C_2\}$. This case is symmetrical to case c), and hence $V(\{A_0, C_2\}) = (a_3 + c_4)\tilde{v}_2(b, 0)$, where $\tilde{v}_2(b, 0)$ is a solution of the following problem $\max_{v_2}((a_3 + c_4)\tilde{v}_2)$ subject to $v_2 A_3 \leq (b, 0)$, $v_2 \geq 0$.

Note that $\tilde{v}_2(b, 0) \neq v_2^*(b, 0)$ (see (4. 11)).

e) $S = \{A_0, B, C_1\}$. In this case player A_0 allocates his all resources between players B and C_1, whereas B allocates his all products to C_1, and

$$V(\{A_0, B, C_1\}) = (a_1 + c)\tilde{w}(\tilde{u}_3) + (a_2 + c_3)\tilde{v}_1(\tilde{u}_1, \tilde{w}^{(1)}(\tilde{u}_3)),$$

where $((\tilde{u}_1, \tilde{u}_3), \tilde{v}_1, \tilde{w})$ is a solution of the problem

$$\max_{u_1, u_3} \max_{v_1} \max_{w}[(a_1 + c)w(u_3) + (a_2 + c_3)v_1(u_1, w(u_3))]$$

subject to $(w = w_{(1)} + w_{(2)})$.

$$wA_1 \leq u_3, vA_2 \leq (u_1, w), \qquad u_1 + u_3 \leq b, \qquad w, v_1, u_1, u_3 \geq 0.$$

Obviously, $\tilde{w}(\tilde{u}_3) \neq \tilde{w}^*(\tilde{u}_3^*)$ (see (4.12)) and $\tilde{v}_1(\tilde{u}_1, \tilde{w}(\tilde{u}_3)) \neq v_1^*(u_1^*, w^{(1)*}(u_3^*))$ (see (4.10))

f) $S = \{A_0, B, C_2\}$. This case is symmetrical to case e), and hence

$$V(\{A_0, B, C_2\}) = (a_1 + c)\tilde{w}(\tilde{u}_3) + (a_3 + c_4)\tilde{v}_2(\tilde{u}_2, \tilde{w}(\tilde{u}_3)),$$

where $((\tilde{u}_2, \tilde{u}_3), \tilde{v}_2, \tilde{w})$ is a solution of the problem

$$\max_{u_2, u_3} \max_{v_2} \max_{w}[(a_1 + c)w(u_3) + (a_3 + c_4)v_2(u_2, w(u_3))]$$

subject to $(w = w_{(1)} + w_{(2)})$.

$$wA_1 \leq u_3, \qquad v_2 A_3 \leq (u_2, w), \qquad u_2 + u_3 \leq b, \qquad w, v_2, u_2, u_3 \geq 0.$$

g) $S = \{A_0, C_1, C_2\}$. Player A_0 allocates his all resources to C_1 and C_2, whereas player B supplies no resources to players C_1 C_2:

$$V(\{A_0, C_1, C_2\}) = (a_2 + c_3)\tilde{v}_1(\tilde{u}_1, 0) + (a_3 + c_4)\tilde{v}_2(\tilde{u}_2, 0),$$

where $((\tilde{u}_1, \tilde{u}_2), \tilde{v}_1, \tilde{v}_2)$ is a solution of the problem

$$\max_{u_1, u_2} \max_{v_1} \max_{w_2} [(a_2 + c_3)v(u_1, 0) + (a_3 + c_4)v_2(u_2, 0)]$$

subject to

$$v_1 A_2 \leq (u_1, 0), \qquad v_2 A_3 \leq (u_2, 0), \qquad u_1 + u_2 \leq b, \qquad v_1, v_2, u_1, u_2 \geq 0.$$

Obviously, $\tilde{v}_1(\tilde{u}_1, 0) \neq v_1^*(u_1^*, 0)$ (see (4.15)) and $\tilde{v}_2(\tilde{u}_2, 0) \neq v_2^*(u_2^*, 0)$ (see (4.11)).

h) $S = \{A_0, B, C_1, C_2\}$.

$$V(\{A_0, B, C_1, C_2\}) = \max_{u} \max_{v_1} \max_{v_2} \max_{w} [(a_1 + c)w(u_3) +$$

$$(a_2 + c_3)v_1(u_1, w^{(1)}) + (a_3 + c_4)v_2(u_2, w^{(2)})]$$

subject to

$$wA_1 \leq u_3, \qquad v_1 A_2 \leq (u_1, w_{(1)}(u_3)), \qquad v_2 A_3 \leq (u_2, w_{(2)}(u_3)),$$

$$u_1 + u_2 + u_3 \leq b, \qquad w, v_1, v_2, u_1, u_2, u_3 \geq 0.$$

By defining for each coalition $S \subset \{A_0, B, C_1, C_2\}$ its guaranteed payoff $V(S)$ as the value of zero sum game, we have defined a super additive function V in terms of which we may consider the relevant cooperative game.

2. We shall construct the characteristic function V' in terms of the equilibrium (4.14). Here the preceding cases also hold.

1) For all $S \subset \{B, C_1, C_2\}$, i.e. for those coalitions which do not contain A_0, we obtain $V'(S) = 0$.

2) $S \subset \{A_0, B, C_1, C_2\} : A_0 \in S$.

a) $S = \{A_0\} : V'(A_0) = 0$;

b) $S = \{A_0, B\} : V'(\{A_0, B\}) = (a_1 + c)w^*(b)$, where $w^*(b)$ is a solution of the problem (4.12) for $u_3 = b$;

c) $S = \{A_0, C_1\} : V'(\{A_0, C_1\}) = (a_2 + c_3)v_1^*(b, 0)$, where $v_1^*(b, 0)$ is a solution of problem (4.10) for $u_1 = b$, $w^{(1)} = 0$;

d) $S = \{A_0, C_2\} : V'(\{A_0, C_2\}) = (a_3 + c_4)v_2^*(b, 0)$, where $v_2^*(b, 0)$ is a solution of problem (4. 11) for $u_2 = b$, $w^{(2)} = 0$;

e) $S = \{A_0, B, C_1\}$. In order to compute the values of the characteristic function for this case, we shall consider an auxiliary noncooperative game Γ_1 for three persons A_0, B and C_1 and construct therein a Nash equilibrium.

In the game Γ_1, player A_0 allocates resources to players B and C_1. Having received a supply of resources u_{31} from player A_0, player B delivers his products

w_1 to playerC_1. Player C_1 receives a supply of resources u_{11} from A_0 and uses them to manufacture final products v_{11}. Double indices in parameters u_{11}, u_{31}, v_{11} and a subscript in w_1 show that a decision is made in the game Γ_1.

In the game Γ_1, the set of strategies for player A_0 is

$$\{(u_{11}, u_{31}) | u_{11} \geq 0,\ u_{31} \geq 0,\ u_{11} + u_{31} \leq b,\ u_{11}, u_{31}, b \in R^l\}.$$

The strategies of player B are functions of the form $w_1(u_{31})$ with values in the set

$$\{w_1 | w_1 A_1 \leq u_{31},\ w_1 \geq 0,\ w_1 \in R^n,\ A_1 \geq 0\}.$$

The strategies of player C_1 are functions $v_{11}(w_1, u_{11})$ with values in the set $\{v_{11} A_2 \leq (u_{11}, w_1),\ u_{11} \geq 0,\ A_2 \geq 0\}$.

In order to construct an equilibrium in the game Γ_1, we shall consider the following three problems:

$$\max(c_3 v_{11}) \tag{4.15}$$

subject to $v_{11} A_2 \leq (u_{11}, w_1), v_{11} \geq 0, A_2 \geq 0$;

$$\max(c_1 w_1) \tag{4.16}$$

subject to $(w_2 + w_1) A_1 \leq u_{31}, w_1 \geq 0, u_{31} \geq 0, w_2 \geq 0, A_1 > 0$;

$$\max[a_1 \overline{w}_1(u_{31}) + a_2 \overline{v}_{11}(u_{11}, \overline{w}_1(u_{31}))] \tag{4.17}$$

subject to $u_{11} + u_{31} \leq b, u_{11} \geq 0, u_{31} \geq 0, b \geq 0$, where $\overline{v}_{11}, \overline{w}_1$ are solutions of the linear parametric programming problems (4.15), (4.16). Unlike the former two problems, problem (4.17) is a nonlinear programming problem.

L e m m a 4. The situation $((\overline{u}_{11}, \overline{u}_{31}), \overline{w}_1, \overline{v}_{11})$ made up of the solutions of (4.17), (4.16),(4.15), respectively, is equilibrium in the game Γ_1.

This Lemma can be proved in much the same way as Lemma 3.

We now assume that

$$V'(\{A_0, B, C_1\}) = (a_1 + c)\overline{w}_1(\overline{u}_{31}) + (a_2 + c_3)\overline{v}_{11}(\overline{u}_{11}, \overline{w}_1(\overline{u}_{31}))$$

is the total payoff to players A_0, B, C_1 in the Nash equilibrium in the game Γ_1 $(c = c_1 + c_2)$.

f) $S = \{A_0, B, C_2\}$. In order to compute the values of the characteristic function for this case, we shall consider an auxiliary noncooperative game Γ_2 for three persons A_0, B and C_2. In the game Γ_2, the Nash equilibrium is constructed in the same way as in the preceding case (in the game Γ_1). Let

$((\overline{\overline{u}}_{22}, \overline{\overline{u}}_{32}), \overline{\overline{w}}_2, \overline{\overline{v}}_{22})$ be such an equilibrium. We set $V'(\{A_0, B, C_2\})$ equal to the total payoff to players A_0, B, C_2 in the Nash equilibrium in the game Γ_2:

$$V'(\{A_0, B, C_2\}) = (a_1 + c)\overline{\overline{w}}_2(\overline{\overline{u}}_{32}) + (a_3 + c_4)\overline{\overline{v}}_{22}(\overline{\overline{u}}_{22}, \overline{\overline{w}}_2(\overline{\overline{u}}_{32})).$$

g) $S = \{A_0, C_1, C_2\}$. As in the two preceding games, we shall consider an auxiliary noncooperative game Γ_3 involving three players A_0, C_1, and C_2, and construct therein a Nash equilibrium.

Let $((\hat{u}_{13}, \hat{u}_{23}), \hat{v}_{13}, \hat{v}_{23})$ be an equilibrium in the game Γ_3. Set $V'(\{A_0, C_1, C_2\})$ equal to the total payoff to the players in this equilibrium:

$$V'(\{A_0, C_1, C_2\}) = (a_2 + c_3)\hat{v}_{13}(\hat{u}_{13}) + (a_3 + c_4)\hat{v}_{23}(\hat{u}_{23}).$$

h) $S = \{A_0, B, C_1, C_2\}$:

$$V'(\{A_0, B, C_1, C_2\}) = (a_1 + c)w^*(u_3^*)+$$

$$+(a_2 + c_3)v_1^*(u_1^*, w^{(1)*}(u_3^*)) + (a_3 + c_4)v_2^*(u_2^*, w^{(2)*}(u_3^*)),$$

i.e. the value of the characteristic function for the maximum coalition is the total payoff to the players in the Nash equilibrium (4.14) in the game Γ.

L e m m a 5. The function V' is super additive.

This Lemma is proved in much the same way as Lemma 2.

The payoff vector

$$\xi = (a, w^*(u_3^*) + a_2v_1^*(u_1^*, w^{(1)*}(u_3^*))a_3v_2^*(u_2^*, w^{(2)*}(u_3^*));$$

$$cw^*(u_3^*); c_3v_1^*(u_1^*, w^{(1)*}(u_3^*)); c_4v_2^*(u_2^*, w^{(2)*}(u_3^*))),$$

whose components are the players' payoffs in the equilibrium (4.14), is an imputation in the game Γ. In fact,

$$\sum_{i=1}^{4} \xi_i = V'(A_0, B, C_1, C_2), \quad \xi \geq 0, \quad i = 1, ..., 4,$$

$$V'(\{A_0\}) = V'(\{B\}) = V'(\{C_1\}) = V'(\{C_2\}) = 0.$$

Unlike a simple diamond-shaped hierarchical control system (Theorem 1), we cannot claim here that the imputation ξ belongs to the core of the game $\Gamma_{V'}$.

4.4   Dynamic Hierarchical Control Systems

Dynamic allocation problem. In section 1 of this chapter we discussed a static two-level control system with one administrative center A_0 and n manufacturing divisions $B_1, B_2, \ldots, B_n$. For this system we found Nash-optimal controls, constructed a characteristic function, and defined the condition for belonging of the player's payoff vector to the core of cooperative game.

In this section we shall consider the functioning of the control system in time or, more precisely, on the interval $[0, T]$, assuming that the parameter t ranges over a discrete set of values $0 = t_1 < t_2 < \ldots < t_m = T$. We assume that all the parameters in this problem vary with time, i.e. the variables $b, A_i, c_i, a_i, \alpha_i, i = 1, \ldots, n$, are functions of time: $b(t), A_i(t), c_i(t), a_i(t), \alpha_i(t), i = 1, \ldots, n$.

The administrative center A_0 and manufacturing divisions $B_1, B_2, \ldots, B_n$ seek to maximize the profit that is total for the entire functioning period of the system, i.e. the payoffs to players $A_0, B_1, \ldots, B_n$ are respectively

$$\sum_{k=1}^{m} \sum_{i=1}^{n} (a_i(t_k), v_i(t_k)), \ \sum_{k=1}^{m} (c_1(t_k), v_1(t_k)), \ldots, \ \sum_{k=1}^{m} (c_n(t_k), v_n(t_k)),$$

where $v_i(t_k) = v_i(u, t_k)$ is the production program which is approved by division B_i at time t_k and satisfies the constraints

$$v_i(t_k) A_i(t_k) \leq u_i(t_k) + \alpha_i(t_k), \qquad v_i(t_k) \geq 0,$$

following from the choice of resources allocation

$$u(t_k) = (u_1(t_k), \ldots, u_n(t_k)), \qquad \sum_{i=1}^{n} u_i(t_k) \leq b(t_k), \qquad u_i(t_k) \geq 0$$

made by the administrative center A_0 at the time t_k; $\alpha_i(t_k)$ is the vector of resources available to division B_i at the time t_k.

Denote by $\Gamma(t_k)$ a static game considered for the year t_k, where the players' payoffs are

$$\sum_{i=1}^{n} (a_i(t_k), v_i(t_k)), \ (c_1(t_k), v_1(t_k)), \ \ldots, \ (c_n(t_k), v_n(t_k)).$$

We shall consider the current games $\Gamma(t_k, T)$, $t_k \in [0, T]$, along with the games $\Gamma(t_k)$, on the time interval $[t_k, T]$. The players' payoffs in $\Gamma(t_k, T)$ are

$$\sum_{l=k}^{m} \sum_{i=1}^{n} (a_i(t_l), v_i(t_l)), \ \sum_{l=k}^{m} (c_1(t_l), v_1(t_l)), \ \ldots, \ \sum_{l=k}^{m} (c_n(t_l), v_n(t_l)),$$

Let $u^*(t_k), v_1^*(u, t_k), \ldots, v_n^*(u, t_k)$ be Nash equilibria in the static game $\Gamma(t_k)$. Using the line of reasoning of section 1 in this chapter, we may show that the Nash equilibrium in the game $\Gamma(t_k, T)$ consists of players' using each year t_l, $(l \geq k)$ those strategies which form the Nash equilibrium in the static game $\Gamma(t_l)$, i.e. it is of the form

$$(u_{t_k}^*(t), v_{1,t_k}^*(u, t), \ldots, v_{n,t_k}^*(u, t)),$$

where

$$u_{t_k}^*(t) = \begin{cases} u^*(t_k), t \in [t_k, t_{k+1}), \\ \cdots\cdots\cdots\cdots\cdots, \\ u^*(t_{m-1}), t \in [t_{m-1}, T), \\ u^*(T), t = T, \end{cases}$$

$$v_{i,t_k}^*(u, t) = \begin{cases} v_i^*(u, t_k), t \in [t_k, t_{k+1}), \\ \cdots\cdots\cdots\cdots\cdots, \\ v_i^*(u, t_{m-1}), t \in [t_{m-1}, T), \\ v_i^*(T), t = T, \end{cases}$$

Denote $N = \{A_0, B_1, \ldots, B_n, \}$. In the game $\Gamma(t_0, T)$, we define the function $V(S, t_0, T)$, $S \subset T$, using the payoffs and strategies in the Nash equilibrium. The construction of the function $V(S, t_0, T)$ is similar to that of the characteristic function (4.4) but for a few differences in the form of payoffs to players in static and dynamic games. For this reason, the relevant formulas are given without proof:

1) for A_0 $V(A_0, t_0, T) = 0$;

2) for $S \subset \{B_1, \ldots, B_n\}$

$$V(S, t_0, T) = \sum_{l=1}^{m} \sum_{i \in S} (c_i(t_l), v_i^*(0, t_l)); \tag{4.18}$$

3) for $S(A_0 \in S)$

$$V(S, t_0, T) = \sum_{l=1}^{m} \sum_{i \in S} [a_i(t_l) + c_i(t_l)] v_i^*(u^{*S}(t_l), t_l),$$

where $u^{*S}(t_l)$ is a solution of the nonlinear programming problem

$$\max_{u} \sum_{l=1}^{m} \sum_{i \in S} a_i(t_l) v_i^*(u(t_l), t_l)$$

subject to $\sum_{i \in S} u_i(t_l) \leq b(t_l)$, $u_i(t_l) \geq 0$, $i \in S$, $l = 1, \ldots, m$.

Since the controls $u_i(t_l)$ for various l are selected independently, the function $V(S, t_0, T)$ is equal to the sum of characteristic functions in static games $\Gamma(t_l)$, $l = 1, \ldots, m$, i.e. we have the following representation (compare (4.4) and (4.18)):

$$V(S, t_0, T) = \sum_{l=1}^{m} V(S, t_l), \qquad S \subset N, \tag{4.19}$$

where $V(S, t_l)$ is a characteristic function in the static game $\Gamma(t_l)$ defined by (4.4). From (4.19) it immediately follows that the function $V(S, t_0, T)$ is super additive in S, since this property, as indicated above, is possessed by the function $V(S, t_l)$, $l = 1, \ldots, m$. Hence, $V(S, t_0, T)$ is the characteristic function and generates a cooperative game $\Gamma_V(t_0, T)$.

We shall now construct an $(n + 1)$ vector

$$\eta^0 = \Big(\sum_{l=1}^{m} \sum_{i=1}^{n} (a_i(t_l) v_i^*(u^*(t_l), t_l))\Big),$$

$$\sum_{l=1}^{m} (c_1(t_l), v_1^*(u^*(t_l), t_l)), \; \ldots,$$

$$\sum_{l=1}^{m} (c_n(t_l) v_n^*(u^*(t_l), t_l))\Big),$$

whose components are respectively equal to the payoffs of players $A_0, B_1, \ldots, B_n$ in a Nash equilibrium. Also, it will be shown that this vector is an imputation in the cooperative game $\Gamma_V(x_0, T)$ in the form of characteristic function $V(S, t_0, T)$. Let us examine the vector

$$\eta^0 = \sum_{l=1}^{m} \xi^{t_l}, \tag{4.20}$$

where the $(n + 1)$ vector ξ^{t_l} is $\xi^{t_l} = (\sum_{i=1}^{n} a_i(t_l) v_i^*(u^*(t_l), t_l)), c_1(t_l) v_1^*(u^*(t_l), t_l),$ $\ldots, c_n(t_l) v_n^*(u^*(t_l), t_l))$.

As discussed earlier (see (4. 5) in sec. 2), the ξ^{t_l} is an imputation in the static cooperative game $\Gamma_V(t_l)$ in the form of characteristic function $V(S, t_l)$, i.e.

1) $\xi_i^{t_l} \geq V(\{i\}, t_l)$, $i \in N$;
2) $\sum_{i \in N} \xi_i^{t_l} = V(N, t_l)$, $l = 1, \ldots, m$.

From this we have

$$\sum_{l=1}^{m} \xi_i^{t_l} \geq \sum_{l=1}^{m} V(\{i\}, t_l); \qquad i \in N;$$

$$\sum_{l=1}^{m} \sum_{i \in N} \xi_i^{t_l} = \sum_{l=1}^{m} V(N, t_l),$$

or, applying (4.19) and (4.20),

$$\eta_i^0 \geq V(\{i\}, t_0, T), \qquad i \in N; \qquad \sum_{i \in N} \eta_i^0 = V(N, t_0, T).$$

Hence, η^0 is actually an imputation in the game $\Gamma_V(t_0, T)$. Further, using the line of reasoning from section 1 in this chapter, it can be shown that the sharing η^0 belongs to the core $C_V(t_0, T)$ of the game $\Gamma_V(t_0, T)$ if

$$\sum_{i \in S} a_i(t_l) v_i^*(u^{*S}(t_l), t_l) \geq$$

$$\geq \sum_{i \in S} (a_i(t_l) + c_i(t_l))[v_i^*(u^{*S}(t_l), t_l) - v_i^*(u(t_l), t_l)] \qquad (4.21)$$

for all $l = 1, \ldots, m$ and $S : A_0 \in S$. From this it follows that if the players every year t_l share the profits according to an imputation ξ^{t_l}, and condition (4.21) is satisfied (it is interpreted in the same economic terms as the relevant condition from section 2 in this chapter), then their dynamic stable (time-consistent) functioning is guaranteed.

We shall now consider the functioning of the diamond-shaped system (see Fig.5 in sec. 3) on the interval $[t_0, T]$. Suppose that Δ is an arbitrary partitioning of the interval $[l_0, T]$ by the points t_k, $k = 0, 1, \ldots, m$. Let $\Gamma(t_0, T)$ be the relevant game, where $t_0 = 0$.

The payoffs to players A_0, B_1, B_2, C in $\Gamma(t_0, T)$ are respectively

$$J_i(t_0, v(t)) = \sum_{k=0}^{m} f_i(t_k, v(t_k)), \qquad i = 1, \ldots, 4,$$

where $v(t_k) \in C(w_1(t_k), w_2(t_k))$ is a production program for player C at the time $t_k \in \Delta$; $w_i(t_k, u_i(t_l))$ is a control for player B_i at the time t_k, and $u(t_k) = (u_1(t_k), u_1(t_k))$ is a control for player A_0 at that time.

We shall define the static noncooperative game $\Gamma(t_k)$ with payoffs $f_i(t_k), i = 1, \ldots, 4$ at the time t_k. Let

$$(v^*(t_k), w_1^*(t_k), w_2^*(t_k), u^*(t_k)) \qquad (4.22)$$

be a Nash equilibrium in the game $\Gamma(t_k)$. The strategies from (4.22) are determined by solving problems (4.6)–(4.8), where all parameters are determined at the time t_k. Then the situation

$$(v_{t_0}^*(t), w_{1t_0}^*(t), w_{2t_0}^*(t), u_{t_0}^*(t))$$

where

$$v_{t_0}^*(t) = \begin{cases} v^*(t_0), \text{if} \quad t \in [t_0, t_1), \\ \dots\dots\dots\dots, \\ v^*(t_{m-1}), \text{if} \quad t \in [t_{m-1}, T), \\ v^*(T), \text{if} \quad t = T, \end{cases}$$

is equilibrium in the game $\Gamma(t_0, T)$ (see sec. 2 in this chapter). Strategies w_1^*, w_2^*, u^* are determined in a similar manner. Making use of (4.22) and payoffs (4.21) in this situation, we construct a characteristic function (see sec. 1 in this chapter).

Now we have a representation

$$V'(S, t_0, T) = \sum_{k=0}^{m} V'(S, t_k), \qquad S \subset \{A_0, B_1, B_2, C\},$$

where $V'(S, t_k)$ is the characteristic function for $\Gamma(t_k)$ constructed in the same way. By Lemma 5, $V'(S, t_k)$ is super additive in S, and hence $V'(S, t_k, T)$ is also super additive in S. Moreover, it follows from this representation that $V'(S, t_k, T)$ is additive in t_k. Therefore the assertion that the imputation

$$\xi = \{J_i(t_0, v_{t_0}^*(t))\}$$

belongs to the core of the game and its dynamic stability, can be proved by reference to Theorem 1.

The development planning of closed ecosystems should take into account the major and minor components of system which may be large in number even in the simplest cases. When the development of system is governed by legislative acts or by allocating resources and capital investments, the interaction of components can be modelled by a hierarchical game on a finite graph of inter-component relations. Because of a large number of participants whose interests do not necessarily coincide, the hierarchical games under consideration prove to be non zero sum games involving many players, and hence the basic challenge here is to formulate an acceptable optimality principle. We examined the simplest of hierarchical games: tree-like, diamond-shaped, diamond-shaped with additional relations, etc. When analyzing the feasibility of optimal behavior, we compared in each case various optimality principles: the Nash equilibrium and the core constructed by employing various forms of characteristic functions. We thus obtained effective methods for finding optimality principles where their existence is ensured by suitable analytic conditions. In spite of effectiveness of constructions, in the above-mentioned simplest cases the actual computations of optimal behavior may prove to be rather complicated. The approach discussed above can be extended to more general hierarchical games modelling the interaction of closed ecosystems with a large number of major components. At the same time, large dimension of problem may hamper provision of specific recommendations for optimal behavior. For this reason, the most acceptable seems to be only that model which correctly selects a few major (controlled) components of the system.

Chapter 5

MULTICRITERIA OPTIMIZATION MODELS

5.1 Development Models of Closed Ecosystems

This chapter deals with mathematical models for development of environmentally closed regions.

It is well known that environmental problems arise not by themselves, but in close relation to other problems of control and development. Creative activities of man in the last decades have resulted in environmental changes that are comparable to those which proceeded during millions of years.

Some of the most beautiful landscapes are man-made. These are flowering meadows, woods and pastures in the mountains of Europe, terraces and rice fields in South-East Asia, pampases and savannas in southern Africa developed to prepare hunting areas. Human activities in creation and maintenance of genetic diversity are difficult to overestimate. The results of such activities are observed, e.g., where the species diversity of domestic animals (sheeps, cattle, dogs, fur-bearing animals) is increased. Some species became extinct because man could not prevent them from spreading at a proper time, which undermined a food supply in their natural habitat.

Thus, in order to preserve natural diversity, we need to take into account the principle of active control. Development of environmentally closed regions resulting from human activities is objective reality, and hence should not be perceived as something prohibitive or undesirable.

Environmental protection and preservation of existing ecosystems may pose acute problems where the long-range development planning of industrial and agricultural production is concerned. If environmental aspects of development are to be taken into account, we need to introduce additional development objectives which are in keeping with specific environmental requirements.

To give an objective assessment of development results, it would appear natural to employ several independent criteria some of which satisfy the requirements for environmental protection and preservation of existing ecosystems. For the most part the "ecological" group of criteria is hardly compatible with the "economic" group and thus combination (scalarization) of such criteria is not justified. This leads to statement of multicriterial problems of optimal control which are still poorly known. When the parties seeking to establish environmental criteria can exert strong influence on development, we arrive at the conflict-controlled processes described by non zero sum differential games.

Qualitative assessment of any development program must take into account the time factor which may bring about changes in development objectives, and hence cause the chosen solution to lose dynamic stability. Referring to [19], we have numerous examples of assessment of development results using environmental criteria which lead to multicriteria optimization problems. These assessments are not detailed in this section. It should be noted, however, that they are static and fail to take account of the time factor.

Islands and isolated mountain are the most fragile ecosystems. At the same time they provide convenient areas for studies of ecological consequences of development. Because of the boundedness of a region of studies, it is relatively easy to identify components which play a decisive role in man-environment interactions. A moderate number of parameters permits the use of simple mathematical models and the amount of data to be processed can be readily handled by modern computers. In the most general cases, the results of modeling may provide a framework for qualitative recommendations.

One of the most fragile ecosystems in our country is represented by Commander Islands (Komandorskie Islands) which are a unique natural complex. These Islands are part of Aleutians stretching from Alaska Peninsula to Kamchatka. Ecological disturbances in these islands are irreversible, because their ecosystem refers to the northern biocenosis with a small number of components. The islands are valued for the close association of the land biocornosis. They are currently inhabited by seal, sivuch, kalan and other valuable animals. Beaches and cliffs are densely colonized by numerous birds.

Since the discovery of Commander Islands by Vitus Bering (in 1741) and until the early twentieth century the hunting here was totally uncontrolled.

Kalans and fur-seals were on the verge of extinction and Steller's sea-cows became extinct. In these islands the annual output of sealskins throughout the nineteenth century accounted for 20 to 30 thousand pieces, with the result that the number of seal-rookeries was substantially reduced in the early twentieth century.

The Soviet Government implemented specific projects to restore the number of seals and kalans by providing state protection for these species. For the most part this problem was successfully solved and good conditions were provided for rational use of natural resources. Nowadays, however, a sharp increase is observed in economic activities which may disturb ecological balance of this unique natural complex. For this reason, it is vital to determine the proper ways for development of the island economy by taking into account the importance of these islands to our country. To do this, we need to establish scientific criteria and provide rationales for the objectives which may form the basis for economic activities.

The corresponding criteria are difficult to establish for purposes of evaluating alternative developments. For this reason, we shall follow a different route. The state of an environmentally closed region can be described by the vector $x = (x_1, \ldots, x_n)$ whose components are the quantitative states of industries and major activities: number of inhabitants, animal species density, plant state, etc. Based on the analysis of the island situation and with due regard for their own interests, the organizations which are concerned about island development and bear responsibility for the development of major economic activities may propose their own interpretation of the "ideal" state of the island economy by determining a target point M_i (the point M_i is selected by the i-th organization) in the space of all possible states X. From the point of view of a given organization the island development should be oriented to this point.

Depending on the number of organizations concerned we obtain the set of targets $M_1, \ldots, M_i, \ldots, M_m$. Suppose that at the end of a long-term planning period T implementation of one of the alternative development projects caused the island state to pass from point x_0 to point $x(T)$. Then the development criterion is naturally chosen to be the vector criterion

$$[\varrho(x(T), M_1), \ldots, \varrho(x(T), M_i), \ldots, \varrho(x(T), M_m)],$$

where ϱ is the euclidean distance to be minimized between the state resulting from development and the target points $M_1, \ldots, M_i, \ldots, M_m$. The point $x(T)$ is found by employing mathematical models in accordance with the chosen development project.

5.2   Multicriteria Optimization Problems

The previous example shows the necessity to estimate "ecological" decisions by several independent criteria. Nowadays there is the whole branch of mathematical control theory (multicriterial optimization theory) dealing with problems of this type. For a detailed exposition see [41].

Since the detailed treatment of multicriteria optimization problems is beyond the scope of our discussion, we shall formulate various approaches to construction of optimality principles, examine these principles for dynamic stability, and put forward methods for finding optimal solutions in specific cases.

Given several independent criteria for assessment of managerial decisions, the choice of the best decision becomes a nontrivial problem. It is clear that, in the multicriteria optimization problem with two vector estimates differing from one another only by one component, preference is given to that estimate whose component is larger. However, the vector estimates with distinct components are much more difficult to compare.

Let X be the set of possible decision outcomes. Each of the outcomes $x \in X$ is evaluated by the vector criterion $H(x) = \{H_1(x), \ldots, H_i(x), \ldots, H_m(x)\}$ (the outcome preference degree is assumed to be increasing with increasing components of vector H). Since $H \in R^m$, we introduce on the vector set $\{H\} \in R^n$ a strong preference relation $>$ as it is done for the m-dimensional Euclidean space R^m. We shall say that the vector $H' = \{H_i'\} > H'' = \{H_i''\}$ if and only if $H_i' > H_i''$ for all $i = 1, \ldots, m$. In a similar manner we introduce a weak preference relation $\geq$: we say that the vector $H' = \{H_i'\} \geq H'' = \{H_i''\}$, if $H_i' \geq H_i''$ for all $i = 1, \ldots, m$.

Denote by $K = \{H(x) : x \in X\}$ the set of estimates for all possible values $x \in X$. Obviously, if there is a vector $H^* \in K$ such that $H^* \geq H$ for all $H \in K$, then the solution x^* for which $H(x^*) = H^*$ must be thought of as the best one, since among the solutions $x \in X$ it is the best solution in all components of the vector criterion H.

The vector estimate $H^* \in K$ is called maximal in $\geq$ (in $>$) for K, if there is no estimate $H \neq H^*, H \in K$, such that $H \geq H^*$ ($H > H^*$). The $\geq$ maximal estimate is called a Pareto-optimal (or efficient) estimate, while the relevant solution x^* is called Pareto-optimal (or efficient).

Now the Pareto-optimal solution has the property that there is no other solution $x' \neq x^* \in X$ exceeding it in the order relation $\geq$ over all components of criterion H. In other words, if x^* is the Pareto-optimal solution, then condition $H_i(x') \geq H_i(x^*)$, $i = 1, \ldots, m$, must imply $H_i(x') = H_i(x^*)$, $i = 1, \ldots, m$.

The set of estimates $\widehat{K} \subset K$ satisfying this condition is called the Pareto (or efficient) set, while the set of relevant solutions $P(X) \subset X$ is called the set of efficient solutions or Pareto-optimal set, i.e. $P(X) = \{x \in X : H(x) \in \widehat{K}\}$.

The $>$ maximal vector estimate $\overline{K} \in K$ is called weakly efficient or weak Pareto-optimal or Slaiter-optimal, while the relevant solution $\overline{X}$ is called Slaiter-optimal or weakly efficient. So the Slaiter- optimal solution has the property that there is no other solution $x' \neq \overline{x} \in X$ exceeding it in $>$ over all components of criterion H. In other words, if x is Slaiter-optimal, then there is no $x' \in X$ such that $H_i(x') > H_i(x^*)$, $i = 1, \ldots, m$.

The set of Slaiter-optimal estimates $\overline{K} \subset K$ satisfying this condition is called weakly efficient, while the set of relevant solutions $S(X) \subset X$ is called a weakly efficient solution set, i.e. $S(X) = \{x \in X$: for which there are no $x' \in X$ such that $H_i(x') > H_i(x)\}$.

Since $H > H'$ implies $H \geq H'$, any efficient estimate is weakly efficient, so that $\overline{K} \subset \widehat{K}$ $P(X) \subset S(X)$.

Let the set K[41] be of the form shown in Fig.7 (the case of two criteria). The set $\widehat{K}$ coincides with the "north-eastern" boundary of the set K (curves bc, de without points d and e, hp), while the set $\overline{K}$ is composed of the curve $abcde$ (including e) and hpq.

Multicriteria optimization is largely centered around selection of an optimal solution from the set of all solutions. Clearly the method must be thought of as good when this solution proves to be efficient or weakly efficient. We shall describe two approaches to selection of an optimal solution.

Let $y_i^* = \max\limits_{x \in X} H_i(x)$. Consider the expression

$$\max_{0 \leq i \leq m} \frac{y_i^* - H_i(x)}{|y_i^*|}, \tag{5.1}$$

evaluating the maximal deviation of the estimate H of an arbitrary solution $x \in X$ from the vector $y^* = (y_1^*, \ldots, y_i^*, \ldots, y_m^*)$ which represents the vector of maxima in each criterion. An optimal point $x^* \in X$ can be chosen to be the point x^* minimizing the expression (5.1), i.e.,

$$\max_{0 \leq i \leq m} \frac{y_i^* - H_i(x^*)}{|y_i^*|} = \min_{x \in X} \max_{1 \leq i \leq m} \frac{y_i^* - H_i(x)}{|y_i^*|}. \tag{5.2}$$

It can be shown that the solution x^* is always weakly efficient. If this solution is unique (up to equivalence), then it is efficient.

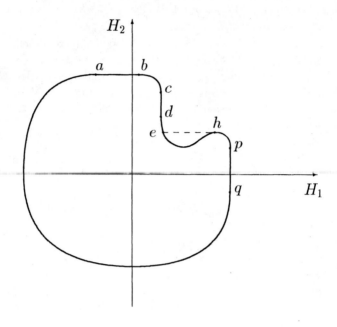

Fig. 7.

Another method of selecting an optimal solution is represented by what are called Nash bargaining schemes. The method is formulated under certain assumptions about the structure of the set K and functions $H_i(x)$, $i = 1, \ldots, n$. It can also be employed in a more general case.

We assume that the set K of all possible estimates is convex and compact in R^m. Let us introduce an initial solution $x^0 \in X$ by which is meant a "conservative" solution to be improved in solving this multicriteria problem. The value of the utility vector H at the point $x^0 \in X$ $H(x^0) = \{H_1(x^0), \ldots, H_m(x^0)\}$ is called a "status quo" point.

By the bargaining scheme is meant the rule φ which places each pair $(K, H(x^0))$ in correspondence with a certain pair $(\overline{H}, \overline{x}) = \varphi(K, H(x^0))$, where $\overline{H} \in \widehat{K}, \overline{x} \in X$ and $\overline{H} = H(\overline{x})$ ($\overline{x}$ is interpreted as an optimal solution).

We shall now formulate for bargaining schemes the axioms to be satisfied by the rule φ which associates each convex closed subset of K and the point $H \in K$ with some pair $(\overline{x}, \overline{H})$:

1) Realizability: $\overline{H} \in K$, $\overline{x} \in X$, $\overline{H} = H(\overline{x})$.

2) Individual rationality: $\overline{H} \geq H(x^0)$.

3) Pareto optimality: if $H \in K$ and $H \geq \overline{H}$, then $\overline{H} = H$.

4) Independence from irrelevant alternatives: if $\overline{H} \in A \subset K$ and $(\overline{H}, \overline{x}) = \varphi(K, H(x^0))$, then $(\overline{H}, \overline{x}) = \varphi(A, H(x^0))$.

5) Linearity: If the set $K' = \alpha K + \beta$ is obtained from K by linear transformation , i.e. $H'_i = \alpha_i H_i + \beta_i$ $(1 \leq i \leq m)$, and $\varphi(K, H(x^0)) = (\overline{H}, \overline{x})$, then $\varphi(K', \alpha H(x^0) + \beta) = (\alpha \overline{H}(\overline{x}) + \beta, \overline{x})$.

The meaning of the first three axioms is sufficiently clear. Axiom 4) means that, with larger opportunities for selecting $(\overline{H}, \overline{x})$, we may agree on the same payoff vector with less opportunities if this vector is realizable. Linearity Axiom states that, in distinct utility measurement scales, we are guided by the same optimality principle in the choice of (H, x).

For simplicity, assume that the set K has the vector H, every i-th coordinate of which is strictly larger than $H_i(x^0)$. Then the following assertion is true (for proof, see [8]). The function

$$\varphi(K, H(x^0)) = \{(\overline{H}, \overline{x})| \max_{H \geq H(x_0), H \in K} g(H, K, H(x^0)) =$$

$$= g(\overline{H}(\overline{x}), K, H(x^0))\},$$

where $g(H, K, H(x^0)) = \prod_{i=1}^{m} (H_i - H_i(x^0))$, satisfies Axioms 1)-4).

We shall now discuss the possibility of scalarization of the vector criterion H. It turns out that in a sufficiently wide class of cases the maximum of the scalarized criterion is in the set of efficient or weakly efficient points, and conversely, each efficient or weakly efficient point in the sense of the vector criterion H can be computed as the maximum of a scalar criterion obtained from H. We shall formulate more precisely the conditions under which this may occur.

D e f i n i t i o n. The set $S \subset R^n$ is called convex if it contains any two points and their connecting line segment, i.e. if $(\lambda x + (1 - \lambda)x') \in S$ for any $x, x' \in S$ and $\lambda \in [0, 1]$.

For each point $y \in R^n$, let $A_y = \{y' : y' \leq y\}$; then the set S is called weakly convex if the set $S_* = \bigcup_{y \in S} A_y$ is convex.

It is apparent that if an estimate H is weakly efficient in the set K, then it is also weakly efficient in the set K_*. Let K be weakly convex. The estimate $H^* \in K$ is weakly efficient if and only if there exists a vector $\mu = (\mu_1, \ldots, \mu_n)$, $\mu_i \geq 0$, $\sum_{i=1}^{m} \mu_i = 1$, $i = 1, \ldots, n$ such that $(\mu, H^*) \geq (\mu, H)$ for all $H \in K$ (

parenthesis denotes the scalar product). The last assertion reduces the problem
of finding weakly efficient points of the set K and weakly efficient solutions to
the problem of finding the maximum of a linear function (μ, H) on the set K.
Exhausting all possible vectors $\{\mu : \sum_{i=1}^{m} \mu_i = 1, \mu_i \geq 0\}$, we obtain the whole
set of weakly efficient solutions.

We shall now examine dynamic multicriteria problems.

5.3   Multicriteria Optimal Control Problems

Suppose the state of an environmentally closed region is described by the vector
$x \in R^n (x \geq 0)$. At the initial time t_0 the region is in the state $x(t_0) = x_0$.
Now the problem is to determine alternative regional developments for a long
term $[t_0, T]$, where T is the end of the planning period. We assume that the
regional development on the time interval $[t_0, T]$ can be described by the system
of differential equations

$$\dot{x} = f(x, u), \quad x \in R^n, \quad u \in U \subset comp R^n,$$

where u is the control interpreted to mean external influences (the rate of
growth of capital investments and resources) whereby the development is controlled. The control u is selected continuously in time and the resulting functions $u(t) \subset U$, $t \in [t_0, T]$ are t-measurable. The conditions ensuring the
existence, continuability and uniqueness of the solution to system

$$\dot{x} = f(x, u(t)) \tag{5.2}$$

under any measurable control $u(t)$ on the time interval $[t_0, T]$ and with initial
condition $x(t_0) = x_0$ are assumed to be satisfied. Each open-loop control $u(t)$
$t \in [t_0, T]$ determines a particular alternative motion $x(t)$, $t \in [t_0, T]$ derived
as a solution to equation (5.2) with initial condition $x(t_0) = x_0$.

Let $C^{T-t_0}(x_0)$ be the reachability set of system (5.2), i.e. the set of points in
R^n at which the solution of (5.2) can arrive from the initial state x_0 at the time
T by employing all possible open-loop controls $u(t)$, $t \in [t_0, T]$. In other words,
the reachability set of system (5.2) is the set of endpoints of trajectories $\{x(T)\}$
emanating from the initial state x_0 under all possible open-loop controls $u(t)$,
$t \in [t_0, T]$.

Let us next assume that the quality of the alternative development is determined by the point $x(T)$ at which the region arrives at the final time T

as a result of this development. Now it is assumed that the vector criterion $H(x(T)) \in R^m, x(T) \in C^{T-t_0}(x_0)$ defining the quality of the trajectory $x(t)$ and the relevant control $u(t)$ is given on the reachability set $C^{T-t_0}(x_0)$ of system (5.2). Thus we are led to the dynamic multicriteria optimization problem examined in the preceding section

$$\chi(x_0, T - t_0) = \{x(T) : x(T) \in C^{T-t_0}(x_0)\}, \tag{5.3}$$

$$K(x_0, T - t_0) = \{H(x(T)) : x(T) \in C^{T-t_0}(x_0)\}. \tag{5.4}$$

Here the sets K and χ are dependent on the parameters x_0, $T - t_0$ representing the initial conditions of the development problem (5.2). Since the formulated dynamic multicriteria optimization problem is dependent on the initial conditions $x_0, T - t_0$ (the initial state of the region and the duration of a planning period), we denote this problem by $\Gamma(x_0, T - t_0)$.

We have thus arrived at the dynamic multicriteria optimization problem $\Gamma(x_0, T - t_0)$, the set of all possible outcomes $\chi(x_0, T - t_0)$ defined in (5.3), and the set of all possible estimates $K(x_0, T - t_0)$ defined in (5.4). Let us assume that $\widehat{K}(x_0, T - t_0) \subset K(x_0, T - t_0)$ is the set of efficient estimates; $\overline{K}(x_0, T - t_0) \subset K(x_0, T - t_0)$ is the set of weakly efficient estimates; $P[\chi(x_0, T - t_0)]$ and $S[\chi(x_0, T - t_0)]$ are the corresponding solution sets.

Dynamic optimization problems lay particular emphasis on dynamic stability of the chosen optimality principle. Although this question is a trivial consequence of the Bellman optimality principle in the case of classical dynamic single-criterion optimization problems, nevertheless it presents serious difficulties where passage is made to multicriteria optimization problems and non zero-sum game problems (see [34,35,38]).

Our dynamic multicriteria optimization problem $\Gamma(x_0, T - t_0)$ is dependent on the initial condition x_0 and the process duration $T - t_0$. To examine this problem for dynamic stability, we imbed it in the family of similar multicriteria optimization problems with initial conditions x and duration $T - t$ $(t_0 \leq t \leq T)$.

As is shown in the preceding section, multicriteria problems are characterized by many principles of optimality. For completeness we shall clarify the requirement for dynamic stability of optimality principles or time consistency of optimality principles when development follows an optimal path. Suppose that at the start of the process, i.e. in the solution of the problem $\Gamma(x_0, T - t_0)$, we employed an optimality principle to construct an optimal trajectory. When moving along this trajectory, we pass from the problem with some initial states to the problem with the other initial states. Although the chosen trajectory is optimal in the problem for initial states of the process, the remaining part of the trajectory (starting with some current time t, $t_0 \leq t \leq T$) may not generally be an optimal trajectory implementing the same optimality principle in the problem for initial states on this trajectory which correspond to the current time t. Therefore, at the time t we may have no reason to follow further the initially chosen optimal trajectory, which may lead to the eventual abandonment of the optimality principle adopted in the original problem, i.e. this may bring about instability of the process as a whole. Dynamic stability requires that the initially chosen motion be preserved in the problems with current initial data on the optimal trajectory.

Dynamically stable optimality principles include Pareto optimality and Slaiter optimality. We shall show dynamic stability of the Pareto optimal set (dynamic stability of the weakly efficient set or the set of Slaiter optimal estimates can be proved in a similar manner). Indeed, suppose $\widehat{K}(x_0, T - t_0)$ is the Pareto optimal set of estimates and $P[\chi(x_0, T - t_0)]$ is the Pareto optimal set of solutions in the dynamic multicriteria optimization problem $\Gamma(x_0, T - t_0)$ from the initial state x_0 with prescribed duration $T - t_0$ and terminal payoff. Let $\{H_i^*\} = H^*$ be the vector of estimates from the set $\widehat{K}(x_0, T - t_0)$. Suppose we have chosen the control $\overline{u}(t)$ and the corresponding trajectory $\overline{x}(t)$ for which the estimate $H^* = \{H_i^*\}$ is realized at the end of the process, i.e.the control $\overline{u}(t)$ is such that $\overline{x}(\tau)$ passes at the time T (at which the process terminates) through the point $\overline{x}(T)$, where $H(\overline{x}(T)) = \{H_i(\overline{x}(T))\}$ is equal to the utility vector $H^* = \{H_i^*\}$. Let $C^{T-t_0}(x_0)$ be the set of reachability of the controlled system from the initial state x_0 at the time T. Considering variations in this set along the trajectory $\overline{x}(\tau)$, we may note that

$$C^{T-\tau_1}(\overline{x}(\tau_1)) \supset C^{T-\tau_2}(\overline{x}(\tau_2)), \qquad t_0 \leq \tau_1 \leq \tau_2 \leq T. \qquad (5.5)$$

From (5.5) we have

$$K(\overline{x}(\tau_1), T - \tau_1) \supset K(\overline{x}(\tau_2), T - \tau_2), \qquad t_0 \leq \tau_1 \leq \tau_2 \leq T.$$

Since the vector $H^* = \{H_i^*\}$ belongs to the Pareto optimal set in the problem with initial state x_0 and duration $T - t_0$, there is no utility vector $H' \neq H^*$ belonging to $K(x_0, T - t_0)$ such that $H_i' \geq H_i^*$ for all $1 \leq i \leq n$. From (5.5) we have that this is especially true for the set $K(\overline{x}(\tau), T - \tau)$, $t_0 \leq \tau \leq T$. Thus the utility vector $H^* = \{H_i^*\}$ is not dominated by any one of the elements of the set $K(\overline{x}(\tau), T - \tau)$ or, in other words, it belongs to Pareto optimal sets of the current problem with initial condition $\overline{x}(\tau)$ and duration $T - \tau$. This means that the utility vector $H^* = \{H_i^*\}$ in all current problems (when moving along the trajectory $\overline{x}(\tau)$) remains Pareto optimal. The fact that the vector H^* was arbitrarily chosen from the set $K(x_0, T - t_0)$ implies dynamic stability of the Pareto optimal set.

The static case, however, shows that the Pareto optimal set can't uniquely determine a cooperative solution; we need a correct method of selecting a terminal point from the Pareto optimal set, since only one outcome of development can actually be realized.

We shall now consider various approaches to selecting a particular efficient (weakly efficient) solution from the set of all efficient (weakly efficient) solutions mentioned in the preceding section. Moreover, we shall examine them for dynamic stability.

The weakly efficient solution x^* selected from the condition

$$\max_{1 \le i \le m} \frac{y_i^* - H_i(x^*)}{|y_i^*|} = \min_{x \in C^{T-t_0}(x_0)} \max_{1 \le i \le m} \frac{y_i^* - H_i(x)}{|y_i^*|}$$

in the problem $\Gamma(x_0, T - t_0)$ is denoted by $x^*(x_0, T - t_0)$, and the relevant estimate $H(x^*)$ by $H(x^*) = H^*(x_0, T - t_0)$. This lays emphasis on the dependence on the initial conditions of the problem. Note that $y_i^* = \max_{x \in C^{T-t_0}(x_0)} H_i(x)$, where max is taken over the reachability set $C^{T-t_0}(x_0)$, is also dependent on the initial conditions x_0, $T - t_0$ (taken to be parameters). Therefore, the condition for selection of a point $x^*(x_0, T - t_0)$ can be written in full form as follows:

$$\max_{1 \le i \le m} \frac{\max\limits_{x \in C^{T-t_0}(x_0)} H_i(x) - H_i(x^*(x_0, T - t_0))}{|\max\limits_{x \in C^{T-t_0}(x_0)} H_i(x)|} =$$

$$(5.6)$$

$$\min_{x \in C^{T-t_0}(x_0)} \max_{1 \le i \le m} \frac{\max\limits_{x \in C^{T-t_0}(x_0)} H_i(x) - H_i(x)}{|\max\limits_{x \in C^{T-t_0}(x_0)} H_i(x)|}.$$

Let $\overline{x}(t)$ be an optimal trajectory leading to the point $x^*(x_0, T - t_0)$, i.e. $\overline{x}(t)|_{t=t_0} = x_0$, $\overline{x}(t)|_{t=T} = x^*(x_0, T - t_0)$. We consider the current problem $\Gamma(\overline{x}(t), T - t)$ for $t_0 \le t \le T$. Suppose we wish to verify at the time t whether the selected point $x^*(x_0, T - t_0)$ satisfies the condition (5.6) written for the current problem. And again we need to select a weakly efficient point by employing the previous formula for the current problem. To do this, we compute

$$
\min_{x \in C^{T-t}(\overline{x}(t))} \max_{1 \le i \le m} \frac{\max\limits_{x \in C^{T-t}(\overline{x}(t))} H_i(x) - H_i(x)}{\left| \max\limits_{x \in C^{T-t}(\overline{x}(t))} H_i(x) \right|}. \tag{5.7}
$$

Suppose that min in (5.7) is attained at the point $x^*(\overline{x}(t), T-t)$. The condition for coincidence of the current weakly efficient points yields

$$
x^*(x_0, T - t_0) = x^*(\overline{x}(t), T - t) \tag{5.8}
$$

for $t \in [t_0, T]$. Obviously, (5.8) holds in rare cases, since the sets $C^{T-t}(\overline{x}(t))$ decrease in inclusion for $t \in [t_0, T]$ and $\max\limits_{x \in C^{T-t}(\overline{x}(t))} H_i(x)$ generally decreases, except for the trivial case, where it is attained for all $1 \le i \le m$ at the same point $\tilde{x}_i^*(x_0, T - t_0)$. This means that the choice of a weakly efficient point by (5.6) is not dynamically stable.

To study dynamic stability of the Nash bargaining scheme, we need to define concretely the notion of a "conservative" solution and a status quo point. Formally, the conservative solution in the problem $\Gamma(x_0, T - t_0)$ can be taken to be any point $x^0(T)$ of the reachability set $C^{T-t_0}(x_0)$. This point $x^0(T)$, however, must be the endpoint of the trajectory $x^0(t), t \in [t_0, T]$, governing the development under some control $\tilde{u}^0(t), t \in [t_0, T]$. Let

$$
(\overline{H}(x_0, T - t_0), \overline{x}(x_0, T - t_0)) = \varphi(K(x_0, T - t_0), H[x^0(x_0, T - t_0)])
$$

be the choice of an efficient point according to the bargaining scheme φ in the problem $\Gamma(x_0, T - t_0)$ with the proviso that the conservative solution is the point $x^0(x_0, T - t_0) \in C^{T-t_0}(x_0)$. As noted before, the point $\overline{H}(x_0, T - t_0), \overline{x}_0(x_0, T - t_0)$ is determined from the condition (see sec. 9 in this chapter)

$$
\varphi(K(x_0, T - t_0), H[x^0(x_0, T - t_0)]) = \{(\overline{H}(x_0, T - t_0), \overline{x}(x_0, T - t_0))|
$$

$$
\max_{\substack{H \ge H[x^0(x_0, T - t_0)] \\ H \in K(x_0, T - t_0)}} \prod_{i=1}^{m} (H_i - H_i[x^0(x_0, T - t_0)]) =
$$

$$
= \prod_{i=1}^{n} (\overline{H}_i(\overline{x}) - H_i[x^0(x_0, T - t_0)])\}.
$$

Let $x^*(t)$ be the optimal trajectory joining the point x_0 and $\overline{x}(x_0, T - t_0)$, i.e. $x^*(t)|_{t=t_0} = x_0$, $x^*(t)|_{t=T} = \overline{x}(x_0, T - t_0)$. Consider the arbitration scheme for the current problem $\Gamma(x^*(t), T - t), t_0 \leq t \leq T$. Let $(\overline{H}(x^*(t), T - t), \overline{x}(x^*(t), T - t))$ be the choice dictated by the bargaining scheme, i.e.

$$\varphi(K(x^*(t), T - t), H[x^0(x^*(t), T - t)]) =$$

$$= \{\overline{H}(x^*(t), T - t), \overline{x}(x^*(t), T - t))|,$$

$$\max_{\substack{H \geq H[x^0(x^*(t), T-t)] \\ \overline{H} \in K(x^*(t), T-t_0)}} \prod_{i=1}^{m} (H_i - H_i[x^0(x^*(t), T - t]) =$$

$$= \prod_{i=1}^{n} (\overline{H}_i(\overline{x}) - H_i[x^0(x^*(t), T - t)])\}. \tag{5.9}$$

Dynamic stability means that the condition

$$\overline{x}(x^*(t), T - t) = \overline{x}(x_0, T - t_0) \tag{5.10}$$

holds for all $t \in [t_0, T]$. As is seen from (5.9), this depends on the nature of variations in the "conservative" solution $x^0(x^*(t), T - t)$ and the status quo point $H_i(x^0(x^*(t), T - t))$ along the optimal trajectory $x^*(t)$ for $t \in [t_0, T]$. The preliminary analysis shows that (5.10) holds in extremely rare cases.

As for the method of selecting an efficient (weakly efficient) solution based on the criterion convolution, the problem here reduces to an optimal single-criterion control problem for which the Bellman optimality principle hold. Hence the resulting efficient (weakly efficient) solution is always dynamically stable.

5.4 Constructing a Pareto Optimal Set in the Problem of Approaching Several Target Points

Suppose the state of an environmentally closed region at the time t_0 is described by the vector $x_0 \in R^n$ $(x_0 \geq 0)$. We assume that the regional development on the time interval $[t_0, T]$ can be described by the system of differential equations.

$$\dot{x} = f(x, u), \qquad x \in R^n, \qquad u \in U \subset R^l, \qquad u \geq 0 \tag{5.11}$$

where u is the control vector interpreted to mean investments that are allocated to ensure development of the region. The component x_i in the state

vector describes the quantitative state of the i-th industry or the i-th direction
of the regional development, while the i-th component of the control vector
u_i indicates capital investments in the i-th industry or direction. Further it is
assumed that investments are allocated in a centralized manner by an external control center A_0. Under standard conditions on the right part of system
(5.11), for every initial condition $x(t_0) = x_0$ and a measurable open-loop control $u(t)$ for $t \in [t_0, T]$ there a single trajectory of regional development defined
over the time interval $[t_0, T]$.

Let $C^{T-t_0}(x_0)$ be the reachability set of system (5.11), i.e. the set of states
$x(T)$, in which the region R may appear at the time T under all possible
controls employed by center A_0. In what follows this set is assumed to be
convex and compact.

Suppose the result of regional development is evaluated by several "experts" $B_1, \ldots, B_m$, representing the interests of environmental departments,
industries, or directions of regional activities.

Each of the experts B_i, $i = 1, \ldots, m$ is guided by his own vision of regional
problems and thus determines a target point M_i whereto the development is
to be directed when planning allocation of investments over the time interval
$[t_0, T]$. The target points M_i can be lying sufficiently close to one another, but
the assumption of their coincidence would be an unduly strong idealization.

Now the utility of each point $x(T) \in C^{T-t}(x_0)$ (the potential result of
development of region R) can be evaluated by center A_0 from the point of
view of its proximity to target points $M_1, \ldots, M_m$. Thus we are led to the
utility vector related to each point

$$\{-\varrho(x(T), M_i)\} = H_i(x(T)), \qquad (5.12)$$

where ϱ is the Euclidean distance between the points $x(T)$, M_i. (We may
also use other definitions of the distance in R^n, e.g., taking these distances
to be different for different M_i, i.e. considering the functions $H(x(T), M_i)$.
This, however, provides no easy-to-grasp geometric interpretation for optimal
solutions. Needless to say that such a definition precludes application of a
transferable approach, because utility functions are perceived by each of the
"experts" in a strictly individual way.

Mathematically, the problem amounts to finding optimal development paths
in the sense of the vector criterion $H(x)$.

D e f i n i t i o n. The control $\overline{u}(t)$ is called Pareto optimal if there is no
control $u(t)$ such that

$$H_i(\overline{x}(T), \overline{u}(t)) \leq H_i(x(T), u(t)), \quad i = 1, \ldots, m,$$

and for at least one i_0 $H_{i_0}(\overline{x}(T), \overline{u}(t))$ < $H_{i_0}(x(T), u(t))$, where $H(x(T), u(t))$ is the utility vector under control $u(t)$, and $x(t)$ is the corresponding trajectory.

Denote by $\{u^P\}$ the set of Pareto optimal controls and by $\{x^P(t)\}$ the set of the corresponding trajectories.

We shall now define the structure of the Pareto set in our problem. According to our previous assumption, the reachability set $C^{T-t_0}(x_0)$ is convex and compact. For every expert the set $C^{T-t_0}(x_0)$ has the corresponding best point $x(T)$ such that $\varrho(x(T), M_i) = \min\limits_{\xi \in C^{T-t_0}(x_0)} \varrho(\xi, M_i)$. Generally speaking, no one from B_i can ensure that it will be reached. It would be natural to expect that, based on preliminary negotiations, the experts would restrict their consideration to the set of terminal points confined "between" the best points for each from B_i.

We shall show that it is the set of points of such a structure that corresponds to the set of Pareto optimal controls.

For every point $x(T)$ $\in$ $C^{T-t_0}(x_0)$ there is a vector $H(x(T))$ $= (-\varrho(x(T), M_1), \ldots, -\varrho(x(T), M_m))$.

Let $K(x_0, T - t_0) = \{H(x(T)) | x(T) \in C^{T-t_0}(x_0)\}$. The set $K(x_0, T - t_0)$ is the set of all possible payoff vectors realizable at the time T. Denote by $\widehat{K}(x_0, T - t_0)$ a subset of the set $K(x_0, T - t_0)$ corresponding to the set of Pareto controls $\{u^P\}$:

$$\widehat{K}(x_0, T - t_0) = \{H(x^P(T))\}.$$

Let $\widehat{M} = \text{conv}\{M_i, i = 1, \ldots, m\}$, where $\text{conv}\{M_i, i = 1, \ldots, m\}$ is the convex hull of the points M_i. Denote by π the operator of orthogonal projection from the space R^n onto a convex compact set B. By the orthogonal projection of the point $x \in R^n$ onto B $(x \overline{\in} B)$ we mean the point $\pi_B x \in B$:

$$\varrho(x, \pi_B x) = \min\limits_{y \in B} \varrho(x, y). \qquad (5.13)$$

We call this point an image, and the point x a pre-image of the projection operator. By the orthogonal projection of the point $x \in B$ onto B we mean the point x itself. The orthogonal projection $\pi_B A$ of the set A onto the set B is taken to be the set of orthogonal projections of the points appearing in A onto B.

In what follows we need the lemmas given below.

L e m m a 1. Suppose B is a convex closed set in R^n and x is some point which does not belong to B. The inequality $\varrho(\pi_B x, y) \le \varrho(x, y)$ then holds for all $y \in B$.

P r o o f . The point $\pi_B x$ exists (since B is closed) and is bounded. Let us take an arbitrary point $y \in B$, $y \neq \pi_B x$. Since B is convex, we have $\omega_\lambda = \lambda y + (1 - \lambda)\pi_B x \in B$, $0 \leq \lambda \leq 1$. By definition, the point $\pi_B x$ supplies the minimum to the function $\varrho^2(x, \omega_\lambda) = \sum_{i=1}^{n}(x_i - \lambda y_i - (1-\lambda)\pi_B x_i)^2$. Therefore

$$\frac{\partial \rho^2(x, \omega_\lambda)}{\partial \lambda}\bigg|_{\lambda=0} = 2\sum_{i=1}^{n}(\pi_B x_i - y_i)(x_i - \pi_B x_i) \geq 0.$$

From this we have

$$-2((y - \pi_B x)(x - \pi_B x)) \geq 0.$$

Hence, the angle between vectors $y - \pi_B x$, $x - \pi_B x$ is not less than the right angle and is the largest of all interior angles of the triangle with vertices $(x, \pi_B x, y)$, i. e. $\varrho(x, y) \geq \varrho(\pi_B x, y)$. This proves the lemma.

Let $\overline{x}, \overline{\overline{x}} \in \omega_\lambda$, where $\omega_\lambda = \lambda \overline{y} + (1-\lambda)\overline{\overline{y}}$, $\lambda \in [0, 1]$, $\overline{x}, \overline{\overline{x}}, \overline{y}, \overline{\overline{y}} \in R^n$. Introduce the function $F(\lambda) = \varrho(\overline{x}, \omega_\lambda) - \varrho(\overline{\overline{x}}, \omega_\lambda)$.

L e m m a 2. From $F(\lambda) \geq 0$ with $\lambda = 0; 1$ it follows that $F(\lambda) \geq 0$ for all $\lambda \in (0, 1)$.

P r o o f. Since $\varrho(\overline{x}, \omega_\lambda)$ and $\varrho(\overline{\overline{x}}, \omega_\lambda)$ are positive, $\varrho^2(\overline{x}, \omega_\lambda) \geq \varrho^2(\overline{\overline{x}}, \omega_\lambda)$ implies $\varrho(\overline{x}, \omega_\lambda) \geq \varrho(\overline{\overline{x}}, \omega_\lambda)$ for $\lambda \in [0, 1]$. Therefore, for convenience, we may take $F'(\lambda) = \varrho^2(\overline{x}, \omega_\lambda) - \varrho^2(\overline{\overline{x}}, \omega_\lambda)$ instead of $F(\lambda)$.

Let us fix $\lambda = \lambda_1 \in (0, 1)$. Then $\omega_{\lambda_1} = \tilde{x} = \lambda_1 \overline{y} + (1 - \lambda_1)\overline{\overline{y}}$ and

$$F'(\lambda_1) = \sum_{i=1}^{n}(\overline{x}_i - \lambda_1 \overline{y}_i - (1 - \lambda_1)\overline{\overline{y}}_i)^2 - \sum_{i=1}^{n}(\overline{\overline{x}}_i - \lambda_1 \overline{y}_i - (1 - \lambda_1)\overline{\overline{y}}_i)^2 =$$

$$= \sum_{i=1}^{n}[\overline{x}_i^2 - \overline{\overline{x}}_i^2 - 2(1 - \lambda_1)\overline{\overline{y}}_i\overline{x}_i - 2\lambda_1\overline{y}_i\overline{x}_i +$$

$$+ 2(1 - \lambda_1)\overline{\overline{y}}_i\overline{\overline{x}}_i + 2\lambda_1\overline{y}_i\overline{\overline{x}}_i].$$

In view of

$$F'(0) = \sum_{i=1}^{n}(\overline{x}_i^2 - 2\overline{x}_i\overline{\overline{y}}_i - \overline{\overline{x}}_i^2 + 2\overline{\overline{x}}_i\overline{\overline{y}}_i),$$

$$F'(1) = \sum_{i=1}^{n}(\overline{x}_i^2 - 2\overline{x}_i\overline{y}_i - \overline{\overline{x}}_i^2 + 2\overline{\overline{x}}_i\overline{y}_i),$$

we have

$$F'(\lambda_1) = F'(0) + F'(1) + \sum_{i=1}^{m}\{\overline{\overline{x}}_i^2 - \overline{x}_i^2 + 2\overline{x}_i[\lambda_1\overline{y}_i + (1 - \lambda_1)\overline{y}_i] -$$

$$-2\overline{x}_i[\lambda_1\overline{y}_i + (1-\lambda_1)\underline{y}_i]\} = F'(0) + F'(1)+$$

$$+ \sum_{i=1}^{m}(\overline{\overline{x}}_i^2 - \overline{x}_i^2 + 2\overline{x}_i\hat{x}_i - 2\overline{\overline{x}}_i\hat{x}_i),$$

where $(\hat{x}_i = \lambda_1\overline{y}_i + (1-\lambda_1)\underline{y}_i)$ is the point that is symmetrical to the point $\tilde{x}$ with respect to the midpoint of the line segment ω_λ. Performing simple transformations, we obtain

$$\sum_{i=1}^{m}(\overline{\overline{x}}_i^2 - \overline{x}_i^2 + 2\overline{x}_i\hat{x}_i - 2\overline{\overline{x}}_i\hat{x}_i) = \sum_{i=1}^{m}(\overline{\overline{x}}_i - \hat{x}_i)^2 - \sum_{i=1}^{m}(\overline{x}_i - \hat{x}_i)^2 =$$

$$\varrho^2(\overline{\overline{x}}, \hat{x}) - \varrho^2(\overline{x}, \hat{x}) = -F'(1-\lambda_1).$$

Finally, $F'(\lambda_1) = F'(0) + F'(1) - F'(1-\lambda_1)$. Set $\lambda_1 = 1/2$. Then $F'(\frac{1}{2}) = \frac{1}{2}[F'(0) + F'(1)] \geq 0$.

Similarly, we may show for all $\lambda_l = l/2^k$, $k = 1, 2, \ldots$, $l = 1, 2, \ldots, 2^k - 1$ $(\lambda_l \in (0,1))$,

$$F'(\frac{l}{2^k}) = \frac{1}{2}[F'(\frac{l-1}{2^k}) + F'(\frac{l+1}{2^k})] \geq 0.$$

L e m m a 3. Let B^r be an r-dimensional closed convex polyhedron in R^n with vertices $B_1, \ldots, B_q$. Then for all $y \in B^r$ and $x \overline{\in} B^r$ the inequality $\varrho(y, B_i) < \varrho(x, B_i)$ holds for at least one $i \in I = \{1, \ldots, q\}$.

P r o o f (by induction). With $r = 1$, B^1 is a line segment. The lemma is obvious. Suppose it is true for $r = k - 1$. Since B^k is convex, the segment,

$$\omega = [\lambda\xi + (1-\lambda)\pi_{B_k}x] \in B^k, \lambda \in [0,1],$$

where the point $\xi \in B^{k-1}$ is such that $y \in \omega$. By induction, there exists $i_0 \in I$ such that $\varrho(\xi, B_{i_0}) < \varrho(x, B_{i_0})$, where $B_{i_0} \in B^{k-1}$. But

$$\varrho(y, B_{i_0}) = \varrho[\overline{\lambda}\xi + (1-\overline{\lambda})\pi_{B^k}x, B_{i_0}] \leq \overline{\lambda}\varrho(\xi, B_{i_0})+$$

$$+(1-\overline{\lambda})\varrho(\pi_{B^k}x, B_{i_0}) < \overline{\lambda}\varrho(x, B_{i_0}) + (1-\overline{\lambda})\varrho(\pi_{B^h}x, B_{i_0}).$$

Lemma 1 implies $\varrho(\pi_{B^k}x, B_{i_0}) < \varrho(x, B_{i_0})$, therefore

$$\overline{\lambda}\varrho(x, B_{i_0}) + (1-\overline{\lambda})\varrho(\pi_{B^k}x, B_{i_0}) \leq \overline{\lambda}\varrho(x, B_{i_0})+$$

$$+(1-\overline{\lambda})\varrho(x, B_{i_0}) = \varrho(x, B_{i_0}).$$

We thus obtain $\varrho(y, B_{i_0}) < \varrho(x, B_{i_0})$, $i_0 \in I$, which is what we set out to prove.

L e m m a 4. Let B^r be an r-dimensional closed convex polyhedron in R^n with vertices $B_1, \ldots, B_q$, and let x, y be some points that do not belong to B^r.

If there is a point $\overline{\xi} \in B^r$ for which $\varrho(y,\overline{\xi}) < \varrho(x,\overline{\xi})$, then $\varrho(y,B_i) < \varrho(x,B_i)$ for at least one $i \in I$.

P r o o f. For $\overline{\xi} \in B^1$ the lemma is obvious. Suppose the lemma holds for $\overline{\xi} \in B^{k-1}$, and let $\overline{\xi} \in B$. By the definition of B^{k-1} and B^k, there exists an index $i_0 \in I$ such that $B_{i_0} \in B^k \setminus B^{k-1}$. Then there exists a point $\xi_{i_0} \in B^{k-1}$ for which

$$\overline{\xi} \in \omega = [\lambda B_{i_0} + (1 - \lambda)\xi_{i_0}] \subset B^k, \quad \lambda \in [0,1]$$

Suppose that $\varrho(y, B_{i_0}) \geq \varrho(x, B_{i_0})$. If $\varrho(y,\xi_{i_0}) < \varrho(x,\xi_{i_0})$, then by induction, there exists $B_i \in B^{k-1} \subset B^k$ such that $\varrho(y,B_i) < \varrho(x,B_i)$.

If $\varrho(y,\xi_{i_0}) \geq \varrho(x,\xi_{i_0})$, then by Lemma 2 $\varrho(\xi,y) \geq \varrho(\xi,x)$ for all $\xi \in \omega = \lambda\xi_{i_0} + (1 - \lambda)B_{i_0}$, $\lambda \in [0,1]$, which contradicts the condition of the lemma. Hence, $\varrho(y, B_{i_0}) < \varrho(x, B_{i_0})$ for at least one i_0.

Denote $\widehat{M} = \text{conv}\{M_i, i = 1,\ldots,m\}$.

Theorem 1. Let $\widehat{M} \cap C^{T-t_0}(x_0) = \emptyset$. Then

$$\widehat{K}(x_0, T - t_0) = \{H(x) \quad |x \in \pi_{C^{T-t_0}(x_0)}\widehat{M}\}$$

(in this case, target points are unreachable; see Fig.8)

P r o o f. Let $y' \in \pi_{C^{T-t_0}(x_0)}\widehat{M}, x \in C^{T-t_0}(x_0), x \neq y'$. Let us introduce the function $F(\xi) = \varrho(y',\xi) - \varrho(x,\xi), \xi \in \widehat{M}$, and the set $Y = \{y \in \widehat{M}|y' = \pi_{C^{T-t_0}(x_0)}y\}$. Take $\overline{y} \in Y : \varrho(y',\overline{y}) = \min_{y\in Y} \varrho(y',y)$. Such a point exists, since Y is compact. By the definition of the point $\overline{y}$, the inequality $F(\overline{y}) < 0$ holds for all $x \in C^{T-t_0}(x_0)$. Lemma 4 then implies $\varrho(y',M_i) < \varrho(x,M_i)$ for at least one $i = 1,\ldots,m$, i.e.

$$H_i(y') > H_i(x). \tag{5.14}$$

for at least one i. And this means that $H(y') \in \hat{\kappa}(x_0, T - t_0)$.

We shall show that the set $C^{T-t_0}(x_0)$ has no other points possessing the property (5.14) than the points of the set $\pi_{C^{T-t_0}(x_0)}\widehat{M}$. This means that for any $x \in C^{T-t_0}(x_0) \setminus \pi_{C^{T-t_0}(x_0)}\widehat{M}$ there is a point at which

$$H_i(\tilde{y}) \geq H_i(x) \quad \text{for all} \quad i = 1,\ldots,m \tag{5.15}$$

Let us consider the sets

$$\widehat{M}_1 = \text{conv}(\widehat{M}, \pi_{C^{T-t_0}(x_0)}\widehat{M}), \widehat{M}_2 = \text{conv}\pi_{C^{T-t_0}(x_0)}\widehat{M}.$$

Obviously, $\widehat{M}_2 \subset \widehat{M}_1$. By Lemma 1, for any $x \in C^{T-t_0}(x_0) \setminus \widehat{M}_1$ there exists a point $\tilde{y} \in \pi_{\widehat{M}_1}x \in \widehat{M}_1$ satisfying (5.15).

Now let $x \in \widehat{M}_2 \setminus \pi_{C^{T-t_0}(x_0)}\widehat{M}$ and let $\pi_{\widehat{M}}x$ be its projection onto $\widehat{M}$. Since the set $C^{T-t_0}(x_0)$ is convex by definition and $\pi_{C^{T-t_0}(x_0)}\widehat{M} \subset C^{\overline{T-t_0}(x_0)}$ (because of the emptiness of the set $\widehat{M} \cap C^{\overline{T-t_0}}(x_0)$, where $C^{\overline{T-t_0}}(x_0)$ is the boundary of the set $C^{T-t_0}(x_0)$), there exists a point $x' \in \pi_{C^{T-t_0}(x_0)}\widehat{M} \cap \omega$, $\omega = \lambda x + (1-\lambda)\pi_{\widehat{M}}x$, $\lambda \in [0,1]$. This point is the required one, since by Lemma 1, it satisfies inequality (5.15).

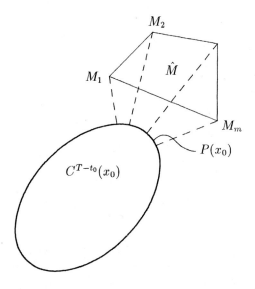

Fig. 8.

Now only the points of the set $\pi_{C^{T-t_0}(x_0)}\widehat{M}$ possess the property (5.15). Hence,

$$\widehat{K}(x_0, T - t_0) = \{H(y)|y \in \pi_{C^T {}^{t_0}(x_0)}\widehat{M}\}.$$

Theorem 2. Let $\widehat{M} \subset C^{T-t_0}(x_0)$. Then

$$\widehat{K}(x_0, T - t_0) = \{H(x)|x \in \pi_{C^{T-t_0}(x_0)}\widehat{M}\} = \widehat{M}$$

(in this case all target points are reachable; see Fig.9).

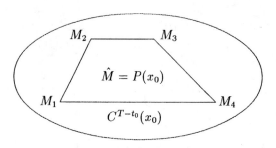

Fig. 9.

P r o o f. For any $x \in \widehat{M}$ and all $y \in \widehat{M}$ the inequality $H_i(y) > H_i(x)$ holds for at least one i.

We have thus established that only the payoff vector on the set $\widehat{M}$ can be Pareto optimal. Show that all vectors of this set are Pareto optimal. Let $x, y \in \widehat{M}$, $x \neq y$. With $r = 1$, $\widehat{M}$ is the line segment with endpoints M_1, M_2. We have

$$\varrho(M_1, M_2) = \varrho(M_1, y) + \varrho(y, M_2) = \varrho(M_1, x) + \varrho(x, M_2).$$

But since $x \neq y$, $\varrho(M_1, y) < \varrho(M_1, x)$ or $\varrho(M_2, y) < \varrho(M_2, x)$. Therefore $H(y) \in \widehat{K}(x_0, T - t_0)$.

Suppose the theorem is true for $r = k - 1$. Consider the ray Z_x originating in the point x and passing through y, if $r = k$. Then there exists a point $\overline{z} \in Z_x$ such that $\varrho(x, \overline{z}) = \max\limits_{z \in \widehat{M} \cap Z_x} \varrho(x, z)$. Obviously, $\overline{z}$ lies on the boundary of $\widehat{M}$, i.e. it belongs to the $(k-1)$-dimensional face of the k-dimensional polyhedron $\widehat{M}$. By induction, $H(z) \in \widehat{K}(x_0, T - t_0)$. Then by definition of the Pareto optimal set, there exists at least one i_0 for which $H_{i_0}(\overline{z}) > H_{i_0}(x)$, or, what is the same, $\varrho(\overline{z}, M_{i_0}) < \varrho(x, M_{i_0})$.

Since $y \in \omega = \lambda x + (1 - \lambda)\overline{z}, \lambda \in [0, 1]$, we have

$$\varrho(y, M_{i_0}) = \varrho(\overline{\lambda} x + (1 - \overline{\lambda})\overline{z}, M_{i_0}) \leq \overline{\lambda}\varrho(x, M_{i_0}) + (1 - \overline{\lambda})\varrho(\overline{z}, M_{i_0}) <$$

$$< \overline{\lambda}\varrho(x, M_{i_0}) + (1 - \overline{\lambda})\varrho(x, M_{i_0}) = \varrho(x, M_{i_0}),$$

i.e. $\varrho(y, M_{i_0}) < \varrho(x, M_{i_0})$. Hence $H(y) \in \widehat{K}(x_0, T - t_0)$.

If we interchange x and y, we have that
$H(x) \in \widehat{K}(x_0, T - t_0)$. Thus, for all $y \in \widehat{M} \equiv \pi_{C^{T-t_0}(x_0)}\widehat{M}$ and only for them,
$H(y) \in \overline{K}(x_0, T - t_0)$. This completes the proof of the theorem.

Theorem 3. Let the points $M_i, i = 1, \ldots, m$ be arranged so that $\widehat{M} \supset C^{T-t_0}(x_0)$. Then

$$\widehat{K}(x_0, T - t_0) = \{H(x) | x \in \pi_{C^{T-t_0}(x_0)}\widehat{M} = C^{T-t_0}(x_0)\} = \Xi(x_0, T - t_0)$$

(in this case all target points are unreachable, but the experts' objectives differ from one another; see Fig.10).The proof follows from Theorem 2 if the sets $\widehat{M}$ and $C^{T-t_0}(x_0)$ are interchanged.

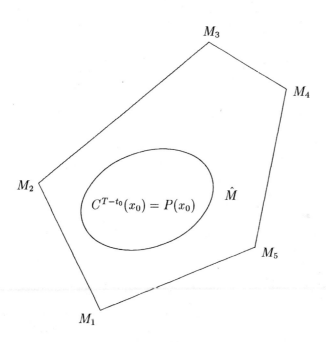

Fig. 10.

Let us consider the general case of arrangement of the points M_i, $i = 1, \ldots, m$ relative to the set $C^{T-t_0}(x_0)$ (Fig.11).

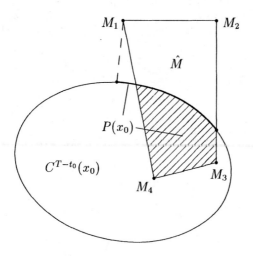

Fig. 11.

Suppose there exists a partition $\tau = (N_1, N_2)$ of the set N ($N_1 \cup N_2 = N$, $N_1 \cap N_2 \neq \emptyset$), such that

$$N_1 = \{i \in N | M_i \in C^{T-t_0}(x_0)\}, N_2 = \{i \in N | M_i \overline{\in} C^{T-t_0}(x_0)\}$$

Theorem 4. In the considered case $\widehat{K}(x_0, T-t_0) = \{H(x) | x \in \pi_{C^{T-t_0}(x_0)}\widehat{M}\}$.

P r o o f. If $N_1 = \emptyset$, then the conditions of Theorem 1 or Theorem 3 are respectively satisfied when $\widehat{M} \cap C^{T-t_0}(x_0) = \emptyset$ or $C^{T-t_0}(x_0) \subset \widehat{M}$ (there is also the case where $M_i \overline{\in} C^{T-t_0}(x_0)$, $C^{T-t_0}(x_0) \not\subset \widehat{M}$, $C^{T-t_0}(x_0) \cap \widehat{M} \neq \emptyset$). If $N_2 = \emptyset$, then $\widehat{M} \subset C^{T-t_0}(x_0)$ and we have the conditions of theorem 2.

We assume that $N_1, N_2 \neq \emptyset$. Introduce the notation $M_1 = \widehat{M} \cap C^{T-t_0}(x_0)$, $\widehat{M}_2 = \widehat{M} \setminus \widehat{M}_1$. Then $\pi_{C^{T-t_0}(x_0)}\widehat{M} = \widehat{M}_1 \cup \pi_{C^{T-t_0}(x_0)}\widehat{M}_2$.

Let

$$y' \in \pi_{C^{T-t_0}(x_0)}\widehat{M}, \ x \in C^{T-t_0}(x_0), \ x \neq y' \tag{5.16}$$

We show that

$$H_i(y') > H_i(x) \tag{5.17}$$

for at least one i. To this end, we consider two cases:

1) $y' \in \widehat{M}_1$. In this case, inequality (5.17) is proved in the same way as Theorem 2;

2) $y' \in \pi_{C^{T-t_0}(x_0)}\widehat{M} \setminus \widehat{M}_1 = \pi_{C^{T-t_0}(x_0)}\widehat{M}_2$. The inequality $\varrho(y', \overline{y}) < \varrho(x, \overline{y})$ then holds for any x from(5.16) and $\overline{y} \in Y$, where $Y = \{y \in \widehat{M}_2 | \pi_{C^{T-t_0}(x_0)}y = y'\}$. Hence, inequality (5.17) follows from Lemma 4.

Now the set $\pi_{C^{T-t_0}(x_0)}\widehat{M}$ consists only of the points satisfying condition(5.17). We shall show that the set $C^{T-t_0}(x_0)$ has no other points possessing the property (5.17) than the points of the set $\pi_{C^{T-t_0}(x_0)}\widehat{M}$. In particular, we show that for any $x \in C^{T-t_0}(x_0) \setminus \pi_{C^{T-t_0}(x_0)}\widehat{M}$ there is a point $\widetilde{y} \in \pi_{C^{T-t_0}(x_0)}\widehat{M}$ where $\varrho(\widetilde{y}, M_i) < \varrho(x, M_i)$ for all $i \in N$. Let us consider the set $\widehat{M}_3 = \mathrm{conv}\pi_{C^{T-t_0}(x_0)}\widehat{M}$. By Lemma 3, for any $x \in C^{T-t_0} \setminus \widehat{M}_3$ there exists a point $\widetilde{y} \in \pi_{C^{T-t_0}(x_0)}\widehat{M}$, such that $\varrho(\widetilde{y}, M_i) < \varrho(x, M_i)$ for all $i \in N$.

Now let $x \in (\widehat{M}_3 \setminus \pi_{C^{T-t_0}(x_0)}\widehat{M})$. If $\widetilde{y} = \pi_{\widehat{M}}x \in \widehat{M}_1$, then the point $\widetilde{y}$ is the required one (see Lemma 3), i.e. $\widetilde{y} = \pi_{\widehat{M}}x$. If, however, $\pi_{\widehat{M}}x \in \widehat{M}_2$, then $\pi_{\widehat{M}}x \overline{\in} \pi_{C^{T-t_0}(x_0)}\widehat{M}$, but there exist $x' \in \pi_{C^{T-t_0}(x_0)}\widehat{M}_2 \cap \omega$, where $\omega = \lambda x + (1 - \lambda)\pi_{\widehat{M}}x$, $\lambda \in [0,1]$, and, by Lemma 3, $\varrho(x', M_i) < \varrho(x, M_i)$ for all $i = 1, \ldots, m$ (if B_k is taken to be $\mathrm{conv}(x'\mathrm{conv}\pi_{C^{T-t_0}(x_0)}\widehat{M}))$, i.e. x' is the required point y.

However,the case where $M_i \overline{\in} C^{T-t_0}(x_0)$, $C^{T-t_0}(x_0) \not\subset \widehat{M}$, but $C^{T-t_0}(x_0) \cap \widehat{M} \neq \emptyset$ is proved in the same way as Theorem 2. This completes the proof of the theorem.

Theorems 1-4 provide a constructive way of constructing the Pareto optimal set for various arrangements of "target" points relative to the domain of reachability.

5.5 A Model for Development Control

In this section we shall construct a mathematical model for development of an environmentally closed region assuming that it comes under the influence of several parties (players) $B_1, \ldots, B_m$ representing the interests of various industries and environmental departments.In this case, the utility (payoff function) of one or another development path for player B_i is derived from (5.12) via the target points $M_i, i = 1, \ldots, m$ determined for each of the parties $B_1, \ldots, B_m$.

We assume that the regional development on the time interval $[t_0, T]$ can be described by the system of differential equations

$$\dot{x} = f(x, u_1, \ldots, u_n), \qquad x \in R^n, \qquad u_i \in U_i \subset \mathrm{Comp}R^l, \qquad (5.18)$$

where $u_i \in U_i$ is the control vector selected by party B_i (the i-th player).

Now we have a non zero-sum game involving m persons $B_1, \ldots, B_m$ (for a detailed formalization of this game, see [38], Ch.4).

We propose an optimality principle which, bearing a resemblance to the principles given in the Neumann-Morgenstern theory, is still free of the assumption that the players' payoffs are transferable. In essence, the payoff non-transferability implies that for every point $x(T) \in C^{T-t_0}(x_0)$ there is a unique imputation. We associate each coalition S to the set composed of all vectors (imputation) that the coalition may guarantee its members. The notions of imputation and dominance will be modified.

Denote by $\Gamma(t_0, x_0)$ the resulting differential non zero-sum game.

D e f i n i t i o n 1. By the imputation in the game $\Gamma(t_0, x_0)$ with terminal payoffs we mean the vector

$$H(x(T)) = \{H_i(x(T)), i = 1, \ldots, m\}, \qquad x(T) \in C^{T-t_0}(x_0).$$

Denote by $E(t_0, x_0)$ the set of imputations that are realizable in the game $\Gamma(t_0, x_0)$, i.e. $E(t_0, x_0) = \{H(x(T)) : x(T) \in C^{T-t_0}x_0\}$. The solution of the game $\Gamma(t_0, x_0)$ is interpreted to mean a subset $M(t_0, x_0) \in E(t_0, x_0)$ of imputations realizable in the game. The way of specifying a subset $M(t_0, x_0)$ governs the choice of a particular optimality principle in the differential game $\Gamma(t_0, x_0)$ with terminal payoffs. In what follows we point out specific forms of the sets $M(t_0, x_0)$.

For each coalition we define the set $V(S)$ to be referred to as the characteristic set of coalition S :

1) $V(\emptyset) = 0$;

2) $V(N) = E(t_0, x_0)$;

3) to define $V(S)$ for $S \neq N \neq \emptyset$, we consider the family of auxiliary zero-sum differential games $\Gamma_y(t_0, x_0, S)$ for $y \in C^{T-t_0}(x_0)$.

The game $\Gamma_y(t_0, x_0, S)$ is a zero-sum differential game between coalition S (the maximizing player) and coalition $N \setminus S$ (the minimizing player). The players' sets of strategies are Cartesian products of strategy sets for coalition members, i.e. the set $D^{(S)} = \prod_{i \in S} D^{(i)}$ for coalition S and the set $D^{(N \setminus S)} = \prod_{i \in N \setminus S} D^{(i)}$ for coalition $N \setminus S$ [38]. The elements of the sets $D^{(S)}$ and $D^{(N \setminus S)}$ are respectively denoted by φ_S and $\varphi_{N \setminus S}$. As before, denote by $x(t)$ the solution of system (5.18) with initial condition x_0. The payoff to player S in each situation $(\varphi_S, \varphi_{N \setminus S})$ is determined as follows: $J(t_0, x_0, \varphi_S, \varphi_{N \setminus S}) = -\varrho(x(T), y)$, where $x(t)$ is a trajectory in situation $(\varphi_S, \varphi_{N \setminus S})$ from the initial state x_0. The payoff to player $N \setminus S$ is set equal to $-K$. It is well known that the value of such a game always exists in the class of piecewise open-loop strategies (see [39]). Denote it by $val\Gamma_y(t_0, x_0, S)$. Let

$$Y(S) = \{y \in C^{T-t_0}(x_0) | val\Gamma_y(t_0, x_0, S) = 0\}.$$

The definition of the game value (see [33], [39]) and the set $Y(S)$ implies that for all $y \in Y(S)$ coalition S can guarantee for any $\varepsilon > 0$ an ε-approach to y.

We shall now define the set $V(S) : V(S) = \{H(x(T)) | x(T) = y \in Y(S)\}$, i.e. $V(S)$ is the set of those imputations that coalition S can guarantee with any previously specified accuracy of $\varepsilon > 0$. We have thus defined for each coalition S the characteristic set $V(S)$.

L e m m a 5. The characteristic sets of coalition have the following properties :

1) $V(\emptyset) = \emptyset$;
2) $V(R \cup S) \supset V(R) \cup V(S)$, if $R \cap S \neq \emptyset$;
3) $V(S) \subset V(N)$ for all $S \subset N$.

P r o o f. Properties 1) and 3) follow immediately from the definition of $V(S)$. To prove property 2), let us assume that the imputation H belongs to $V(S)$. Then there exists $y \in Y(S)$ such that $H_i = H_i(y), i = 1, \ldots, m$. We will show that for any $S' \supset S$ $Y(S') \supset Y(S)$.

Indeed, let $y \in Y(S)$; and this means that $val\,\Gamma_y(t_0, x_0, S) = 0$. Since $S' \supset S$, we have $val\,\Gamma_y(t_0, x_0, S') = 0$. For if coalition S guarantees that the y will be approached within a distance shorter than ε, then this can be guaranteed by any coalition $S' \supset S$ (the following strategy is always possible: players from S use a strategy that is ε-optimal in the game $\Gamma_y(t_0, x_0, S)$ and players from $S' \setminus S$ use in this game a truncation of the ε-optimal strategy of coalition $N \setminus S$ on the set $S' \setminus S$). Hence we have that $Y(S') \supset Y(S)$, which yields $Y(R \cup S) \supset Y(S)$, i.e. $y \in Y(R \cup S)$. By the definition of the set $V(R \cup S)$, this means that the imputation $H = \{H_i(y), i = 1, \ldots, n\} \in V(R \cup S)$.

We have thus shown that $V(S) \subset V(R \cup S)$. Replacing S by R, we obtain $V(R) \subset V(S \cup R)$, and finally $V(R \cup S) \supset V(S) \cup V(R)$.

Let H' and H'' be imputations and S some coalition.

D e f i n i t i o n 2. We say that the imputation H' dominates the imputation H'' in coalition $S(H' \succ_S H'')$ if $H' \in V(S)$ and $H'_i > H''_i$ for all $i \in S$;

the imputation H' dominates the imputation $H''(H' \succ H'')$ if there exists a coalition S such that $H' \succ_S H''$.

This understanding of dominance enables one to extend notions of the core and NM-solution from the Neumann-Morgenstern cooperative theory to differential games without any changes [5,33].

Suppose the player's payoff in $\Gamma(t_0, x_0)$ is of the form (5.12). It turns out that in a number of cases the Pareto optimal imputation set $\widehat{K}$ coincides with the core and NM-solution. To simplify further computations, we assume that $\widehat{M} \cap C^{T-t_0}(x_0) = \emptyset$. Let $R_i = \max\limits_{x \in \pi \widehat{M}} \varrho(x, M_i)$, $i = 1, \ldots, m$, and let $C(M_i, R_i)$ be a closed sphere with M_i as its center and R_i as its radius (in the following, $\pi \widehat{M} = \pi_{_cT-t_0(x_0)}\widehat{M}$). Then the following theorem is true.

Theorem 5. In order that, in the game $\Gamma(t_0, x_0)$ with payoff (5.12), the core coincide with the Pareto optimal imputation set $\widehat{K}$, it is sufficient that

$$\left[\bigcap_{i \in S} C(M_i, R_i)\right] \bigcap Y(S) = \emptyset \tag{5.19}$$

for all $S \subset N, S \neq N$.

P r o o f. Let the condition of the theorem be satisfied. Prove that the core exists and coincides with the set $\widehat{K}$. To do this, it suffices to show that no imputation from $\widehat{K}$ is dominated.

Suppose the opposite is true. Let the imputation $H'(x)$ $(x \in \pi \widehat{M})$ be dominated by some imputation $H''(y)$, $y \in C^{T-t_0}(x_0)$. This means that there exists a coalition $S \subset N(S \neq N)$ such that

$$H''(y) \in V(S), \qquad H_i''(y) > H_i'(x) \tag{5.20}$$

for all $i \in S$. Since $H''(y) \in V(S)$, we have $y \in Y(S)$, and condition (5.19) implies

$$-H_i''(y) = \varrho(y, M_i) > R_i$$

for at least one $i \in S$. For all $x \in \pi \widehat{M}$, however $\varrho(x, M_i) = -H_i'(x) \leq R_i$, which contradicts (5.20). The fact that the point $x \in \pi \widehat{M}$ has been chosen arbitrarily proves the theorem.

Theorem 6. In order for the game $\Gamma(t_0, x_0)$ with payoffs (5.12) to have HM-solution L, it is sufficient that

$$Y(N \setminus \{i\}) \cap \overline{C^{T-t_0}(x_0)} = \emptyset \tag{5.21}$$

for all $i = 1, \ldots, m$, where $\overline{C^{T-t_0}(x_0)}$ are boundary points of the set $C^{T-t_0}(x_0)$. In this case, the Pareto optimal solution set $\widehat{K}$ coincides with NM-solution, i.e. $L = \widehat{K}$.

P r o o f. Clearly, $\pi\widehat{M} \subset C^{\overline{T-t_0}}(x_0)$. The condition of the theorem, in particular, implies that $Y(S) \cap \pi\widehat{M} = \emptyset$ for all $S \neq N$, since with $S \neq N$ $S \subset N \setminus \{i\}$ for some $i \in N$.

Let $H', H'' \in \hat{K}(x_0, T - t_0)$. Show that they cannot dominate one another. It follows from the definition of $\widehat{K}$ that the imputations H', H'' do not dominate one another in coalition N. If, however, $H' \succ_s H''$ in some coalition $S \subset N$ $(S \neq N)$, then $H'(y) \in V(S)$ by the definition of dominance. But this is impossible, since by the definition of $V(S)$, here $y \in Y(S)$ and $H' \in \widehat{K}$, hence $y \in \pi\widehat{M}$. This results in $Y(S) \cap \pi\widehat{M} \neq \emptyset$ for some $S \neq N$, which contradicts (5.21). The second property of NM-solution always holds for the set $\widehat{K}(x_0, T - t_0)$.

Theorems 5, 6 provide a constructive way of defining the Pareto optimal set, the core, and NM-solution.

D e f i n i t i o n 3. Let $y \in M(t_0, x_0)$. The control $\overline{u}(t)$ and its related trajectory $\overline{x}(t)$ are called conditionally optimal if $\overline{x}(t_0) = x_0, \overline{x}(T) = y$.

Let us consider the current games $\Gamma(t, \overline{x}(t))$ and the related solutions $M(t, \overline{x}(t))$. By definition, for all $t_0 \leq t \leq T$ $M(t, \overline{x}(t)) \subset E(t, \overline{x}(t))$, where $E(t, \overline{x}(t)) = \{H(x) : x \in C^{T-t}(\overline{x}(t))\}$. In view of the payoff nontransferability, $E(t, \overline{x}(t)) \subset E(t_0, x_0)$ for all $t > t_0$. In general, it is easy to show that for all $t_0 \leq t' < t'' \leq T$ $E(t'', \overline{x}(t'')) \subset E(t', \overline{x}(t'))$.

D e f i n i t i o n 4. The solution $M(t_0, x_0)$ is called dynamically stable in the game $\Gamma(t_0, x_0)$ with terminal payoffs if for every $H(y) \in M(t_0, x_0)$ there is at least one conditionally optimal trajectory $\overline{x}(t) = x_0, \overline{x}(T) = y$ such that

$$H(y) = \bigcap_{t_0 < t \leq T} M(t, \overline{x}(t)).$$

The conditionally optimal trajectories corresponding to the imputations from a dynamic stable solution are called optimal trajectories.

Dynamic stability of solution guarantees that the motion along the optimal trajectory $\overline{x}(t)$ is rational at each time instant, since for all $t \in [t_0, T]$ the imputation in a finite state y continues to satisfy the same optimality principle. i.e. $H(y) \in M(t, \overline{x}(t))$ for all $t \in [t_0, T]$. Violation of this condition may cause players to change the cooperative decision (the imputation $H(y)$) at any time t, when $H(y) \overline{\in} M(t, \overline{x}(t))$.

Let $\overline{x}(t), \overline{x}(t_0) = x_0, \overline{x}(T) = y, y \in \pi\widehat{M}$ be an optimal trajectory. Denote by $\pi\widehat{M}(t)$ the projection of the set $\widehat{M}$ onto the set $C^{T-t}(\overline{x}(t))$. Since $y \in \pi\widehat{M}$, it is the point in the set $C^{T-t_0}(x_0)$ that is the nearest to some point $z \in \widehat{M}$, i.e.

$$\varrho(z, y) = \min_{y' \in C^{T-t_0}(x_0)} \varrho(z, y').$$

Since $C^{T-t_0}(\overline{x}(t)) \subset C^{T-t_0}(x_0)$, $y \in C^{T-t}(\overline{x}(t))$, the point y continues to be the nearest in the set $C^{T-t}(\overline{x}(t))$ to the point z for all $t \in [t_0, T]$, i.e. for all $t \in [t_0, T]$ it is the projection of z onto the set $C^{T-t}(\overline{x}(t))$, and hence $y \in \pi \widehat{M}(t)$ for all $t \in [t_0, T]$.

Theorem 4 implies that the Pareto optimal imputation set in the game $\Gamma(t, \overline{x}(t))$ is of the form $\widehat{K}(\overline{x}(t), T-t) = \{H(y') | y' \in \pi \widehat{M}(t)\}$. Since $y \in \pi \widehat{M}(t)$ for all $t \in [t_0, T]$, we have $H(y) \in \widehat{K}(x(t), T - t)$ for all $t \in [t_0, T]$. From this we obtain the following theorem for stability of Pareto optimal imputations.

Theorem 7. For any conditionally optimal trajectory $\overline{x}(t)$ in the game $\Gamma(x_0, t_0)$ with terminal payoff the imputation

$$H(y) = \{H_i(\overline{x}(T)) = H_i(y) | y \in \pi \widehat{M}, \qquad i = 1, \ldots, m\}$$

belongs to the Pareto optimal imputation set $\widehat{K}(\overline{x}(t), T - t)$ for all current games $\Gamma(t, \overline{x}(t))$ for all $t \in [t_0, T]$, i.e. the Pareto optimal imputation set is dynamically stable.

Note that this theorem is a consequence of a more general result on dynamic stability of Pareto optimal solutions.

Let $Y_t(S) = Y(S, t, \overline{x}(t))$. The following theorems are consequences of Theorems 5-7. In these theorems, the core in the game with nontransferable payoffs is interpreted to mean the set of imputations that are nondominated in the sense of Definition 2 (in contrast to the definition of dominance for the game with transferable payoffs, here dominance is possible in the set of all players). Similarly, allowing for dominance in the set of all players, the concept of NM-solution (for definition, see [5,33]) is extended to cover the game with nontransferable payoffs.

Theorem 8. If for all $S \subset N$, $S \neq N$ there is

$$\left[\bigcap_{i \in S} C(M_i, R_i(t))\right] \cap Y_t(S) = \emptyset, \quad t_0 \leq t \leq T,$$

then the core in the game with payoffs (5.12) is dynamically stable. Here $R_i(t) = \max_{x \in \pi M(t)} \varrho(x, M_i)$, $i = 1, \ldots, m$.

Theorem 9. If $Y_t(N \setminus \{i\}) \cap C^{T-t}(\overline{x}(t)) = \emptyset$ for all $i = 1, \ldots, m$ and $t \in [t_0, T]$, then NM-solution in the game with payoffs (5.12) is dynamically stable.

Another example of dynamically stable solutions is provided by the set of imputations in the Nash equilibrium.

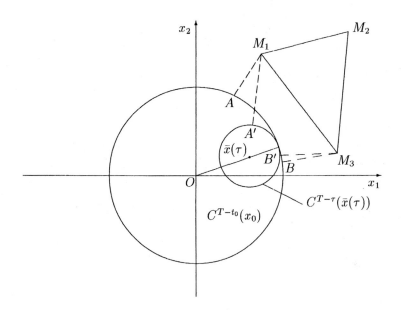

Fig. 12.

E x a m p l e. Suppose system (5.18) has the form

$$\dot{x} = u_1 + u_2 + u_3, \ x = (x_1, x_2) \in E_2,$$

$$u_i = \{u_1^i, \ u_2^i\}, \ |u_i| \leq 1, \ i = 1, 2, 3, \ x(0) = x_0 = 0,$$

$$N = \{1, 2, 3\}, \ M = \{M_1, M_2, M_3\}, \ \widehat{M} \cap C^{T-t_0}(x_0) = \emptyset, \ T = 1.$$

The reachability set $C^{T-t_0}(x_0)$ (Fig.12) is the circle of radius $R = 3$ centered at the point $x(0) = 0$. The set $\pi\widehat{M}$ coincides with arc AB.

Let $y \in AB$, $\overline{x}(t) = Oy$ be an optimal trajectory. For $\tau \in [0, 1]$ the set $C^{T-\tau}(\overline{x}(\tau))$ is the circle tangent to the set $C^{T-t_0}(x_0)$ at the point y; the set $\pi\widehat{M}(\tau)$ coincides with arc $A'B'$ that is the orthogonal projection of a triangle $\widehat{M} = \triangle M_1 M_2 M_3$ onto the circle $C^{T-\tau}(x(\tau))$. Since the conditions of Theorems 8,9 are here explicitly satisfied, we have

$$H(y) = \{-\varrho(y, M_1), -\varrho(y, M_2), -\varrho(y, M_3)\} \in \widehat{K}(\overline{x}(t), T - t)$$

for all $\tau \in [0,1]$, i.e. there exist a dynamically stable core and NM-solution.

The optimal planning problems incorporating the ecological factor are essentially multicriteria problems. Studies of multicriteria optimal control problems bring to light a nontrivial question of dynamic stability of optimality principles which is virtually absent in classical single-criterion problems. It turns out that the set of Pareto optimal solutions is dynamically stable, although the procedure of selecting a particular solution from this set may not be dynamically stable.

The construction of Pareto optimal sets generally involves serious problems. Such problems, however, are found to be solvable in the long-term planning for environmentally closed regions with finitely many target points.In this case the set of Pareto optimal solutions is constructed as the projection of a convex hull of target points onto the reachability set of the system of ordinary differential equations describing development processes. It is possible to use the techniques of non zero sum differential games where several parties are concerned about development.This enables one to find effective ways of constructing optimality principles in order to solve the problems of approaching a finite number of target points.

5.6   Regularization of Optimality Principles

Multicriteria optimal control problems are distinguished by multiplicity of optimality principles borrowed from the static theory of multicriteria optimization. As in the theory of non zero-sum differential games, the use of optimality principles borrowed from the static theory leads to contradictions arising from the loss of dynamic stability or strong dynamic stability. This fact was initially noted in [34],[64], where the corresponding notions were introduced.In the English speaking countries the literatures subsequently transformed these terms into "time consistency" and "strong time consistency".

Dynamic stability of the optimality principle means that any segment of an optimal trajectory determines the optimal motion with respect to the relevant initial states of the process. Strong dynamic stability means that any optimal extension in the current problem of the multicriteria optimal control together with the optimal motion at the origin of the process is an optimal trajectory.

Both properties hold for the overwhelming majority of classical optimal control problems (a single-criterion case) and follow from the Bellman optimality principle [65].

The absence of dynamic or strongly dynamic stability in the optimality principle basically involves the possibility that the previous "optimal" decision will be abandoned at some current time, thereby making meaningless the very problem of seeking an optimal control.That is the reason that particular emphasis is placed on the construction of optimality principles possessing dynamic or strongly dynamic stability. This specifically applies to long-term managerial decisions on development of complex ecosystems. In fact, the performance of each such system is evaluated by a set of parameters and the question of long-term management of its development is incorporated into the framework of multicriteria optimal control. The choice of a dynamically unstable principle of development is incorporated into the framework of multicriteria optimal control. The choice of a dynamically unstable principle of development may endanger at some intermediate instant of time further movement along the initially chosen "optimal" path, because new paths may be found to be optimal for the current state of system development. In practice, however, we often observe deviations from the initial decisions and failure to implement long-term development programs.

We propose to construct strong dynamically stable optimality principles for multicriteria optimal control problems on the basis of "regularization" of optimality principles from the static theory of multicriteria decision-making. The idea of regularization consists in expanding the family of optimal trajectories to cover all possible envelopes of optimal motions in the current subproblems [67].

When the construction of similar envelopes is found to be impossible, it is proposed to construct δ-approximating trajectories resulting in δ-dynamically stable and δ-strong dynamically stable motions.

Let us consider the simplest problem of optimal control $\Gamma(x_0, T - t_0)$ on a fixed time interval $[t_0, T]$ with terminal payoff

$$\dot{x} = f(x, u), \quad x(t_0) = x_0, \tag{5.22}$$

where $u \in U \subset \text{Comp} R^l$; $x \in R^m$, $t \in [t_0, T]$. The payoff vector is dependent on the process state at the time T and is defined as

$$H(x(T)) = \{H_1(x(T)), \ldots, H_n(x(T))\}.$$

The class of admissible open-loop controls comprises all possible piecewise continuous functions given on $[t_0, T]$ with values in U.

Let $X(x_0, T - t_0)$ be the set of trajectories of system (5.22) that are considered on the interval $[t_0, T]$, emanate from the initial state x_0 and can be obtained by using all possible admissible controls $u(t)$.

The optimality principle of problem $\Gamma(x_0, T - t_0)$ is interpreted to mean a subset of trajectories $D(x_0, T - t_0) \subset X(x_0, T - t_0)$. The trajectories $x^*(t) \in D(x_0, T - t_0)$ are called optimal trajectories.

Let $x^*(t) \in D(x_0, T - t_0)$ be a fixed optimal trajectory. We consider the family of multicriteria optimal control subproblems $\Gamma(x^*(T), T-t)$, $t \in [t_0, T]$ with the initial state $x^*(t)$ on the optimal trajectory $x^*(\tau)$ that are defined on the time interval $[t, T]$. Recall the notion of dynamic stability or strongly dynamic stability for the optimality principle.

The optimality principle $D(x_0, T - t_0)$ is called dynamically stable if for every trajectory $x^*(t) \in D(x_0, T - t_0)$ the trajectory $x_\tau^*(t) = x^*(t)$, $t \in [\tau, T]$ belonging to the set $X(x^*(\tau), T - \tau)$ of admissible trajectories in the subproblem $\Gamma(x^*(\tau), T - \tau)$, also belongs to $D(x^*(\tau), T - \tau)$ that is the optimality principle of the subproblem $\Gamma(x^*(\tau), T - \tau)$.

The optimality principle $D(x_0, T - t_0)$ is called strong dynamically stable if for every trajectory $x^*(t) \in D(x_0, T - t_0)$, for every subproblem $\Gamma(x^*(\tau), T - \tau)$, $\tau \in [t_0, T]$, and for every trajectory $\tilde{x}(t) \in D(x^*(\tau), T - \tau)$, a trajectory of the form

$$\overline{x}(t) = \begin{cases} x^*(t), & t \in [t_0, \tau), \\ \tilde{x}(t), & t \in [\tau, T) \end{cases}$$

belongs to the set $D(x_0, T - t_0)$.

Conceptually, dynamic stability implies that the segment of an optimal trajectory $x_\tau^*(t) = x^*(t)$ in the problem $\Gamma(x_0, T - t_0)$ for $t \in [t_0, T)$ is an optimal trajectory in the subproblem $\Gamma(x^*(\tau), T - \tau)$.

Strong dynamic stability implies that any trajectory composed of the segment of an optimal trajectory $x^*(t)$ for $t \in [t_0, \tau)$ and from the optimal trajectory in the subproblem $\Gamma(x^*(\tau), T - \tau)$ is an optimal trajectory in the problem $\Gamma(x_0, T - t_0)$.

It is easy to see that the set of Pareto optimal trajectories $P(x_0, T - t_0)$ in the problem $\Gamma(x_0, T - t_0)$ is a dynamically stable principle, but is not strong dynamically stable.

In applications, our interest is in the strong dynamically stable optimality principles, because movements along the corresponding optimal trajectories in the current subproblems do not produce new optimal motions unpossible of deriving from the optimality principle in the main problem $\Gamma(x_0, T - t_0)$.

However, among the well-known optimality principles in the theory of multicriteria optimal control there are no strong dynamically stable optimality principles except perhaps those which can be reduced by convolution of criteria to a single criterion, but this leads to a classical single-criterion problem.

The optimality principle $\overline{D}(x_0, T - t_0)$ is called regularization of the optimality principle $D(x_0, T - t_0)$, if $x(t) \in \overline{D}(x_0, T - t_0)$ when

$$\frac{dx(t)}{dt} = \frac{dy(t)}{dt}, \qquad (5.22)$$

where $y(\tau) \in D(x(t), T - t)$, $\tau \in [t, T]$ belongs to the optimality principle in the subproblem $\Gamma(x(t), T - t)$.

In other words, the trajectory belonging to a regularized optimality principle at each time t has the same direction as an optimal trajectory in the subproblem for which this instant of time t is initial.

The question now arises as to whether there exist any trajectories possessing this property.

It turns out that if the optimality principle $D(x_0, T - t_0)$ is dynamically stable, then $\overline{D}(x_0, T - t_0) \supset D(x_0, T - t_0)$ and hence the set $\overline{D}(x_0, T - t_0)$ is nonempty.

We consider $D(x_0, T - t_0)$ to be Pareto optimal trajectories in the problem $\Gamma(x_0, T - t_0)$. Since Pareto optimal trajectories are dynamically stable [65], the Pareto optimal solution regularization $\overline{D}(x_0, T - t_0)$ is nonempty.

It can be verified that the optimality principle regularization $\overline{D}(x_0, T - t_0)$ is always a strong dynamically stable principle of optimality.

E x a m p l e 1. Let us consider the controlled system

$$\dot{x} = u_1 + u_2 + u_3,$$

$$x(t_0) = x_0, \qquad (5.23)$$

where $|u_i| \leq 1$, $x \in R^2$, $u \in R^2$, $t \in [t_0, T]$. $H_i(x(T)) = -\varrho(x(T), M_i)$, $M_i \in R^2$, $i = 1, 2, 3$ is a specified system of points.

Let $C^{T-t_0}(x_0)$ be a reachability set of system (5.23). It represents a circle of radius $R = 3(T - t_0)$ centered at point x_0. Suppose the convex hull $\widehat{M}$ of points M_1, M_2, M_3 does not intersect $C^{T-t_0}(x_0)$.

Let $D(x_0, T - t_0)$ be a Pareto optimal set; then the endpoints of Pareto optimal trajectories in $\Gamma(x_0, T - t_0)$ lie on arc $\overset{\smile}{AB}$ (Fig. 13). In subproblem $\Gamma(x^*(\tau), T - \tau)$ the endpoints of Pareto optimal trajectories from the local Pareto optimal set $D(x^*(\tau), T - \tau)$ lie on arc $A'B'$. It can be seen that the set of trajectory endpoints of the regularized criterion $\overline{D}(x_0, T - t_0)$ coincides with the shaded set $\widehat{D}$. Here one may see that the interior point from $\widehat{D}$ is not Pareto optimal and is dominated on arc $\overset{\smile}{AB}$, which implies a performance degradation (some payoff losses), but this is offset by the strongly dynamic stability of the optimality principle $\overline{D}(x_0, T - t_0)$.

However, we cannot always claim that there exists a nonempty $\overline{D}(x_0, T - t_0)$. Let us consider another example.

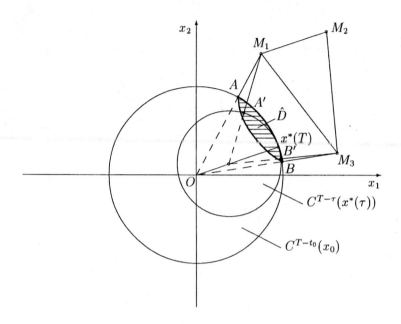

Fig. 13.

E x a m p l e 2. There are many ways of selecting a particular Pareto optimal solution from the set of all Pareto optimal solutions. We revert to one of the previously discussed methods.

Let $C^{T-t_0}(x_0)$ be the reachability set of system (5.23). It is proposed to select a Pareto optimal point $\overline{x}(x_0, T - t_0)$ such that

$$\min_{x \in C^{T-t_0}(x_0)} \max_i \frac{\max\limits_{x' \in C^{T-t_0}(x_0)} H_i(x') - H_i(x)}{\max\limits_{x' \in C^{T-t_0}(x_0)} H_i(x')}. \qquad (5.24)$$

is attained.

Obviously, min in (5.24) depends on the input parameters x_0, $T - t_0$ of problem $\Gamma(x_0, T - t_0)$. Let $x^*(t)$ be an optimal trajectory sending x_0 to the point $\overline{x}(x_0, T - t_0)$. Suppose the optimality principle $D(x_0, T - t_0)$ in problem $\Gamma(x_0, T - t_0)$ is made up of a single trajectory $x^*(t)$ (the trajectory $x^*(t)$ is Pareto optimal). It can be readily seen that, in the current problems $\Gamma(x^*(\tau), T - \tau)$, to find the corresponding points $\overline{x}(x^*(\tau), T - \tau)$, it is necessary to compute the minimum of the expression

$$\min_{x \in C^{T-\tau}(x^*(\tau))} \max_i \frac{\max\limits_{x' \in C^{T-\tau}(x^*(\tau))} H_i(x') - H_i(x)}{\max\limits_{x' \in C^{T-\tau}(x^*(\tau))} H_i(x')}. \tag{5.25}$$

Clearly, the point $\overline{x}(x^*(\tau), T - \tau)$, where the minimum is attained in (5.25), does not generally coincide with the point $\overline{x}(x_0, T - t_0)$, where the minimum is attained in (5.23), i.e.

$$\overline{x}(x^*(\tau), T - \tau) \neq \text{const}, \quad \tau \in [t_0, T].$$

This means that the trajectory $x^*_\tau(t) \in D(x^*(\tau), T - \tau)$, joining $x^*(\tau)$ and $\overline{x}(x^*(\tau), T - \tau)$, does not coincide with the segment of trajectory $x^*(t)$, $t \in [t_0, T]$, that is optimal in $\Gamma(x_0, T - t_0)$. That is to say, here the optimality principle $D(x_0, T - t_0)$ is dynamically unstable.

In order to regularize $D(x_0, T - t_0)$, we need to construct a trajectory $\widehat{x}(t)$ such that

$$\frac{d\widehat{x}(\tau)}{d\tau} = \frac{dx^*_\tau(t)}{dt}\bigg|_{t=\tau},$$

where $x^*_\tau(t) \in D(\widehat{x}^*(\tau), T - \tau)$, $t \in [\tau, T]$, $\tau \in [t_0, T]$.

The trajectory $\widehat{x}(\tau)$, $\tau \in [t_0, T]$ is found to be the envelope of a certain family of trajectories $x^*_\tau(t)$ in subproblems $\Gamma(\widehat{x}^*(\tau), T - \tau)$ that is tangent to them at the initial point. The existence of such an envelope depends on differential properties of the family of optimal trajectories $x^*_\tau(t)$ in initial data, but this question calls for special investigation. To avoid the related difficulties, we shall introduce a weaker notion of δ-strongly dynamic stability.

Let us consider the partitioning Δ of the interval $[t_0, T]$ by points $t_0 < t_1 < \ldots < t_k = T$. In this case, $t_{i+1} - t_i = \delta > 0$, $i = 0, \ldots, k - 1$.

The optimality principle $D(x_0, T - t_0)$ is called δ-dynamically stable if for the trajectory $x^*(t) \in D(x_0, T - t_0)$ a trajectory of the form $x^*_{t_i}(t) = x^*(t)$, $t_i \in \Delta$, $t \in [t_i, T]$, belonging to $X(x^*(t_i), T - t_i)$ that is the set of admissible trajectories in subproblem $\Gamma(x^*(t_i), T - t_i)$, also belongs to $D(x^*(t_i), T - t_i)$ that is an optimality principle in subproblem $\Gamma(x^*(t_i), T - t_i)$.

The optimality principle $D(x_0, T - t_0)$ is called δ-strong dynamically stable if for every trajectory belonging to $D(x_0, T - t_0)$, for every subproblem

$\Gamma(x^*(t_i), T - t_i)$, $t_i \in \Delta$, and for $\tilde{x}(t) \in D(x^*(t_i), T - t_i)$ a trajectory of the form

$$\overline{x}(t) = \begin{cases} x^*(t), & t \in [t_0, t_i), \\ \tilde{x}(t), & t \in [t_i, T] \end{cases}$$

belongs to $D(x_0, T - t_0)$.

We revert to Example 2. Suppose $x_1^*(\tau) = x^*(\tau)$ sends the point x_0 to the point $\overline{x}(x_0, T - t_0)$. Let us consider the point $x_1^*(t_1)$ and let $x_2^*(\tau)$ be an optimal trajectory in subproblem $\Gamma(x^*(t_1), T - t_1)$ sending the point $x_1^*(t_1)$ to the point $\overline{x}(x_1^*(t_1), T - t_1)$. Let $x_k^*(\tau)$ be an optimal trajectory in subproblem $\Gamma(x_{k-1}^*(t_{k-1}), T - t_{k-1})$ sending the point $x_{k-1}^*(t_{k-1})$ to the point $\overline{x}(x^*(t_{k-1}), T - t_{k-1})$.

We construct a trajectory with $x_\delta^*(\tau) = x_i^*(\tau)$, $i = 1, \ldots, k - 1$, for $\tau \in [t_{i-1}, t_i)$. Suppose $\overline{D}(x_0, T - t_0)$ is made up of a single trajectory $x_\delta^*(\tau)$, $\tau \in [t_0, T]$. From the definition of the trajectory $x_\delta^*(\tau)$, its uniqueness, and the explicit observation that $\overline{D}(x_0, T - t_0)$ is δ-dynamically stable, it follows that $\overline{D}(x_0, T - t_0)$ is also δ-strong dynamically stable.

Similarly, a δ-strong dynamically stable principle of optimality can be constructed in terms of the set of Pareto optimal trajectories in problem $\Gamma(x_0, T - t_0)$.

Let $D(x_0, T - t_0)$ be the set of Pareto optimal trajectories $x^*(t)$ in problem $\Gamma(x_0, T - t_0)$.

Let $x_1^*(\tau) \in D(x_0^*(t_0), T - t_0)$, $x_2^*(\tau) \in D(x_1^*(t_1), T - t_1), \ldots, x_k^*(\tau) \in D(x_{k-1}^*(t_{k-1}), T - t_{k-1})$. We construct a trajectory of the form $x_\delta^*(\tau) = x_i^*(\tau)$, $i = 1, \ldots, k - 1$, for $\tau \in [t_{i-1}, t_i)$.

Exhausting the arbitrary Pareto optimal trajectories $x_1^*(\tau), x_2^*(\tau), \ldots, x_k^*(\tau)$ in the subproblems $D(x_0^*(t_0), T - t_0)$, $D(x_1^*(t_1), T - t_1), \ldots, D(x_{k-1}^*(t_{k-1}), T - t_{k-1})$, we obtain various trajectories $x_\delta^*(\tau)$. Denote the set of all such trajectories by $\overline{D}(x_0, T - t_0)$.

From the construction it follows that the optimality principle $\overline{D}(x_0, T - t_0)$ is δ-strong dynamically stable.

Chapter 6

EVOLUTIONARY GAMES

6.1   Hawk-Dove Game

The theory of games was initially developed as the theory of rational behavior in conflict situations. Its major fields of applications have been and still are economics and social sciences. In the classical theory of noncooperative games, the major principle of solution based on the idealized notion of rationality of participants is a Nash equilibrium. Applications of such an approach, however, often fail to produce satisfactory results. If the Nash equilibrium principle is to be successful, one has not only to assume that the players wish to optimize their behavior, but also to ensure a sufficiently high degree of harmonization among actions and expectations of all participants of a game [68]. This generated a need for alternative concepts of solution. The most promising among the approaches recently developed is the principle developed in the theory of evolutionary games.

The advent of the theory of evolutionary games was dictated by the necessity to model situations where the participants of a conflict have no ability of rational thinking.The evolution of nature provides an example of such a process. Maynard Smith and J.Price show (see [69]) that the rivalry of animals can be described as a game and that the theory of games can be successfully used in biology. In this case, particular emphasis is laid not on the extent to which the actions of an individual contending party are rational, but on the problem of achieving an equilibrium as a result of evolution.

Conflicts persist in nature when animals contend for limited resources such as territory, food or partners. Although all of such encounters can be described as a game, nevertheless animals cannot consciously maximize some utility function,. because they have no conscious rationality. But the evolutionary laws operating in nature provide some prerequisites for optimization. An individual exhibiting the maximum survival ability is eliminated in the process of natural selection. All individuals are expected to display an equal maximum ability to survive when the evolution is in equilibrium. Thus, in the biological theory of games, the rationality criterion of the classical theory of games is replaced by the Darwinian function of utility of productivity.

Biologically, the strategy is a behavioral phenotype which is peculiar to and uncontrolled by an individual. The phenotype completely determines the behavior of an animal in all possible situations. Thus the theory of evolutionary games allows an analysis of the evolutionary process without a detailed study of the corresponding genetic mechanism. The strategy is assumed to be inheritable : if an individual displays a certain phenotype(a behavioral strategy), then its offsprings are characterized by the same phenotype. Note that this implies asexual reproduction. It also seems reasonable to assume that there exist mixed phenotypes (strategies) : if an individual displays a mixed phenotype and has a certain advantage, then this phenotype must be secured in the process of evolution at the genetic level.

The theory of evolutionary games lays a particular emphasis on strategies rather than players. A player is regarded as an individual in a population which is chosen in a random way. The basic principle of solving a game is an evolutionary stable strategy. A strategy is called evolutionary stable if all members of a population use this strategy so that no stable group of individuals using the other strategy can appear in the population in the process of natural selection [70]. Note that this concept is applicable to monomorphic population, where individuals can use only pure strategies, although coexistence of various phenotypes is possible.

In order to formulate more precisely the definition of an evolutionary stable strategy and the mathematical conditions for its existence, it is convenient to discuss a specific example. To this end, we shall make some assumptions about the nature of the population discussed. As an illustrative example, we may consider the Hawk-Dove game proposed by Maynard Smith and J. Price [69]. Note that the words "hawk" and "dove" are used to characterize strategies and bear no relation to biological species. The model is based on the following assumptions : 1)the population is infinite; 2) reproduction is asexual; 3) symmetric pairwise encounters occur; 4) mixed strategies exist and are inheritable; 5) the set of strategies is finite, so that the game can be represented in matrix form.

Suppose that two representatives of the same population contend for a resource whose reproductive value is V. The implication of the reproductive value is that the Darwinian utility function (the expected number of offsprings) of an individual which obtained a resource is increased by V. This is not to say that an individual which failed to obtain a resource has zero reproductivity. We may assume that the resource is a territory in the most favorable habitat and a similar area exists in a less favorable habitat, where losers can reproduce as well. Suppose that an animal in the favorable habitat has on the average 5 offsprings while an animal in the unfavorable conditions has 3 offsprings. The resource reproductive value V then is 5-3=2. Thus, V is the increment of the utility function of the resource owner, while the loser's utility function is zero. During the encounter an animal may take one of the three courses of action: "observe", "attack", or "retreat".

In real situations animals may switch from one type of behavior to the other in a very intricate way. For the present, however, we assume that each individual has a fixed strategy. For simplicity, only two pure strategies are assumed to be feasible, namely Hawk and Dove. Hawk attacks until his opponent stampedes into a retreat or he himself receives a wound and is forced to retreat. Dove demonstrates his intention to capture a resource, observes his opponent's reactions, and effects a retreat as soon as his opponent delivers an attack. Suppose that the wound reduces the utility function by the magnitude of C. We shall analyze the game without considering the difference in the size and age of individuals, although it may significantly affect the outcome of the encounter and the choice of behavior strategy.

In the case of an encounter of two Hawks, the opponents continue to fight until one of them receives a wound and is forced to retreat. Let a random variable ρ with the space of values $\{I, II\}$ denote the winner. Since we agreed upon the equality of the opponents' forces, it would appear reasonable that each of them would have equal chances to win the fight, i.e. $\text{Prob}\{\rho = I\} = \frac{1}{2} = \text{Prob}\{\rho = II\}$. Now the payoff to the winner is V and the payoff to the loser is $-C$. Then the expected payoff to each of the opponents is

$$V\text{Prob}\{\rho = I\} + (-C)\text{Prob}\{\rho = II\} - \frac{V - C}{2}. \qquad (6.1)$$

When one of the opponents is Dove and the other is Hawk, Dove effects a retreat as soon as Hawk stages an attack. Hawk receives the disputable resource and his payoff is equal to V. Dove's payoff taken as an increment of his utility function is zero. But this is not to say that Dove in the Hawks population has a zero utility function. The point is that Dove's utility function is not affected by the encounter with Hawk.

of his utility function is zero. But this is not to say that Dove in the Hawks population has a zero utility function. The point is that Dove's utility function is not affected by the encounter with Hawk.

Two Doves can share a resource among themselves. If, however, the resource is indivisible, then the opponents demonstrate their intentions to capture the resource, but neither of them decides on the attack against this opponent. Sooner or later one of the opponents gets tired and gives up the resource. Let ρ denote the player who conceded the resource. Then ρ is a random variable with the space of events $\{I, II\}$. It would appear reasonable that $\text{Prob}\{\rho = I\} = \frac{1}{2} = \text{Prob}\{\rho = II\}$. The payoff to the player who conceded the resource is 0 and the payoff to the player who captured the resource is V. Thus, the expected payoff to Pigeon is

$$0\text{Prob}\{\rho = I\} + V\text{Prob}\{\rho = II\} = \frac{V}{2}. \tag{6.2}$$

if his opponent is also Dove. From the above discussion it follows that the Hawk-Dove game can be represented as a symmetric bimatrix game with the payoff matrix of the form

$\dfrac{V-C}{2}$ $\quad$ $\dfrac{V-C}{2}$	V $\quad$ 0
0 $\quad$ V	$\dfrac{V}{2}$ $\quad$ $\dfrac{V}{2}$

Now the question is: which of the strategies will dominate in the population or, in other words, which of the strategies will be evolutionary stable. For an arbitrary strategy I to be evolutionary stable, it must possess the following property. If almost all members of the population use a strategy I, then the utility function of an individual using the strategy I in this population must be greater than the utility function of an individual using any other strategy: otherwise an increasing number of mutants may appear in the population and the strategy I will be unstable.

If in our example $V > C$, then the combination (H,H) is a unique Nash equilibrium. The strategy of Hawk is strictly dominant and hence is stable. In the mixed population of Hawks and Doves, Hawks have a greater reproductive

If however, $V < C$, then the combination (H,H) is no longer Nash equilibrium. Hence the monomorphic population of Hawks is not stable. If Doves appear by chance in such a population, then the proportion of Doves in the population increases, because their utility function is found to be greater than that of Hawks. Similarly, the population made up of Doves is not stable, because the occasional Hawks in this population are reproductively more successful than Doves. If $V < C$, then the Hawk-Dove game has a unique Nash equilibrium in mixed strategies. We define strategy I as follows: Hawk's strategy is used with probability p_H and Dove's strategy is used with probability $1 - p_H$. In the process of reproduction the progeny inherits probability p_H. This brings up the question: what is the value of p_H which may ensure that the strategy I is evolutionary stable? To answer this question, we shall prove Theorem 1.

Theorem 1 [71]. Let $E(i, j)$ be the payoff to an individual using a strategy i resulting from an encounter with an individual using a strategy j. If the mixed strategy I with the spectrum $a, b, c, \ldots$ is evolutionary stable, then $E(a, I) = E(b, I) = \ldots = E(I, I)$.

P r o o f. Let a belong to the spectrum of I and

$$E(a, I) < E(I, I)$$

We may represent I as $I = Pa + (1 - P)x$, i.e., a is used with probability P and the pure or mixed strategy x with no a in its spectrum is used with probability $1 - P$. Then

$$E(I, I) = PE(a, I) + (1 - P)E(x, I) < PE(I, I) + (1 - P)E(x, I).$$

Hence $E(I, I) < E(x, I)$, which contradicts the definition of an evolutionary stable strategy. This means that our assumption is not true. If I is evolutionary stable, then $E(a, I) > E(I, I)$ can not be satisfied. Hence, for any strategy a from the spectrum of I

$$E(a, I) = E(I, I).$$

This completes the proof of the theorem

Thus, according to Theorem 1, there must be

$$E(H, I) = E(D, I),$$

or

$$P_H E(H, H) + (1 - P_H)E(H, D) = P_H E(D, H) + (1 - P_H)E(D, D).$$

or

$$P_H E(H, H) + (1 - P_H)E(H, D) = P_H E(D, H) + (1 - P_H)E(D, D).$$

From this we get

$$\frac{1}{2}(V - C)P_H + V(1 - P_H) = \frac{1}{2}V(1 - P_H)$$

and

$$P_H = \frac{V}{C} \tag{6.3}$$

Now, if the Hawk-Dove game has a mixed evolutionary stable strategy I then $P_H = \frac{V}{C}$ by (6.3). We shall verify whether this strategy is evolutionary stable. Suppose that a mutant using a strategy $J(J \neq I)$ appears in a population. Then $E(J, I) < E(I, I)$, because I is a mixed strategy that is Nash equilibrium. If $E(J, I) < E(I, I)$, then it is clear that the mutants using the strategy J cannot appear in the population. If, however, $E(J, I) = E(I, I)$, then the condition for evolutionary stability of the strategy I requires that $E(I, J) > E(J, J)$. Let p be the probability of using Hawk's strategy in the mixed strategy J. Then

$$E(J, J) - E(I, J) = (pE(H, J) + (1 - p)E(D, J)) -$$

$$- \left(\frac{V}{C}E(H, J) + (1 - \frac{V}{C})E(D, J) \right) =$$

$$= \left(p - \frac{V}{C} \right) E(H, J) + \left(\frac{V}{C} - p \right) E(D, J) =$$

$$= \left(p - \frac{V}{C} \right) \left(\frac{V}{2} - \frac{pC}{2} \right) =$$

$$= -\frac{1}{2C}(V - pC)^2 < 0.$$

Hence I is a unique evolutionary stable strategy when $V < C$.

In the general case, for the symmetric bimatrix game of dimension 2×2 with the matrix

$$\begin{pmatrix} a & b \\ c & d \end{pmatrix}, \tag{6.4}$$

there exists a unique mixed evolutionary stable strategy (if $a < c$ and $d < b$) prescribing the choice of the first row with probability

$$p = \frac{b - d}{b + c - a - d}. \tag{6.5}$$

6.2 Formal Mathematical Definition of ESS

Referring to section 1, we have the Hawk-Dove game represented as a symmetric bimatrix game. We shall now consider a more general case. Suppose that $\Phi_1 = \{1, 2, \ldots, m\}$ is Player 1's set of pure strategies. Player 2's set of pure strategies I coincides with $II = I$. Let $A = \{a_{ij}\}$, $A' = \{a'_{ij}\}$, $i = 1, 2, \ldots, m$, $= 1, 2, \ldots, m$ be payoff matrices for Players 1 and 2, respectively. Following [72], we shall consider this game. Player 1's payoff matrix A is called the game utility matrix. Since the matrix A completely determines the game, we are dealing with the game A. Mixed strategies for each of the players are elements of the simplex S^m

$$S^m := \{x \in R^m; \sum_i x_i = 1; x_i \geq 0, \}.$$

If Players 1 and 2 use their respective strategies, x and y, then the payoff to Player 1 is

$$xAy = \sum_{i,j} x_i a_{ij} y_j,$$

with x as a row and y as a column denoting the respective mixed strategies. In what follows we will write this quadratic form in place of a less convenient, but more exact representation xAy^T. For the mixed strategy $p \in S^m$, we denote by $C(p)$ the spectrum p and by $B(p)$ the set of pure strategies that provide the best responses against p in the game A:

$$C(p) = \{i; p_i > 0\}, \quad B(p) := \{i; e_i Ap = \max_j e_j Ap\},$$

where e_i is the i-th unit vector. Suppose that, in the game with the utility matrix A, all members of the monomorphic population use a mixed strategy p and a group of mutants using a strategy q appears in this population. In other words, a small fraction ε of members of the population use the strategy q. If the population is to return to the initial state, the utility function of an individual using the strategy q must be less than that of an individual using the strategy p when the population is perturbed. If occasional pairwise encounters take place among the members of the population, then

$$qA((1 - \varepsilon)p + \varepsilon q) < pA((1 - \varepsilon)p + \varepsilon q), \tag{6.6}$$

where $\varepsilon > 0$ is sufficiently small. If (6.5) holds for all strategies $q \neq p$, then the strategy is evolutionary stable. Evidently, p is an evolutionary stable strategy if and only if for all $q \neq p$

$$qAp \leq pAp,$$

and if $qAp = pAp$, then $qAq < pAq$.   (6.7)

We may now provide a formal mathematical definition of an evolutionary stable strategy.

D e f i n i t i o n 1. The mixed strategy p is evolutionary stable in symmetric bimatrix game with matrix A if it is Nash equilibrium, i.e.,

$$qAp \leq pAp, \quad q \in S^m,$$ (6.8)

and satisfies the stability condition

$$\text{if} \quad q \neq p \quad \text{and} \quad qAp = pAp, \quad \text{then} \quad qAq < pAq.$$ (6.9)

Remember that this definition can be applied only to the above problem which is based on the assumption of the nature of the population studied (see sec. 1). Extensions or modifications of this model bring about changes in the definition of an evolutionary stable strategy.

6.3 Field Game (Sex Ratio)

Our model is based on the assumption that each member of a population takes part in one or more pairwise encounters, and the result of an encounter is determined from the utility matrix. Such a model can be used in the case where a member of the population contends for some resource in a pairwise manner. However, there are many situations where a payoff to a player depends not on the result of an encounter with an individual opponent but on the average characteristics of the whole population or some part of this population. In such cases we are dealing with a "field game". An example of such a game is provided by competition among plants: the survival of each plant depends on the level of development of all its neighbors. In fact, the field games are more widely spread than pairwise encounters. Therefore it may be wise to consider the question: what is the strategy which is evolutionary stable in the field game?

Denote by $W(A, B)$ the utility function value for the player using a strategy A in a population all member of which use a strategy B. Evidently, if for all $J \neq I$: $W(J, I) < W(I, I)$, then the strategy I is evolutionary stable.

If, however, $W(J, I) = W(I, I)$, then for the strategy I to be evolutionary stable it is necessary that the utility function $W(J, P_{q,J,I})$ of an individual using the strategy J in the population, where almost all members use the strategy I and only a small part q uses the strategy J, be less than the utility function $W(I, P_{q,J,I})$ of an individual using the strategy I in the same population. Thus, the strategy I is evolutionary stable if for any $J \neq I$

$$W(J, I) < W(I, I),$$

$$\text{if} \quad W(J, I) = W(I, I),$$

$$\text{then for small} \quad q \quad W(J, P_{q,J,I}) < W(I, P_{q,J,I}).$$

If only two pure strategies can be used, then the utility matrix of the game can be written as follows

		Population	
		I	J
Mutant	I	$W(I, I)$	$W(I, J)$
	J	$W(J, I)$	$W(J, J)$

If $W(J, I) < W(I, I)$, then the strategy I is evolutionary stable; if $W(I, J) < W(J, J)$, then J is an evolutionary stable strategy. If neither condition is satisfied, then a mixed strategy with spectrum $\{J, I\}$. is evolutionary stable. But this strategy is not necessarily given by (6.5). This is true only for the case where the utility function of an individual using the strategy I in the population whose members use strategies I and J in the relationship of P and $1 - P$, is a linear combination $PW(I, I) + (1 - P)W(I, J)$. But this is not necessarily the case.

The above assertions can be illustrated by the field game considered as the game of sex ratio in a population [73].

Suppose that N is the number of offsprings produced by a female individual, including sN males and $(1 - s)N$ females. We consider the number s as a strategy of the individual. Since the sex ratio in the progeny apparently has no effect on the number of offsprings in the first generation, we take the utility function to be the expected number of the second-generation offsprings produced by that individual.

We shall consider a population in which all individuals use a strategy s' , i.e.,the progeny of each individual includes $s'N$ male offsprings. Let d be the number of female offsprings and s the number of male offsprings in the progeny. Suppose that females can always find male partners, since males can have more than one female partners in case $d > s$. If, however, $d < s$, then all males have equal chances to find a female partner. Now the number of female partners for each male is a random variable the mean value of which is $d/s = (1 - s')/s'$. Then the utility function of the individual using a strategy s in the population, where the average sex ratio is s', is expressed as

$$W(s, s') = NN(1 - s) + NNs\frac{1 - s'}{s'}, \tag{6.10}$$

since $N(1 - s)$ is the number of female offsprings, Ns is the number of male offsprings, each of the female offsprings always has N descendants, and each of the male offsprings has n descendants from each of his female partners. Thus we have

$$W(s, s') = N^2\left[1 - s + s\frac{1 - s'}{s'}\right],$$

and

$$W(s', s') = 2N^2(1 - s'). \tag{6.11}$$

Further, we assume that each of the female in the population has one of the two strategies: either $s_1 = 0.1$ or $s_2 = 0.6$. Then we have the following game utility matrix

		Population	
		$s_1 = 0.1$	$s_2 = 0.6$
Mutant	$s_1 = 0.1$	1.8	0.967
	$s_2 = 0.6$	5.8	0.8

It is clear that neither s_1 no s_2 is an evolutionary stable strategy. If we use (6.5) to determine a mixed evolutionary stable strategy, then we have that the strategy s_1 must be used with probability 1/25 and the strategy s_2 must be used with probability 24/25 with the result that the proportion of males in the population is 0.5. Actually this ratio must be 0.5 when the population is stable.

Let $\hat{s}$ be the proportion of males in the evolutionary stable population. Then

$$W(s_1, \hat{s}) = W(s_2, \hat{s}), \quad \text{or}$$

$$1 - 0.1 + 0.1(1 - \hat{s})/\hat{s} = 1 - 0.6 + 0.6(1 - \hat{s})/\hat{s},$$

$$\text{or} \quad \hat{s} = 0.5.$$

This means that the evolutionary stable strategy must be $0.2s_1 + 0.8s_2$.

In the general case, we assume that the quantity s_1, characterizing the strategy of a female is an arbitrary number from 0 to 1. Let us find the value of s^* corresponding to the evolutionary stable strategy in that a mutant using a strategy $s \neq s^*$ cannot appear in the population; that is to say, for any $s \neq s^*$ there must be $W(s^*, s^*) > W(s, s^*)$. Assuming that the function W is differentiable, we may find the value of s^* from the condition

$$\left[\frac{\partial W(s, s^*)}{\partial s}\right]_{s=s^*} = 0.$$

Applying this condition to equation (6.10), we obtain, as before, $s^* = 0.5$. We may use equation (6.9) to test the value $s^* = 0.5$ for stability as follows. Let $s' = qs + (1 - q)s^*$, where $s \neq s^*$. From equation (6.10) we then have

$$W(s, s') = N^2[1 - s + s\frac{(1 - s')}{s'}],$$

and

$$W(s^*, s') = N^2[1 - s^* + s^*\frac{(1 - s')}{s'}].$$

Hence it can be readily seen that $W(s, s') < W(s^*, s')$ for $s \neq s^*$.

Thus, the expanded model of the field game has strategy I that is evolutionary stable if condition (6.10) is satisfied. If in the game with two pure strategies, I and J, neither strategy satisfied the conditions (6.10), then the evolutionary stable strategy is a mixed one, but the ratio of strategies, I and J, cannot be derived from equation (6.5); it can be computed from the equation $W(I, P_{op}) = W(J, P_{op})$, where P_{op} denotes the equilibrium of the population. If the set of strategies is continuous, then the evolutionary stable strategy can be obtained from an equation of the form (6.12).

In the analysis of the field game it important to write out correctly the utility function (similar to (6.11)) of the mutant in a population with the known strategy distribution.

6.4 Existence of Evolutionary Stable Strategies

Reverting to the definition of an evolutionary stable strategy given in section 3, we define conditions under which the Nash equilibrium strategy is evolutionary stable. Let us consider the map

$$p \to \{q \in S^m; \quad C(q) \subset B(p)\}.$$

This map satisfies all conditions of the Kakutani fixed point theorem. Hence it has a fixed point. If p is a fixed point, then (p,p) is a symmetric Nash equilibrium in the game A. We have thus proved the following lemma.

L e m m a 1.[74]. Every symmetric bimatrix game has a symmetric Nash equilibrium.

D e f i n i t i o n. If the set of best responses against a strategy p comprises only one strategy p, i.e. $\{p\} = B(p)$, then (p,p) is said to be a strict equilibrium.

If (p,p) is a strict equilibrium, then for any $q \in S^m$ there is always $qAp < pAp$ and condition (6.9) is satisfied in a trivial way. Hence we have the Lemma given below.

L e m m a 2. If (p,p) is a strict equilibrium, then p is an evolutionary stable strategy.

A strict equilibrium does not necessarily exist in every game and, for the equilibrium in mixed strategies, the condition (6,9) can be readily violated with the result that the game has no evolutionary stable strategy. For example, if A is a 2×2 matrix all elements of which are 1, then $pAq = 1$ for all p, q, the and condition (6.9) is not satisfied. But this matrix is singular. The game with a nonsingular matrix always has an evolutionary stable strategy.

Theorem 2.   If A is a 2×2 utility matrix such that $a_{11} \neq a_{21}$ $a_{12} \neq a_{22}$, then the corresponding symmetric bimatrix game has an evolutionary stable strategy.

P r o o f. If $a_{11} > a_{21}$ (or $a_{22} > a_{12}$), then the conditions of Lemma 2 are satisfied. This implies existence of an evolutionary stable strategy. Therefore, it is assumed that $a_{11} < a_{21}$ and $a_{22} < a_{12}$. In this case the game has a unique symmetric equilibrium (p,p) such that $C(p) = B(p) = \{1.2\}$. If $q \neq p$ and $qAp = pAp$, then

$$qAq - pAq = (q-p)Aq = (q-p)A(q-p) =$$

$$= (q_1 - p_1)^2(a_{11} - a_{21} + a_{22} - a_{12}) < 0.$$

Hence condition (6.9) is satisfied and strategy p is evolutionary stable.

In what follows we show that the game with 3 or more pure strategies may have no evolutionary stable strategy. We revert to the Hawk-Dove game incorporating more complex strategies. For convenience we replace algebraic payoffs V and C by numerical values.Since only validity of inequalities is essential, such a replacement is admissible and facilitates further discussion. Let $V = 2$ and $C = 4$. The mixed evolutionary stable strategy then prescribes the use of each strategy with probability $1/2$ and the payoff matrix is of the form

$$
\begin{array}{c}
 \\
H \\
D
\end{array}
\begin{array}{cc}
H & D \\
\left(\begin{array}{cc} -1 & 2 \\ 0 & 1 \end{array}\right)
\end{array}
$$

Suppose that the third strategy - Imitator (I) - is feasible. Imitator is acting as Dove when his opponent is Dove and as Hawk when his opponent is Hawk. The payoff matrix for such a game is of the form

$$
\begin{array}{c}
H \\
P \\
I
\end{array}
\begin{array}{ccc}
H & P & I \\
\left(\begin{array}{ccc} -1 & 2 & -1 \\ 0 & 1 & 1 \\ -1 & 1 & 1 \end{array}\right)
\end{array}
$$

Dove and Imitator are identical in the absence of Hawk. In this game, however, the strategies of Dove and Imitator are identical where there is no Hawk. Therefore it may be more realistic to consider the game with the payoff matrix as

$$
\begin{array}{c}
H \\
D \\
I
\end{array}
\begin{array}{ccc}
H & D & I \\
\left(\begin{array}{ccc} -1 & 2 & -1 \\ 0 & 1 & 0.9 \\ -1 & 1.1 & 1 \end{array}\right)
\end{array}
$$

Such a game implies that, in the encounter between Dove and Imitator, Imitator may somehow learn that his opponent has no wish to deliver an attack, and a payoff to Imitator appears to be a little greater than that to Dove. Evidently, I is an evolutionary stable strategy, since $E(I, I)$ is greater than $E(D, I)$ and $E(H, I)$. Thus, I is the best response against I and, according to Lemma 2, I is an evolutionary stable strategy.

We shall now find out whether this game has any other evolutionary stable strategies. In particular, we shall consider the strategy $i = (\frac{1}{2}, \frac{1}{2}, 0)$. As a general rule, we find

$$
E(H, i) = -\frac{1}{2} + \frac{1}{2} 2 = \frac{1}{2},
$$

$$
E(D, i) = \frac{1}{2} 0 + \frac{1}{2} = \frac{1}{2},
$$

and hence $E(i,i) = 1/2$. The necessary condition for the mixed evolutionary stable strategy, $E(H,i) = E(D,i)$, is satisfied and

$$E(I,i) = -\frac{1}{2} + 1.1\frac{1}{2} = 0.05.$$

Thus, the considered game has two evolutionary stable strategies: $(\frac{1}{2}, \frac{1}{2}, 0)$ and I . In the general case, however, the game with three or more pure strategies may have no evolutionary stable strategy.

6.5   Evolutionary Dynamics

Up to now, we have used the assumption that the genotypes corresponding to the use of mixed strategies can exist. In what follows we eliminate such a possibility and use a population whose individuals can use only pure strategies, although the population can be polymorphic. This leads to the notion of an evolutionary stable state of the population. Further, we shall consider the stability of population equilibrium and the relationship between the concepts of evolutionary stable strategy and evolutionary stable state.

Suppose we have a sufficiently large population each individual of which has some strategy $i \in \{1, \ldots, m\}$. Let x_i be the proportion of individuals using a strategy i in the population; hence $x = (x_1, \ldots, x_m) \in S^m$. Also, suppose that pairwise encounters occur among the members of this population, each individual takes part only in one encounter, and the payoff (the utility function, the expected number of offsprings) to the individual using a strategy i which results from the encounter with the individual using a strategy j, is the element a_{ij} of an $m \times m$ matrix A. Then the expected payoff to the individual using the strategy i is $e_i A x$, while the average payoff to the population is $x A x$. It appears natural that if $e_i A x > x A x$, then the proportion of the next-generation individuals x_i using this strategy increases. If, however, $e_i A x < x A x$, then the frequency of strategy i in the population decreases in such a way that the ratio between the individuals using the strategy i in the two subsequent generations is $\frac{e_i A x}{x A x}$ or, what is the same,

$$x_i' = x_i \frac{e_i A x}{x A x}.$$

Hence, fluctuations in the population occur according to the difference equation

$$x_i' - x_i = x_i \frac{e_i A x - x A x}{x A x}, \qquad i = 1, \ldots, m. \tag{6.13}$$

Assuming that changes in the populations are insignificant, we turn to the differential equation

$$\dot{x}_i = x_i \frac{e_i A x - x A x}{x A x}, \qquad i = 1, \ldots, m. \tag{6.14}$$

Since the right-hand sides of (6.14) contain the division by the same number xAx, the trajectories and stationary points of a solution to the system of differential equations (6.14) are the same as for the simplified system of equations:

$$\dot{x}_i = x_i(e_i A x - x A x), \qquad i = 1, \ldots, m. \tag{6.15}$$

In the following it is this system that will be considered. Note that such a replacement of (6.14) by (6.15) can be made only for symmetric games.

The equations (6.15) were originally proposed by Taylor and Jonker [75] and Zeeman [76] for describing continuous evolutionary dynamics. Similar equations were used by Eingen and Schuster [77] to describe the molecule concentration in the process of life origination. This coincidence is not surprising, since in both cases we are dealing with the evolution of sexually reproducing populations.

It is clear that if the equations (6.15) are to be used for modelling evolutionary processes occurring in a population, it is necessary that any trajectory originating in S^m should stay in S^m. In order to show the validity of this condition, we find

$$\sum_{i=1}^{m} \dot{x}_i = \sum_{i=1}^{m} x_i(e_i A x - x A x) = x A x - \left(\sum_{i=1}^{m} x_i\right) x A x = 0.$$

Hence the plane $\sum_{i=1}^{m} x_i = 1$ is invariant under equation (6.15). Moreover, from $x_i = 0$ we have $\dot{x}_i = 0$. Hence, not only the simplex S^m but also its sides are all invariant.

We say that $p \in S^m$ is a dynamic equilibrium if $\dot{x}_i = 0$, $i = 1, \ldots, m$, i.e., if p is the rest point of the dynamics (6.15). The dynamic equilibrium of p is stable if for any neighborhood U of the point p in the simplex S^m there exists a neighborhood V of this point in S^m such that the trajectories of system (6.15) originating in V always stay in U. The equilibrium state of p is called asymptotically stable if there exists a neighborhood U of the point p in S^m such that any trajectory of system (6.15) originating in U converges to p as $t \to \infty$. Evidently the asymptotic stability requirement is stronger than the stability requirement.

Now $p \in S^m$ is a dynamic equilibrium in the game with the matrix A if and only if $\dot{x}_i = 0$ for any $i = 1, \ldots, m$ or, what is the same, for all $p_i > 0$

$$e_i A p = p A p. \tag{6.16}$$

Hence, if (p, p) is a symmetric Nash equilibrium in the game A, then p is an equilibrium in A. Since any pure strategy satisfies equation (6.16), the reverse is not true.

L e m m a 3. If (p, p) is a Nash equilibrium, then p is a dynamic equilibrium and the reverse is not true.

It can be shown, however, that under certain restrictions the reverse also holds,

D e f i n i t i o n. If the set of best responses against p coincides with the spectrum of p, i.e., $C(p) = B(p)$, then (p, p) is said to be a quasistrict equilibrium.

The following assertion holds for the thus improved notion of a Nash equilibrium.

L e m m a 4. If p is a dynamic equilibrium such that $p_i > 0$ for $i = 1, \ldots, m$, then (p, p) is a quasistrict Nash equilibrium.

P r o o f. By the condition of the lemma $C(p) = \{e_1, e_2, \ldots, e_m\}$. From (6.16) it follows that for $i = 1, \ldots, m$ $e_i A p = p A p$, i.e., the set of best responses against p $C(p)$ coincides with the spectrum of p $B(p) = \{e_1, e_2, \ldots, e_m\}$. But this means that p is a quasistrict equilibrium.

Denote by $F : R^m \to R^m$ the map given by the right-hand sides of equation (6.15). Then $F = (F_1, \ldots, F_m)$

$$F_i(x) = x_i(e_i A x - x A x). \tag{6.17}$$

The Jacobian of system (6.15) can be written for $x \in R^m$:

$$DF_{ij}(x) = \delta_{ij}(e_i A x - x A x) + x_i(a_{ij} - e_j A x - x A e_j),$$

where

$$\delta_{ij} = \begin{cases} 1, & \text{if } i = j, \\ 0, & \text{if } i \neq j. \end{cases}$$

Therefore, if p is a dynamic equilibrium, then

$$DF_{ij}(p) = \begin{cases} p_i(a_{ij} - e_j A p - p A e_j), & i \in C(p), \\ \delta_{ij}(e_i A p - p A p), & i \notin C(p). \end{cases} \tag{6.18}$$

Hence it follows that $e_i Ap - pAp$ for $i \notin C(p)$ are proper numbers of the first approximation system corresponding to the system of differential equations (6.15). Now, if p is a stable equilibrium, then the inequality (6.19)

$$e_i Ap - pAp \leq 0 \quad i \notin C(p) \tag{6.19}$$

must hold for $i \in C(p)$ (see[78]).

Combining (6. 19) and (6. 16), we obtain

$$e_i Ap = pAp \text{ for } i \in C(p), \quad e_i Ap < pAp \text{ for } i \notin C(p).$$

Hence it follows that (p, p) is a Nash equilibrium. We have thus proved the first part of the following lemma.

L e m m a 5. If p is a stable equilibrium of dynamics (6.15), then (p, p) is a Nash equilibrium, and the reverse is not true.

In order to show the validity of the second part of the lemma, we consider the game with the matrix

$$\begin{pmatrix} 1 & 0 \\ 0 & 0 \end{pmatrix}.$$

It is clear that the situation, where both players use the second strategy, is Nash equilibrium. But this equilibrium is not stable, since any trajectory converges to the first strategy.

In what follows it will be shown that the evolutionary stable strategy (which, by definition, is the stable state of monomorphic population) also is the stable state of polymorphic population, where only pure strategies can exist. But all the stable states of the polymorphic population are not necessarily evolutionary stable strategies.

Theorem 3. [75]. Every evolutionary stable strategy is an asymptotically stable dynamic equilibrium, and the reverse is not true.

P r o o f. Let p be an evolutionary stable strategy in the game with the utility matrix A. It can be shown that there exists a neighborhood U of the point p in S^m such that $pAp > xAx$ for all $x \in U, x \neq p$. Furthermore, we assume that the inequality $x_i > 0$ holds for all $x \in U$ $i \in C(p)$. We define the map $z : U \to R$ as follows:

$$Z(x) = \prod_i x_i^{p_i}. \tag{6.20}$$

Then $Z(x) > 0$ for all $x \in U$ and p is the unique global maximum of the map Z. We show that Z is the Liapunov function for system (6.15), i.e.,

$$\nabla Z(x)(p - x) > 0 \quad \text{and} \quad \dot{Z}(x) > 0 \quad \text{for all} \quad x \in U, \quad x \neq p. \tag{6.21}$$

These conditions ensure that p is the unique local maximum Z on U, and Z increases along the trajectory of system (6.15). Hence the conditions (6.21) guarantee that the trajectories originating in U converge to p, i.e., that p is an asymptotically stable equilibrium. Note that if $x \in U$, then

$$\frac{\partial Z}{\partial x_i} = \begin{cases} Z(x)\dfrac{p_i}{x_i}, & \text{if } i \in C(p), \\ 0, & \text{if } i \neq C(p). \end{cases}$$

Hence, if $x \neq p$, then

$$\nabla Z(x)(p - x) = \sum_{i \in C(p)} \frac{\partial Z}{\partial x_i}(p_i - x_i) = Z \sum_{i \in C(p)} \frac{p_i}{x_i}(p_i - x_i) =$$

$$= Z \sum_{i \in C(p)} \frac{(p_i - x_i)^2}{x_i} + Z\Big(1 - \sum_{i \in C(p)} x_i\Big) > 0,$$

Thus the first condition in (6.21) is satisfied. In order to verify the validity of the second condition, we find for $x \neq p$

$$\dot{Z}(x) = \nabla Z \dot{x} = Z \sum_{i \in C(p)} p_i \frac{\dot{x}_i}{x_i} =$$

$$= Z \sum_{i \in C(p)} p_i(e_i A x - x A x) = Z(pAx - xAx) > 0,$$

where the inequality follows from the conditions of selection of a neighborhood U.

We have thus shown that every evolutionary stable strategy is an asymptotically stable equilibrium.

To show that there exist asymptotically stable equilibria that are not evolutionary stable strategies, we consider the game with the matrix

$$\frac{1}{9}\begin{pmatrix} 0 & 1 & 1 \\ -2 & 0 & 4 \\ 1 & 1 & 0 \end{pmatrix}.$$

This game has a unique symmetric equilibrium strategy $p = (\frac{1}{3}, \frac{1}{3}, \frac{1}{3})$. But this strategy is not evolutionary stable. For the strategy $x = (0, \frac{1}{2}, \frac{1}{2})$ we have $xAp = pAp$ $xAx > pAx$. On the other hand, the Jacobian of $DF(p)$ is the matrix

$$\begin{pmatrix} -1 & -1 & -4 \\ -7 & -4 & 5 \\ 2 & -1 & -7 \end{pmatrix}.$$

with the eigenvalues $-\frac{1}{3}, -\frac{1}{3}, -\frac{2}{3}$. Since the eigenvalues have negative real parts, the equilibrium p is asymptotically stable.

For the games of dimension 2, it can be shown that the evolutionary stability requirements of strategy completely coincide with the asymptotic stability requirements of equilibrium.

It is not surprising that for the game with three or more pure strategies the evolutionary stability turns out to be a stronger requirement than the asymptotic stability. The asymptotic stability has been defined for a population under the assumption that only pure strategies can be used. In fact, it seems more appropriate to consider the question of whether the evolutionary stable strategy corresponds to the stable state of the polymorphic population, where different mixed strategies can coexist. Such a population can be represented by the distribution density of f over S^m. Again, using the assumption that the rate of growth is equal to a difference in the utility function, the evolution of such a population is modelled by

$$\dot{f}(x) = f(x)[xA\mu_f - \mu_f A\mu_f] \quad (x \in S^m), \tag{6.22}$$

where μ_f denotes the mean value of the population, $\mu_f = \int f(x)dx$, with $f(x)$ as density. This dynamics was studied by Zeeman [76], but since the equations (6.22) are much more complex than the equations (6.15), their study is still far from being complete.

6.6 Evolutionary Games in Extensive Form

Up to this point the interactions among the members of a population have been represented as a game in normal form. This approach, however, cannot always provide an adequate description of the interactions recurring in a population. To properly allow for the sequential nature of encounters among animals, it is often more appropriate to represent the conflict as a game in extensive form.

In the above discussion, we had to deal only with symmetric games, where (prior to an encounter) contenders were in the same conditions and had the same sets of strategies. Actual conflicts, however, are mostly nonsymmetric: among the contenders there are differences in size, sex, age, and status that can bring some influence to bear on their behavior.In the biological literature on the theory of games, such games are also reduced to symmetric games in normal form, for which the existence of evolutionary stable strategies is studied. The thus constructed symmetric game in normal form may have no evolutionary

stable strategy, whereas the original game has a stable state. Therefore, for
asymmetric games, the evolutionary stability must be formulated in terms of
behavior strategies. The evolutionary stability in extensive games has been
adequately treated by Selten in [82].

Reverting to the previously discussed Hawk-Dove game (sec. 2), we now
assume that one of the contenders is the owner of a territory and the other is
the invader. We also assume that since the owner has a better knowledge of
local conditions, the value V of this territory for him is larger than the value
v of the territory for the invader, but these values are less than the quantity
C which evaluates the risk of being wounded in the encounter. Suppose that
a random element determining whether an individual is the owner or the invader is independent of the genes determining a behavior strategy. Then every
individual can become the owner or the invader. As a special case, we set
$V = v = 20$ and $C = 20$. Further it is assumed that for all individuals in the
population the probability of becoming the owner of the territory is equal to
the probability of becoming the invader and the first random move determines
which of the contenders is the owner and which of them is the invader. This
game can then be symmetrized by being represented in extensive form (Fig.
14).

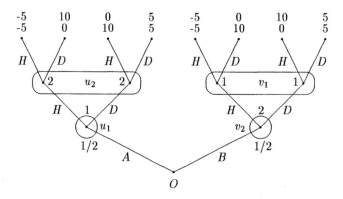

Fig. 14.

Recall that specifying a game in extensive form determines the decision to
be taken by each player, the decision priority order for each player, and the in-

formation on the past course of the game which may become available to every decision-maker. Moreover, the probabilities corresponding to chance move and the payoffs to the players at the end of the game are also determined. Mathematically, a two-person game in extensive form is the $\Gamma = (K, P, U, c, p, a, a')$, where K is the tree graph used to specify an order of moves in the game; P is the partition of the set of positions in the graph into 4 sets: P_i $(i = 1, 2)$ is the priority order set for the i-th player, P_0 is the set of position where a move is randomly made, P_4 is the set of terminal positions; U is a pair (u_1, u_2), where u_i $(i = 1, 2)$ is the partition of player i's priority order set P_i into what are called player i's information sets (the information set is a set of positions such that a decision-maker stationed at one of the points of this set cannot tell exactly at which of the points of the set he is stationed); C is the triple (C_1, C_2, C_3), where C_1 is the set of choices of a chance move, C_i $(i = 1, 2)$ is player i's set of choices determined for each player i's information set; p is the probability distribution over the set of all choices following each position that belongs to the set P_0; finally, a and a' are the payoffs to Players 1 and 2, respectively, determined in terminal positions.

In the extensive-form game (Fig. 14), the players' information sets are shown by dotted lines, and the choices are symbolized by "H" and "D". The figures 0,1,2. indicate the points where the choice is made in a random way and the points where a decision is to be made by Player 1 and Player 2, respectively. The players' choices are shown in columns above the corresponding terminal positions. The chance event "A" implies that Player 1 is the owner of territory, and the probabilities of events "A" and "B" are shown alongside the graph edges.

Although Fig. 14 suggests that decisions should be made sequentially where the first move is made by the owner of the territory, nevertheless Players 1 and 2 choose their strategies simultaneously. However, the fact that the players are acting simultaneously rather than sequentially has no strategic value by itself. Instead, it has only information value. In decision making, neither of the two players is informed about the opponent's choice and this aspect is correctly represented by properly specifying information sets in the extensive-form game.

Reverting to the Hawk-Dove game (Fig.14), we assume that there is no difference between the contenders, although the behavior of animals may be governed by atmospheric conditions. Suppose that weather conditions may affect the value of the territory: it is V in good weather and v in bad weather. As before, let $V = v = 10$ and $C = 20$ and let the probability of occurrence of good weather be equal to the probability of occurrence of bad weather.

Referring to Fig. 14., we may now interpret the chance event "A" as a good (sunny) weather and the chance event "B" as a bad (rainy) weather. Then Fig. 14 represents the Hawk-Dove game, where the payoffs are dependent on weather conditions.

Hence the game tree cannot determine by itself the content of the game in a unique way. In addition, one has to know how the payoffs in the game tree shall be interpreted. In other words, one has to know which of the choices by Player 1 correspond to those by Player 2, i.e., one has to determine the symmetry of the game. The game in Fig. 14 admits of 2 symmetries: the horizontal symmetry corresponding to the owner-invader game (the choice of "H" in the information set v_2) and the vertical symmetry corresponding to the game in which the payoffs are dependent on weather conditions. So, to allow for the game dynamics in a proper way, it is not enough to represent the game in extensive form; one has also to specify the symmetry of that game.

We shall formulate a formal definition of the game symmetry. The symmetry of a two-person game in extensive form is the map T of the set of choices onto the set of choices possessing the following properties (C_i denotes player i's set of choices in the game Γ):

$$\text{if} \quad c \in C_0, \text{then} \quad c^T \in C_0 \quad \text{and} \quad p(c) = p(c^T), \qquad (6.23.a)$$

$$\text{if} \quad c \in C_i, \text{then} \quad c^T \in C_j \quad (i \neq j \in \{1,2\}), \qquad (6.23.b)$$

$$(c^T)^T \text{for all } c, \qquad (6.23.c)$$

for every information set u there exists an information set u^T such that every choice in u is mapped onto the choice in u^T, and for every terminal position z there exists a terminal position z^T such that if z is reached by employing the sequence of choices $c_1, c_2, \ldots, c_k$ then z^T is reached by rearranging the choices $c_1^T, c_2^T, \ldots, c_k^T$, and $a(z) = a'(z^T)$ for every terminal position z.

The symmetric game in extensive form is called a pair (Γ, T), where Γ is the game in extensive form and T is the symmetry of the game Γ (if such a symmetry exists). The game Γ is said to have perfect recall if neither of the two players can forget anything during the game, i.e., every player remembers in every information set all the information that he knew earlier in the game (that is, he remembers all the information sets that he has reached), including all of his own past actions (that is, all the choices that he has made). In what follows, we consider only those games which possess this property.

Let U be the family of information sets for Player 1 and let V be the family of information sets for Player 2. For each $u \in U, v \in V$ we define $b_u(c), b'_v(c)$

to be probability distributions over the set of choices made by a player in the information set $u \in U$ and the information set $v \in V$, respectively.

Let $b = \{b_u(c), u \in U\}$ be the map placing every information set $u \in U$ in correspondence with the probability distribution $b_u(c)$ over the set of its choices in that information set. The map b is called Player 1's behavioral strategy and the images of this map $b_u(c)$ are called the behavior of that player in the information set $u \in U$.

Let $b' = \{b_v(c), v \in V\}$ be the map placing every information set $v \in V$ in correspondence with the probability distribution $b_v(c)$ over the set of its choices in that information set. The map b' is called Player 2's behavioral strategy and the images of this map $b'_v(c)$ are called the behavior of Player 2 on the information set $v \in V$.

Denote Player 1's set of all behavioral strategies by B. In a symmetric extensive-form game, the set B is the same for both players. Furthermore, if the game has perfect recall, an equilibrium exists in the class of behavioral strategies (Kuhn,1953). Therefore, to determine evolutionary stable strategies, it suffices to restrict one's consideration to the class of behavioral strategies.

Let $b, b' \in B$, then for every terminal position z there is the probability $P^{b,b'}(z)$ that the point z will be reached when Players 1 and 2 use the behavioral strategies b and b', respectively. Hence each pair of strategies generates the probability distribution $P^{b,b'}$ over the set Z of all terminal positions. We can now formulate the definition of an evolutionary stable strategy for extensive-form games.

D e f i n i t i o n . Player 1's behavioral strategy $\bar{b}$ is evolutionary stable if it satisfies the following conditions:

1. $E(\bar{b}, \bar{b}^T) = \max\limits_{b \in B} E(b, \bar{b}^T)$,

2. if $b \in B, E(b, \bar{b}^T) = E(\bar{b}, \bar{b}^T)$ and $P(b, \bar{b}^T)$ is not identical to $P(\bar{b}, \bar{b}^T)$, then $E(b, b^T) < E(\bar{b}, b^T)$, where E is the expected payoff in a behavioral strategy situation and b^T is a strategy image in the game with symmetry T.

We shall provide other definition contained in the work of Van Damme.

D e f i n i t i o n . The behavioral strategy situation $(\bar{b}, \bar{b})$ is called a direct ESS if

$$E(\bar{b}, \bar{b}) = \max\limits_{b \in B} E(b, \bar{b})$$

and if for some behavioral strategy $b \in B, E(b, \bar{b}) = E(\bar{b}, \bar{b})$, then $E(b, b) < E(\bar{b}, b)$.

Note that the definition of a direct ESS substantially narrows the ESS set, because here the inequality $E(b, b) < E(\bar{b}, b)$ is required in all cases where $E(b, \bar{b}) = E(\bar{b}, \bar{b})$, but not on a subset of behavioral strategies which require not only $E(b, \bar{b}) = E(\bar{b}, \bar{b})$, but also that the probability measures coincide in the situations $b, \bar{b}$ and $\bar{b}, b$ on the set of all terminal positions in the game. The direct ESS is rare in occurrence, as can be seen from the example below.

E x a m p l e . Let us consider a two-stage game $\bar{\Gamma}$. The following symmetric bimatrix game Γ is played at each stage:

$$\Gamma = \begin{array}{c} a \\ b \end{array} \begin{pmatrix} \overset{A}{(20, 20)} & \overset{B}{(5, 19)} \\ (19, 5) & (1, 1) \end{pmatrix}.$$

A positional two-stage game $\bar{\Gamma}$ is of the form shown in Fig. 15.

The payoff in $\bar{\Gamma}$ is determined as the sum of payoffs in two plays of the game Γ.

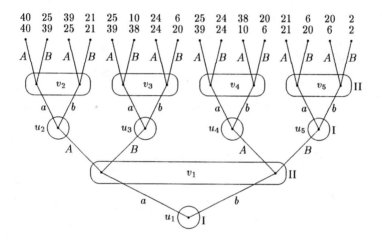

Fig. 15.

The game symmetry is determined by the map aA, bB (Aa, Bb). Then for every terminal node z there is a symmetric node z' such that the payoff to Player 1 at z is equal to the payoff to Player 2 at z', and vice versa. For example, the play (a, A, b, A) with symmetry corresponds to the play (a, A, a, B).

The correspondence between information sets of the players is as follows: $u_1 v_1$ $(v_1 u_1)$, $u_2 v_2$ $(v_2 u_2)$, $u_3 v_4$ $(v_4 u_3)$, $u_5 v_5$ $(v_5 u_5)$. This generates a correspondence between strategies. For example, the strategy $b_1 = (a, a, b, a, b)$ corresponds to the strategy $b'_1 = (A, A, B, A, B)$, and the strategy $b_2 = (b, b, a, a, b)$ corresponds to the strategy $b'_2 = (B, B, A, A, B)$.

Thus, there exists a normal form of the game $\bar{\Gamma}$, that is a symmetric bimatrix game. It can be readily seen that, in the game studied, repetition of the situations (a, A), i.e., situations of the form $\{(a, a, \ldots), (A, A, \ldots)\}$, are not direct ESS, although they may give rise to ESS two times in the game. The reason is that the second condition of the direct ESS is not satisfied. If, however, the ESS is defined as in our case, then any situation of the form $\{(a, a, \ldots), (A, A, \ldots)\}$ is ESS, which appears quite natural. It is easy to see that the direct ESS in the game $\bar{\Gamma}$ dose not exist.

Chapter 7

REGULATION OF CO_2 EMISSION. GAME-THEORETIC APPROACH

7.1 Description of a Model

Considerable recent attention has been focussed on the mathematical modeling of atmospheric pollution due to CO_2 emission. Such models, however, are predominantly descriptive. We shall present here the game-theoretic model proposed by E.Hopfinger [79] in 1979 that is based on the study of a Nash equilibrium and other optimality principles involved in a multistage conflict-controlled process which describes an actual social and ecological situation arising from CO_2 emissions. The conflict-controlled process can be described by a three-person game in extensive form or, more specifically, by a stochastic game. A component game with perfect information whose parameters are completely determined by the stage of the game is played at each stage of stochastic game. The players' choices may influence the payoffs and the probabilities of transition to the next stage wherefrom a new game starts. For each of the players, transition probabilities are evaluated individually and the "critical pollution level" is evaluated differently for different players.

The state set of the game is

$$S = \{(C, L)|C_P \geq C \geq 0, \quad L \geq 0\} \cup \{k \geq 0\},$$

where C is CO_2 concentration in air; C_p is the maximum CO_2 emission if the fuel is all burnt; L is the upper limit of emission during a specified period (at one stage of the game); k is the critical value of C resulting in an ecological disaster.

Let (C^1, L^1) be the initial state. Here C^1 is the presence of CO_2 in air and L^1 is the maximum possible emission of CO_2 in the initial period.

The component game with perfect information is defined as follows.The game involves three players, namely: R as a managerial organ (regulator), P as a producer, and I as the party suffering from pollution (population).

The set of controls (player R's choices) at the state (C, L) is

$$M_R(C, L) = \{l : 0 \leq l \leq L\},$$

where l denotes the upper limit of permissible emission for player P.

Once the quantity $l \in M_R(C, L)$ has been chosen by player R, the amount of emission is selected by player P from the set

$$M_P(C, L, l) = \{a : 0 \leq a \leq l, \quad a \leq (C_P - C)/\beta\},$$

where the quantity $0 < \beta < 1$ will be determined later. Player I makes the next move by selecting a parameter p, depending on (C, L, l, a), from the set

$$M_I(C, L, l, a) = \{p : 0 \leq p \leq 1\}.$$

The variable p defines the pressure that player I may bring to bear on player (regulator) R (which can be a percentage of population votes that may influence R).

With $C = k$, players' emission sets change to the empty sets (i.e.,after a disaster has occurred)

$$M_R(k) = \varnothing, \ M_P(k, 0) = \varnothing, \ M_I(k, 0, 0) = \varnothing.$$

If the choices (l, a, p) have been made in the state (C, L), the game passes into one of the following states

$$(C + \beta a, L), \ (C + \beta a, L/2), \ (k \geq C).$$

The first component of the first two states implies that the CO_2 amount has increased by $\beta\alpha$, with β lying in the interval $[0.01, 0.5]$. In this case the quantity $(1 - \beta)a$ is assumed to disappear in the atmosphere. The second component implies that the former value is still retained or is halved. It is assumed that the probability of L being replaced by $L/2$ is $p\nu$ (p is the choice of I) if the disaster has not yet occurred. The three players individually evaluate the variable k and this fact may influence the transition probability. For simplicity, we assume that the variable k is evaluated as C_R by player R, as C_P by player P, and as C_I by player I. In this case it is assumed that $C_R < C_P$, $C_I < C_P$.

The subjective transition probabilities R_R, P_P, P_I from the state C, L to new states are determined by the Table.

New position t	$P_R(t\mid C, L, l, a\ p)$	$P_P(t\mid C, L, l, a\ p)$	$P_I(t\mid C, L, l, a\ p)$
$(C + \beta a, L)$	0, if $C \le C_R < C + \beta a$ or $C_R < C < C + \beta a$ $1 - p\nu$, if $C + \beta a \le C_R$ or $C_R < C = C + \beta a$	$1 - p\nu$	0, if $C \le C_I < C + \beta a$ or $C_I < C < C + \beta a$ $1 - p\nu$, if $C + \beta a \le C_I$ or $C_I < C + \beta a$
$(C + \beta a, \frac{L}{2})$	0, if $C \le C_R < C + \beta a$ or $C_R < C < C + \beta a$ $p\nu$, if $C + \beta a \le C_R$ or $C_R < C = C + \beta a$	$p\nu$	0, if $C \le C_I < C + \beta a$ or $C_I < C < C + \beta a$ $p\nu$, if $C + \beta a \le C_I$ or $C_I < C = C + \beta a$
C_R	1, if $C \le C_R < C + \beta a$ 0 otherwise	0	1, if $C \le C_R = C_I < C + \beta a$ 0 otherwise
C_I	1, if $C \le C_I = C_R < C + \beta a$ 0 otherwise	0	1, if $C \le C_I < C + \beta a$ 0 otherwise

In what follows, the players are designated by the index $j(j = R, P, I)$. If $C \le C_j < C + a\beta$, then player j with probability 1 may assume that the disaster has occurred, since the emission a brings the state of the game beyond the critical level. The state k remains unchanged, so that $P_j(k; k, 0, 0, 0) = 1$.

We shall consider the players' payoffs to be linear functions, because we do not know how to determine such payoffs.

Let us denote by $U_j(s; l, a, p, t)$ the payoff to player $j (j = R, P, I)$ when transition is made from the state s to the state t and controls l, a, p are selected in this state by players R, P, I, respectively.

$$U_R(C, L; l, a, p; C + \beta a, M) = c_1 l + c_2 a + c_3 p, \qquad (M = L, L/2);$$

$$U_R(C, L; l, a, p; k) = c_1 l + c_2 \frac{k - C}{\beta} + c_3 p + c_R;$$

$$U_R(k; 0, 0, 0; k) = 0;$$

$$U_P(C, L; l, a, p; C + \beta a, M) = c_4 a, \qquad (M = L, L/2);$$

$$U_P(C, L; l, a, p; k) = c_4 \frac{k - C}{\beta} + c_P;$$

$$U_P(k; 0, 0, 0; k) = 0;$$

$$U_I(C, L; l, a, p; C + \beta a, M) = c_5 a + c_6 p, \qquad (M = L, L/2);$$

$$U_I(C, L; l, a, p; k) = c_5 \frac{k - C}{\beta} + c_6 p + c_I;$$

$$U_I(k; 0, 0, 0; k) = 0.$$

It is assumed that the parameters $c_1 \geq 0$, $c_2 > 0$, $c_3 < 0$, $c_4 > 0$, $c_5 > 0$, $c_6 < 0$, $c_j (j = R, P, I)$ provide an extra payoff to player j if the disaster occurs. Therefore, it is assumed to be equal to a sufficiently large negative number. The variable $(k - c)/\beta$ implies that power production is worthwhile until a particular critical level is reached.

A play in the game is given by the infinite sequence

$$\pi = (s^1, l^1, a^1, p^1; s^2, l^2, a^2, p^2; \ldots)$$

of states and controls for players R, P, I respectively, in each component game. By the definition of transition probabilities, only those plays are possible in which $C^1 \leq C^i \leq C_P$ and $L^i \in \{L^1, L^1/2, L^1/4, \ldots\}$, and $a^i = (C^{i+1} - C^i)/\beta$, if $s^{i+1} = (C^{i+1}, L^{i+1})$.

Further, if $s^i = k$, then $s^m = k$ for all $m > i$. Suppose the payoff resulting from realization of the play π is the sum of payoffs in the component games (without a discount factor)

$$\underline{U}_j(\pi) = \sum_{i=1}^{\infty} U_j(s^i, l^i, a^i, s^{i+1}).$$

To simplify the considerations that follow, we also assume that $c_1 = 0$.

Let $(s^1, l^1, a^1, p^1, \ldots)$ be a play in which $s^i = (C^i, L^i)$ and $s^{i+1} = k$. Then

$$\underline{U}_R(s^1, \ldots) = \sum_{j=1}^{i} (c_2 a^j + c_3 p^j) + c_2 \frac{k - C^i}{\beta} + c_3 p^{i+1} + c_R$$

$$= c_3 \sum_{j=1}^{i+1} p^j + c_2 \frac{k - C^1}{\beta} + c_R.$$

When $s^j = (C^j, L^j)$ for $j = 1, 2$

$$\underline{U}_R(s^1, \ldots) = c_3 \sum_{j=1}^{\infty} p^j + \lim_{j \to \infty} \frac{C^j - C^1}{\beta}.$$

Here the limit is determined, because $C^i \leq C_P$. Following this route, we get

$$\underline{U}_P(\pi) = c_4 \frac{k - C^1}{\beta} + c_P,$$

$$\underline{U}_P(\pi) = c_4 \lim \frac{C^j - C^1}{\beta};$$

$$\underline{U}_I(\pi) = c_5 \frac{k - C^1}{\beta} + c_6 \sum_{j=1}^{i+1} p^j + c_I,$$

$$\underline{U}_I(\pi) = c_5 \lim \frac{C^i - C^1}{\beta} + c_6 \sum_{j=1}^{\infty} p^i;$$

We shall now define strategies. We shall restrict our consideration only to the classes of strategies that are dependent on the game state and previous choices made by other players in this state (i.e., we restrict ourselves to stationary strategies).

D e f i n i t i o n.The strategy σ_R for player R is defined as the map $\sigma_R : S \to R$ such that

$$\sigma_R(C,L) \in M_R(C,L) = \{l : 0 \leq l \leq L\},$$

$$\sigma_R(k,0) = 0.$$

The strategy σ_P for player P is defined as the map

$$\sigma_P : \{(s,l) : s \in S, l \in M_R(s)\} \to R,$$

such that

$$\sigma_P(C,L,l) \in M_P(C,L,l) = \left\{a : 0 \leq a \leq l, \frac{C_P - C}{\beta}\right\},$$

$$\sigma_P(k,0) = 0.$$

The strategy σ_I for player I is defined as the map

$$\sigma_I : \{(s,l,a) : s \in S, l \in M_P(s), a \in M_P(s,l)\} \to [0,1],$$

$$\sigma_I(C,L,l,a) \in [0,1],$$

$$\sigma_I(k,0,0) = 0.$$

Denote the players' strategy sets by $\sum_j (j = R,P,I)$. The definition of transition probabilities implies that infinitely many plays are possible in our game. We define the σ-algebra over the set of all possible plays as the minimal σ-algebra containing cylindrical sets with a finite base. It follows from the measure continuation theorem that there exists a unique continuation of probability measures defined over the algebra of cylindrical sets with a finite base and uniquely determined onto a minimal σ-algebra generated by these sets. Denote these probability measures by $P_j(\cdot : \sigma_R, \sigma_P, \sigma_I), (j = P,R,I)$. The payoff to player j is defined as the expected value of his total payoff taken over the subjective probability measure $P_j(\cdot : \sigma_R, \sigma_P, \sigma_I)$ in the set of all plays in the game.

$$V_j(\sigma_R, \sigma_P, \sigma_I) = \int \underline{U}_j(\pi) dP_j(\pi \mid \sigma_R, \sigma_P, \sigma_I), \quad j = R,P,I.$$

We can determine an exact upper bound for $V_j(\sigma_R, \sigma_P, \sigma_I)$. It follows from the definition of transition probabilities that the set of plays with the state components $s^m = (C^m, L^m)$ such that $C^m > C_R$ has a zero probability measure $P_R(\cdot : \sigma_R, \sigma_P, \sigma_1) = 0$. Therefore it suffices to consider the plays $\pi = (s^1, l^1, a^1, p^1; \ldots)$, where s^m either equals (C^m, L^m), for $C^m < C_R$ or coincides with C_R.

Therefore

$$\underline{U}_R(\pi) = c_3 \sum_{j=1}^{i+1} p^j + c_2 \frac{C_R - C^1}{\beta} + c_R, \quad \text{if} \quad C^i \le C_R < C^i + \beta a^i,$$

or

$$\underline{U}_R(\pi) = c_3 \sum_{j=1}^{i+1} p^j + \lim c_2 \frac{C^j - C^1}{\beta}, \quad \text{if} \quad C^j \le C_R \quad j = 1, \ldots.$$

In both cases it is clear that

$$\underline{U}_R(\pi) \le c_2 \frac{C^R - C^1}{\beta}.$$

Hence

$$V_R(\sigma_R, \sigma_P, \sigma_I) \le c_2 \frac{C_R - C^1}{\beta}.$$

In a similar manner it may be shown that

$$V_I(\sigma_R, \sigma_P, \sigma_I) \le c_5 \frac{C_I - C^1}{\beta}.$$

The inequality

$$\underline{U}_P(\pi) \le c_4 \frac{C_P - C^1}{\beta}$$

implies

$$V_P(\sigma_R, \sigma_P, \sigma_I) \le c_4 \frac{C_P - C^1}{\beta}.$$

All inequalities are unimprovable in that there exist the players' strategies under which they become equalities. To this end, it suffices to set $\sigma_R(C, L) = L$, $\sigma_P(C, L, l) = \min(l, (C_P - C)/\beta)$, $\sigma_I(C, L, l, a) = 0$, then $V_R(\sigma_R, \sigma_P, \sigma_I) = c_4(C_P - C^1)/\beta$.

To simplify the proof of the theorems below, we also assume that the payoff U_I to player I is replaced by $U_{I,r}$, where $U_{I,r}$ is determined in the following way

$$U_{I,r}(C, L; l, a, p; C + \beta a, M) = \begin{cases} c_5 a, & \text{if } M = L, \\ c_5 a + c_6/\nu, & \text{if } M = L/2; \end{cases}$$

$$U_{I,r}(C, L; l, a, p; k) = U_I(C, L; l, a, p; k),$$

$$U_{I,r}(k; 0, 0, 0; k) = U_I(k; 0, 0, 0; k).$$

7.2   Solution of the Game

Let us recall the definition of various optimality principles as applied to our case.

D e f i n i t i o n . The triple $(\sigma_R^*, \sigma_P^*, \sigma_I^*) \in \Sigma_R \times \Sigma_P \times \Sigma_I$ is called a Nash equilibrium if

$$V_R(\sigma_R^*, \sigma_P^*, \sigma_I^*) \geq V_R(\sigma_R, \sigma_P^*, \sigma_I^*), \qquad \sigma_R \in \Sigma_R,$$

$$V_P(\sigma_R^*, \sigma_P^*, \sigma_I^*) \geq V_P(\sigma_R^*, \sigma_P, \sigma_I^*), \qquad \sigma_P \in \Sigma_P,$$

$$V_I(\sigma_R^*, \sigma_P^*, \sigma_I^*) \geq V_I(\sigma_R^*, \sigma_P^*, \sigma_I), \qquad \sigma_I \in \Sigma_I.$$

D e f i n i t i o n . The payoff vector $(V_j(\sigma_R, \sigma_P, \sigma_I))$, $j = R, P, I$, is called Pareto optimal if there is no other vector $(V_j(\tau_R, \tau_P, \tau_I))$, where $\tau_j \in \Sigma_j$, $j = R, P, I$, such that

$$V_j(\sigma_R, \sigma_P, \sigma_I) \geq V_j(\tau_R, \tau_P, \tau_I), \qquad j = R, P, I,$$

where at least one of the preceding inequalities is strict.

The game has a large number of Nash equilibria. We shall formulate only three such equilibria. Two of them shall prove to be Pareto optimal (see [79]).

Theorem 1.   The strategy triples below forms a Nash equilibrium in the game studied

1. $$\sigma_R^1(C, L) = \min(L, \max(0, (C_R - C)/\beta)),$$

$$\sigma_P^1(C, L, l) = l, \tag{7.1}$$

$$\sigma_I^1(C, L, l, a) = 0.$$

The respective payoffs here are

$$V_R(\sigma_R^1, \sigma_P^1, \sigma_I^1) = c_2 \frac{C_R - C^1}{\beta}, \tag{7.2}$$

$$V_P(\sigma_R^1, \sigma_P^1, \sigma_I^1) = c_4 \frac{C_R - C^1}{\beta},$$

$$V_I(\sigma_R^1, \sigma_P^1, \sigma_I^1) = \begin{cases} c_5 \dfrac{C_R - C^1}{\beta}, & \text{if } C_R \leq C_I, \\ c_5 \dfrac{C_I - C^1}{\beta} + c_I, & \text{if } C_R > C_I. \end{cases}$$

2. $$\sigma_R^2(C, L) = \min(L, \max(0, \frac{C_I - C}{\beta})),$$

$$\sigma_P^2(C, L, l) = l,$$

$$\sigma_I^2(C, L, l, a) = \begin{cases} 0, & \text{if } l = \min(L, (C_I - C)/\beta) \quad \text{and} \quad C \leq C_I, \\ 1, & \text{if } l \neq \min(L, (C_I - C)/\beta) \quad \text{and} \quad C \leq C_I. \end{cases}$$

The respective payoffs here are

$$V_R(\sigma_R^2, \sigma_P^2, \sigma_I^2) = \begin{cases} c_2 \dfrac{C_I - C^1}{\beta}, & \text{if } C_I \leq C_R \\ c_2 \dfrac{C_I - C^1}{\beta} + c_R, & \text{if } C_I > C_R. \end{cases}$$

$$V_P(\sigma_R^2, \sigma_P^2, \sigma_I^2) = c_4 \frac{C_I - C^1}{\beta}, \tag{7.3}$$

$$V_I(\sigma_R^2, \sigma_P^2, \sigma_I^2) = c_5 \frac{C_I - C^1}{\beta}.$$

3. The "inoperative" point
$$\sigma_R^3(C, L) = 0,$$
$$\sigma_P^3(C, L, l) = 0, \tag{7.4}$$

$$\sigma_I^3(C, L, l, a) = \begin{cases} 0, & \text{if } l = 0 \text{ and } C = C^1, \\ 1, & \text{if } l > 0 \text{ and } C > C^1; \end{cases}$$

with payoffs

$$V_j(\sigma_R^3, \sigma_P^3, \sigma_I^3) = 0, \qquad j = R, P, I.$$

P r o o f . To avoid cumbersome calculations, we shall merely outline the idea of the proof. We shall first prove that the situation (7.1) is Nash equilibrium. Suppose that $i_R \in 1, 2, \ldots$ is determined from the condition

$$C^1 + \beta(i_R - 1)L^1 \le C_R < C_1 + \beta i_R L^1.$$

It can be shown that

$$C^{i+1} = C^1 + \beta i L^1, \qquad a^i = L^1, \qquad i = 1, \ldots, i_R - 1,$$

$$a^{i_R} = \frac{C_R - C^{i_R}}{\beta},$$

$$C^{i+1} = C_R, \qquad a^i = 0, \qquad i = i_R + 1, \ i_R + 2, \ldots,$$

in the equilibrium. Hence

$$V_R(\sigma_R^1, \sigma_R^2, \sigma_R^3) = c_2 \sum_{i=1}^{i_R - 1} L^1 + c_2 \frac{C_R - C^{i_R}}{\beta} = c_2 \frac{C_R - C^1}{\beta};$$

similarly

$$V_P(\sigma_R, \sigma_P, \sigma_I) = C_4 \frac{C_R - C^1}{\beta}.$$

If $C_R \le C_I$, then the state (C_R, L^1) is the state of the game when $i = i_r + 1, i_r + 2, \ldots$, as it follows from player I's subjective transition probabilities. If, however, $C_R > C_I$, then the disaster C_I is the final state of the game with the payoff

$$c_5 \frac{C_I - C^1}{\beta} + c_I.$$

The equilibrium condition for player R's strategy is explicitly satisfied, because in the equilibrium he receives the maximal possible payoff. Thus it is apparent that P cannot obtain a larger payoff from using other strategies. This also applies to player I if $C_R \le C_I$.

The case $C_R > C_I$ is the only one to be treated in more detail. Denote by σ'_P an arbitrary strategy for player I. Then the play π, in which $\lim C^i \le C_I$, is possible only if the quantity L^i is halved infinitely many times. In this case, however, $\underline{U}_{I,r}(\pi) = -\infty < c_5 \frac{C_I - C^1}{\beta} + c_I$. If the quantity L^1 is reduced finitely many times, then $\underline{U}_{I,r}(\pi) \leq c_5 \frac{C_I - C^1}{\beta} + c_I$. Therefore, no other strategy can increase the amount of payoff to player I.

2. We shall now consider the second equilibrium. Let $C_I < C_R$. In this case, R can increase his payoff only if the states (C^i, L^i), where $C^i > C_I$, occur in the play π with positive subjective probability. In this case, however, $\sigma_I^2(C^i, L^i, l, a) = 1$ (infinitely many times) providing $-\infty$ payoff to player R. Obviously P cannot increase his payoff, while I shall receive a maximal payoff

If $C_I = C_R$, then I and P receive their maximal payoffs, P cannot improve his state as compared with the equilibrium.In case $C_I > C_R$ R may wish to avoid the disaster by employing a strategy similar to the one in the first equilibrium. In this case, however, he is penalized by player$I$ infinitely many times and thus receives a smaller payoff. It is easy to show that P and I cannot improve here their position.

It can also be shown that $(\sigma_R^3, \sigma_P^3, \sigma_I^3)$ is equilibrium.

To determine which of the equilibria is Pareto optimal, we construct the set $D \subset R^3$ containing all Pareto optimal payoffs.

Let $C_R < C_I < C_P$. Then there exist $p_R \geq 0, p_I \geq 0, 1 - p_R - p_I \geq 0$, such that D consists of the points satisfying the inequalities

$$x \leq c_2 \frac{C_R - C^1}{\beta} + (1 - p_R)c_R;$$

$$y \leq c_4 \left\{ p_R \frac{C_R - C^1}{\beta} + p_I \frac{C_I - C^1}{\beta} + (1 - p_R - p_I) \frac{C_P - C^1}{\beta} \right\};$$

$$z \leq c_5 p_R \frac{C_R - C^1}{\beta} + c_5 p_I \frac{C_I - C^1}{\beta} + (1 - p_R - p_I) \left(c_5 \frac{C_P - C^1}{\beta} + c_I \right).$$

Let $(\sigma_R, \sigma_P, \sigma_I)$ be a strategy triple and let $C_R < C_I < C_P$. Denote by p_R the probability $P_R(T : \sigma_R, \sigma_P, \sigma_I)$ of occurrence of event T, i.e., the state sequence (C^i, L^i), where $C^i < C_R$, would be implemented. Let $p_I = P_P(T_I : \sigma_R, \sigma_P, \sigma_I)$ be the probability of occurrence of an event, namely, that there would be implemented the plays (s^i, l^i, a^i, p^i), $i = 1, 2, \ldots$ such that $C^i \leq C_I$ for all i, where $s^i = (C^i, L^i)$, $i = 1, 2, \ldots$ and $C^j > C_R$ for at least one j.

Evidently

$$V_P(\sigma_R, \sigma_P, \sigma_I) \leq c_4 \left\{ p_R \frac{C_R - C^1}{\beta} + p_I \frac{C_I - C^1}{\beta} + \right.$$

$$+(1 - p_R - p_I)\frac{C_P - C^1}{\beta}\Big\};$$

By the definition of transition probabilities for player P, the disaster may occur with probability $1 - p_R$. Therefore

$$V_R(\sigma_R, \sigma_P, \sigma_I) \le c_2\frac{C_R - C^1}{\beta} + (1 - p_R)c_R.$$

The subjective probabilities for player I are such that the state components are less than C_R and are equal to p_R and p_I between C_R and C_I , respectively. Therefore

$$V_I(\sigma_R, \sigma_P, \sigma_I) \le c_5 p_R\frac{C_R - C^1}{\beta} + c_5 I\frac{C_I - C^1}{\beta} +$$

$$+(1 - p_R - p_I)\left(c_5\frac{C_I - C^1}{\beta} + c_I\right).$$

The proof in the remaining cases can be carried out in a similar way.

Hence it follows that the first and the second Nash equilibrium are Pareto optimal. This can be seen from selecting $p_I = 1$ or $p_R = 1$ and $p = 1$, since the payoffs in these situations belong to the plane bounding the set from above.

Thus the Pareto optimality requirement alone cannot uniquely determine an equilibrium.

7.3   Side Payments and Coordination of Environmental Policy

It often turns out that implementation of environmental protection measures affects the interests of a variety of neighboring countries. This is especially true where the environmental pollution caused by industrial discharges in one country largely occurs in the territory of a neighboring country. Thus the acid rains occurring in Canada and Norway are essentially due to industrial discharges from the territory of USA and Great Britain. The wastes discharges to the Rhine in Germany and France impair environmental conditions in Netherlands. In a similar situation, Canada, Norway and Netherlands may claim compensation for damages. However, it may turn out that the amount of damage would significantly exceed the cost of effluent and waste treatment in the territory of the country that is an emission or pollution source. In this case it is unlikely that any damages will be recovered. Then it may be wise to make joint environmental arrangements for deriving benefit from cooperation. Such problems have long been the focus of muchstudies with the emphasis on mathematical models constructed by applying methods of the theory of dynamic games.

We shall describe here the approach presented in [61], [62] for solving the above problems and present our own regularization of this approach.

We shall consider two regions in the territory of which emission sources are located. Suppose that region (player) 1 is polluted by emissions from its own sources and those located in region 2. Region (player) 2 suffers no damage from such a pollution.

Each player wishes to maximize the profit from the products that he turns out. On the other hand, it is desirable to minimize the costs of foul gas treatment.

The joint efforts (i. e., cooperation) made to achieve these goals in the asymmetric situation, in which one of the players has no interest in cooperation, are possible only if the disinterested player may get side payments that would encourage him to take part in cooperation and adhere to the conditions of the agreement on cooperation provided such cooperation has been established.

The agreement on cooperation intended to protect countries against the threat of global heating will be effective if the agreement on joint efforts to purify air of environmentally dangerous gases is dynamically stable or time-consistent and hence is capable of preserving cooperation over a long period of time.

Let Q be a variation in the CO_2 concentration as compared with that in 1990. The losses born by the countries are governed by the level of global pollution. $D_i(Q)$ stands for the total losses sustained by the countries of both categories are respectively

$$\begin{cases} D_1(Q) > 0, & \text{for } Q > 0, \\ D_2(Q) = 0, & \text{for all } Q. \end{cases}$$

The equations of motion are

$$\frac{dQ}{dt} = \alpha(e_1 + e_2) - \beta Q, \qquad (7.5)$$

$$Q(0) = Q_0 = 0,$$

where $Q(t)$ is the level of global pollution, e_i stands for controls, i. e. the amount of environmentally dangerous gases produced by player i $(i = 1,2)$ and α, β are environmental parameters.

In a noncooperative problem, each player minimizes his costs:

$$J_i = \int\limits_{t_0}^{\infty} e^{-\rho_i t}[C_i(e_i) + D_i(Q)]\, dt,$$

where $C_i(e_i)$ — the costs of maintaining the CO_2 emission at the level e_i — is a convex decreasing function that satisfies $C_i(e_i^m) = 0$ for some positive emission at the level e_i^m; $D_i(Q)$ — the amount of losses due to physical damages — is a convex increasing function that satisfies $D_1(0) = 0$; $D_2(Q) = 0$ for all Q; $e^{-\rho_i t}$ is a discount factor. In this model, the discount factor is taken to be different for different players.

The choice of strategies, e_1^0 and e_2^0, determines a noncooperative trajectory $Q^0(t)$.

Suppose that trajectory $Q^0(t)$ is realized by employing strategies (e_1^0, e_2^0). Let $V_i^0(Q_0)$ be the minimal costs that are sustained by player i ($i = 1, 2$) in a noncooperative game and are ensured by the pair of strategies (e_1^0, e_2^0). We assume $V_1^0(Q_0) > 0$. In the noncooperative game, player 2 can always ensure himself the costs $C_2(e_2^m) = 0$ by selecting $e_2^0 = e_2^m$. Thus, his minimal guaranteed costs are $V_2(Q_0) \equiv 0$.

In the cooperative problem, by making joint efforts, the players minimize costs

$$J = J_1 + J_2 = \int\limits_{t_0}^{\infty} \{e^{-\rho_1 t}[C_1(e_1) + D_1(Q)] + e^{-\rho_2 t} C_2(e_2)\}\, dt. \qquad (7.6)$$

Let $Q^*(t)$ be the trajectory resulting from the use of the pair of strategies (e_1^*, e_2^*) which ensure that functional (7.6) attains its minimal value. The motion along this trajectory is governed by the equation (7.5).

Let $V_i^*(Q^*(t_0))$ be the costs that are incurred by player i in the cooperative game and are ensured by the pair of strategies (e_1^*, e_2^*). The solution of the problem of minimizing expenditures on reduction of the air CO_2 concentration involves the question of how such expenditures vary with time and whether or not the agreements on payments to players are dynamically stable. Long-term agreements are most likely to be dynamically unstable, because the players' expenditures depreciate in terms of money as time goes on. Therefore, it may be wise to consider the players' expenditures as a continuous flow of cash whose amount is determined on a small interval of time. In the mathematically stated dynamics of players' expenditures, we consider the motion along the trajectory determining the functional of these expenditures. If the motion is considered to be along the trajectory defined over the interval $[t_0, \infty)$, then at the time

t_0 and at the state Q_0 ($t_0 = 0$; $Q(t_0) = Q_0 = 0$) the players jointly minimize a functional of the form:

$$J = \int_0^\infty \{e^{-\rho_1 t}[C_1(e_1) + D_1(Q)] + e^{-\rho_2 t}C_2(e_2)\}dt,$$

where $e^{-\rho_i t}$ — a discount factor — is a factor that does not appear in the quantity determining the payments, but affects the utility of payments as time goes on. The discount factor defines the payment utility from player i's point of view. At the time $t_0 = 0$ the utility is maximal $e^{-\rho_i t_0} = 1$. As time elapses, the payment utility exponentially decreases with respect to the time at which the game starts.

If the process starts at the time t, then the payment utility is maximal at this time, and for $\tau \geq t$ the discount factor for the i-th player becomes $e^{-\rho_i(\tau - t)}$. It is necessary that at the start of the process the payment utility be maximal and equal to this payment.

It is interesting to note that if we solve the problem of cooperative behavior at an intermediate time from initial states along the cooperative trajectory emanating from t_0, Q_0, then the new cooperative trajectory will be different from the extension of the previous one for i. That is, the dynamic stability of the cooperative trajectory is disturbed.

At the intermediate time $l \in [l_0, \infty)$ it is necessary to find a pair of strategies (e_1^{t*}, e_2^{t*}) and, accordingly a trajectory $[Q^t(\tau)]^*$, $\tau \in [t, \infty)$ that minimizes a functional of the form:

$$J^t = \int_t^\infty \{e^{-\rho_1(\tau - t)}[C_1(e_1) + D_1(Q)] + e^{-\rho_2(\tau - t)}C_2(e_2)\}d\tau,$$

differing from (7.6) by the scalar factors $e^{\rho_1 t}$, $e^{\rho_2 t}$. Hence, each player's strategy supplying a minimum to the functional (7.6) varies with the time at which the agreement becomes effective, i. e.,

$$e_i^{0*}(\tau) \neq e_i^{t*}(\tau) \quad \tau \in [t, \infty).$$

Accordingly, the trajectories $Q^*(\tau) \neq [Q^t(\tau)]^*$, $\tau \in [t, \infty)$, are also distinguished, and this means that the cooperative trajectory is dynamically unstable. Therefore, when the players' discount factors are distinguished, the classical "cooperative trajectory" cannot be used. We shall introduce the notion of a locally cooperative trajectory (that is dynamically stable) and carry out regularization of the problem.

Suppose that the agreement on cooperation is implemented at the time t_0 from some state Q_0.

Let $t_0 = 0$; $Q(t_0) = Q_0 = 0$.

We shall fix the partitioning of the time interval $[t_0, \infty)$ by the points $\Theta : \Theta_0 = t_0 < \Theta_1 < \ldots < \Theta_k < \Theta_{k+1} < \ldots$, where $\Theta_{k+1} - \Theta_k = \delta > 0$. Define (e_1^{0*}, e_2^{0*}) and $Q^{0*}(t)$ to be the pair of strategies and, accordingly, the trajectory that minimize a functional of the form:

$$J^{\Theta_0} = \int_0^\infty \{e^{-\rho_1 t}[C_1(e_1) + D_1(Q)] + e^{-\rho_2 t}C_2(e_2)\}dt,$$

where the trajectory $Q^{0*}(t)$ starts from the state $Q^{0*}(\Theta_0)$.

We define (e_1^{1*}, e_2^{1*}) and $Q^{1*}(t)$ to be the pair of strategies and, accordingly, the trajectory that minimize

$$J^{\Theta_1} = \int_{\Theta_1}^\infty \{e^{-\rho_1(t-\Theta_1)})[C_1(e_1) + D_1(Q)] + e^{-\rho_2(t-\Theta_1)}C_2(e_2)\}dt,$$

where $Q^{1*}(t)$ starts from the state

$$Q^{1*}(\Theta_1) = Q^{0*}(\Theta_1).$$

We define (e_1^{2*}, e_2^{2*}) and $Q^{2*}(t)$ to be the pair of strategies and, accordingly, the trajectory that minimize

$$J^{\Theta_2} = \int_{\Theta_2}^\infty \{e^{-\rho_1(t-\Theta_2)})[C_1(e_1) + D_1(Q)] + e^{-\rho_2(t-\Theta_2)}C_2(e_2)\}dt,$$

where the trajectory $Q^{2*}(t)$ starts from the state

$$Q^{2*}(\Theta_2) = Q^{1*}(\Theta_2).$$

We define (e_1^{k*}, e_2^{k*}) and $Q^{k*}(t)$, $k = 1, 2, \ldots$ to be the pair of strategies and, accordingly, the trajectory that minimize

$$J^{\Theta_k} = \int_{\Theta_k}^\infty \{e^{-\rho_1(t-\Theta_k)})[C_1(e_1) + D_1(Q)] + e^{-\rho_2(t-\Theta_k)}C_2(e_2)\}dt,$$

where the trajectory $Q^{k*}(t)$ starts from the state

$$\dot{Q}^{k*}(\Theta_k) = Q^{(k-1)*}(\Theta_k).$$

The pair

$$(\bar{e}_1^*(t), \bar{e}_2^*(t)), \quad t \in [\Theta_k, \Theta_{k+1}), \quad k = 0, 1, 2, \ldots$$

is called a δ-cooperative solution. Accordingly,

$$\overline{Q}^*(t) = Q^{k*}(t)$$

is called a δ-cooperative trajectory for $t \in [\Theta_k, \Theta_{k+1})$.

D e f i n i t i o n. The procedure for constructing the trajectory $\bar{x}(t)$ is called δ-dynamically stable if the segment of trajectory $\bar{x}^{\Theta_k}(t)$ $(t \geq \Theta_k)$ resulting from application of this procedure at the time Θ_k at the state $\bar{x}(\Theta_k)$ coincides with the trajectory $\bar{x}(t)$ resulting from application of this same procedure at the time Θ_0 from the state $\bar{x}(\Theta_0) = x_0$ for $t \geq \Theta_0$, that is

$$\bar{x}(t) = \bar{x}^{\Theta_k}(t) \quad \text{for} \quad t \geq \Theta_k.$$

The trajectory $\bar{x}(t)$ resulting from application of the δ-dynamically stable procedure is called a δ-dynamically stable trajectory.

The proposed procedure for constructing the δ-cooperative trajectory $\overline{Q}^*(t)$ is δ-dynamically stable, since its application for constructing the δ-cooperative trajectory $\overline{Q}^{k*}(t)$ starting at the time Θ_k from the state $Q^*(\Theta_k)$ implies minimization of the functionals that are minimized at the time instants Θ_l $(l \geq k)$ from the state $Q^*(\Theta_l)$ when $\overline{Q}^*(t)$ is constructed.

The δ-cooperative trajectory thus constructed is δ-dynamically stable by construction.

One of the conditions for maintaining cooperation is provided by the motion along the δ-cooperative trajectory. But the motion along the cooperative trajectory does not automatically ensure the solution of the problem of maintaining cooperation.

We shall now consider the conditions for formation of cooperation assuming that the motion further occurs along the δ-cooperative trajectory.

Player 1 decides on cooperation if his expenditures in the noncooperative game are reduced by cooperation:

$$w_1(Q_0) = V_1^0(Q_0) - V_1^*(Q_0)$$

Player 2 is not interested in cooperation, because he is economically indifferent to the threat of global pollution. Therefore, he enters cooperation, provided the expenses on reduction of CO_2 emissions that he may bear in the case of cooperation are off set to him in advance:

$$V_2^*(Q_0) = \int_0^\infty e^{-\rho_2 t} C_2(e_2^*(\tau)) d\tau.$$

The payoff from cooperation is taken to be the difference in the expenses on CO_2 reduction under noncooperation and cooperation subject to prepayment of expenses to player 2:

$$g(Q_0) = V_1^0(Q_0) - V_1^*(Q_0) - V_2^*(Q_0) \geq 0$$

The problem is to find out how this amount shall be allocated between the players.

The Nash bargaining scheme is taken to be the scheme that is capable of preserving the agreement on cooperation. The bargaining solution implies that the amount of payments shall not exceed the amount of payments that the players may have without entering a coalition.

Thus, the problem formally is to find the best allocation vector $x = (x_1, x_2)$ satisfying the following conditions:

$$\begin{cases} \sum_{i=1}^2 x_i = g(Q_0), \\ x_i \geq 0 \end{cases}$$

The bargaining solution is obtained from the condition $\max_x x_1 x_2$. From this condition we find

$$x_i = \frac{g(Q_0)}{2}.$$

That is, the payoff from cooperation is equally allocated between the players.

Then the expenses born by the players in the cooperative game are

$$\overline{V}_1^*(Q_0) = V_1^*(Q_0) + V_2^*(Q_0) + \frac{g(Q_0)}{2}.$$

$$\overline{V}_2^*(Q_0) = -\frac{g(Q_0)}{2},$$

The players' profits from cooperation (as compared with the noncooperative behavior) are

$$\hat{V}_1(Q_0) = -V_1^0(Q_0, e_1^0, e_2^0) + \frac{g(Q_0)}{2}.$$

$$\hat{V}_2(Q_0) = -V_2^0(Q_0, e_1^0, e_2^0) + \frac{g(Q_0)}{2} = 0 + \frac{g(Q_0)}{2} = \frac{g(Q_0)}{2}$$

The bargaining scheme used to preserve the agreement on cooperation must also be dynamically stable so that the agreement on the allocation resulting from application of this scheme will be preserved during the motion along the δ-cooperative trajectory $\overline{Q}^*(t)$.

The amount of $g(Q(t_0))$ is equally allocated between the players if the Nash bargaining scheme is used. The payoff

$$g(\overline{Q}^*(t_0)) = V_1^0(Q^0(t_0)) - V_1^*(\overline{Q}^*(t_0)) - V_2^*(\overline{Q}^*(t_0)),$$

where $V_1^0(Q^0(t_0))$ is computed along the noncooperative trajectory $Q^0(t)$ from the initial state $\overline{Q}^*(t_0) = Q^0(t_0)$, is equally allocated at the time t_0 at the state Q_0.

The trajectories $Q^0(t)$ and $\overline{Q}^*(t)$ coincide only at the time t_0

$$Q^0(t_0) = \overline{Q}^*(t_0).$$

But at any subsequent time $t' > t_0$, $t \in [t_0, \infty)$ we generally have

$$Q^0(t') \neq \overline{Q}^*(t').$$

The players, once using the bargaining scheme, are prescribed at the initial time t_0 to equally allocate a payoff of the form

$$g(\overline{Q}^*(t_0)) = \int_{t_0}^{\infty} e^{-\rho_1 \tau} [C_1(e_1^0) + D_1(Q^0(\tau))] d\tau -$$

$$- \int_{t_0}^{\infty} e^{-\rho_1 \tau} [C_1(\overline{e}_1^*) + D_1(\overline{Q}^*(\tau))] d\tau - \int_{t_0}^{\infty} e^{-\rho_2 \tau} C_2(\overline{e}_2^*) d\tau =$$

$$= \int_{t_0}^{t} e^{-\rho_1 \tau} [C_1(e_1^0) + D_1(Q^0(\tau))] d\tau -$$

$$- \int_{t_0}^{t} e^{-\rho_1 \tau} [C_1(\overline{e}_1^*) + D_1(\overline{Q}^*(\tau))] d\tau - \int_{t_0}^{t} e^{-\rho_2 \tau} C_2(\overline{e}_2^*) d\tau +$$

$$+ \int_{t}^{\infty} e^{-\rho_1 \tau} [C_1(e_1^0) + D_1(Q^0(\tau))] d\tau -$$

$$-\int_t^\infty e^{-\rho_1\tau}[C_1(\overline{e}_1^*) + D_1(\overline{Q}^*(\tau))]d\tau - \int_t^\infty e^{-\rho_2\tau}C_2(\overline{e}_2^*)d\tau.$$

Thus, the single use of the bargaining scheme prescribes that a payoff of the form

$$g^t(\overline{Q}^*[t,\infty)) = \int_t^\infty e^{-\rho_1\tau}[C_1(e_1^0) + D_1(Q^0(\tau))]d\tau -$$

$$-\int_t^\infty e^{-\rho_1\tau}[C_1(\overline{e}_1^*) + D_1(\overline{Q}^*(\tau))]d\tau - \int_t^\infty e^{-\rho_2\tau}C_2(\overline{e}_2^*)d\tau$$

should be allocated, as from the time $t > t_0$.

If, however, we use the bargaining scheme by taking the time t to be the initial time, then a payoff of the form

$$g(\overline{Q}^*(t)) = \int_t^\infty e^{-\rho_1(\tau-t)}[C_1(e_1^0) + D_1(Q^0(\tau))]d\tau -$$

$$-\int_t^\infty e^{-\rho_1(\tau-t)}[C_1(\overline{e}_1^*) + D_1(\overline{Q}^*(\tau))]d\tau - \int_t^\infty e^{-\rho_2(\tau-t)}C_2(\overline{e}_2^*)_2 d\tau$$

shall be equally allocated.

The amount of $g(\overline{Q}^*(t))$ resulting from the reuse of the bargaining scheme, when the time t and state $\overline{Q}^*(t)$ are taken to be initial data, is different from that of the payoff $g^t(\overline{Q}^*[t,\infty))$ to be allocated because of a single use of the bargaining scheme from the state Q_0 at the time t_0, which implies dynamic unstability of the payoff allocation procedure. This fact was noted by the authors of [62].

We shall use the definition introduced by L. A. Petrosjan and employed for the first time in [80].

D e f i n i t i o n. The bargaining scheme is called δ-dynamically stable if, when the scheme is applied at the time Θ_k from the state $\overline{Q}^*(\Theta_k)$, the payoff allocation over the interval $[\Theta_\ell, \Theta_{\ell+1}]$, $\ell \geq k$, coincides with the allocation over the time interval $[\Theta_\ell, \Theta_{\ell+1}]$, $\ell \geq k$, resulting from application of this scheme at the time t_0 from the state $Q_0 = \overline{Q}^*(\Theta_0)$.

We propose that the Nash bargaining scheme should be regularized to obtain a δ-dynamically stable bargaining scheme.

Recall that the motion occurs along the δ-cooperative trajectory made up of the segments $Q^{0*}(t)$, $Q^{1*}(t)$, ..., $Q^{k*}(t)$. In the following, the segments of the δ-cooperative trajectory are denoted as

$$\overline{Q}^{0*}(t), \overline{Q}^{1*}(t), \ldots, \overline{Q}^{k*}(t)$$

Starting from the time Θ_0, the players apply the bargaining scheme only once and, along the δ-cooperative trajectory, come to an agreement that the amount of $g(Q^0(\Theta_0)) = g(\overline{Q}^*(\Theta_0))$ shall be equally allocated.

We define $g([t_0, \Theta_1), \overline{Q}^{0*})$ as the value to be equally allocated between the players over the time interval $[t_0, \Theta_1)$

$$g([t_0, \Theta_1), \overline{Q}^{0*}) =$$

$$= \int_{\Theta_0}^{\Theta_1} e^{-\rho_1(\tau - \Theta_0)}[C_1(e_1^0) + D_1(Q^0(\tau))]d\tau -$$

$$- \int_{\Theta_0}^{\Theta_1} e^{-\rho_1(\tau - \Theta_0)}[C_1(\overline{e}_1^{0*}) + D_1(\overline{Q}^{0*}(\tau))]d\tau -$$

$$- \int_{\Theta_0}^{\Theta_1} e^{-\rho_2(\tau - \Theta_0)}C_2(\overline{e}_2^{0*})d\tau.$$

Starting from the time Θ_k, $k = 1, 2, \ldots$ the players again apply the bargaining scheme and, along the cooperative trajectory, come to an agreement that the amount of $g(\overline{Q}^*(\tau))$, $(\tau = \Theta_k)$ shall be equally allocated.

We define $g([\Theta_k, \Theta_{k+1}), \overline{Q}^{k*})$ as the value to be allocated between the players over the interval $[\Theta_k, \Theta_{k+1})$

$$g([\Theta_k, \Theta_{k+1}), \overline{Q}^{k*}) =$$

$$= \int_{\Theta_k}^{\Theta_{k+1}} e^{-\rho_1(\tau - \Theta_k)}[C_1(e_1^0) + D_1(Q^0(\tau))]d\tau -$$

$$- \int_{\Theta_k}^{\Theta_{k+1}} e^{-\rho_1(\tau - \Theta_k)}[C_1(\overline{e}_1^{k*}) + D_1(\overline{Q}^{k*}(\tau))]d\tau -$$

$$- \int_{\Theta_k}^{\Theta_{k+1}} e^{-\rho_2(\tau - \Theta_k)}C_2(\overline{e}_2^{k*})d\tau.$$

Here e_1^0 is player 1's optimal strategy in the noncooperative game from the state $\overline{Q}^*(\Theta_k)$; $Q^0(\tau)$ is the noncooperative trajectory starting at the time Θ_k from the initial state $\overline{Q}^*(\Theta_k)$ for $\tau \in [\Theta_k, \Theta_{k+1})$; $\overline{e}_1^{k*}$ is player 1's optimal strategy in the cooperative game from the state $\overline{Q}^*(\Theta_k)$; $\overline{Q}^*(\tau)$ is an optimal strategy if the players use δ-cooperative strategies.

The above regularization of the bargaining scheme prescribes that the payoff $g([\Theta_k, \Theta_{k+1}), \overline{Q}^{k*})$ shall be equally allocated when the motion occurs along the δ-cooperative trajectory.

The proposed regularization of the bargaining scheme is δ-dynamically stable by construction.

Bibliography

[1] Alekseyev and V. B. and Krishev, I. I. *Kinetic Equations for Describing Biocenoses*, Biofizika, 1974, Vol 19, № 4, pp. 754–759.

[2] Berliand, M. E. *Modern Issue of Atmospheric Diffusion and Pollution*, Leningrad, 1975, p 48.

[3] Berzh, K. *Graph Theory and Its Applications*, M., 1962, p 319.

[4] Volterra, V. *Mathematical Theory of Struggle for Existence*, M., 1976, p 288.

[5] Vorobyev, N. N. *Theory of Games: Lectures for Economists-Cyberneticists*, Leningrad, 1973, p 160.

[6] Gorelik, V. A. Kononenko, A. F. *Game-Theoretic Models for Decision-Making in Ecological and Economic Systems*, M.,1982, p 144.

[7] Danilov, N. N. *The Pareto Set in an N-Person Differential Game with Nonstrict Competition*, in Some Issues of Differential and Integral Equations, Yakutsk, 1977, Vol 2, pp. 25–35.

[8] Dyubin, G. N. and Suzdal, V. G. *An Introduction to Applied Theory of Games*, M., 1981, p 336.

[9] Zakharov, V. V. *One Game-Theoretic Model of Environmental Protection* in Some Issues of Differential and Integral Equations, Yakutsk, 1978, Vol 3, pp. 32–37.

[10] Zakharov V. V. *Toward the Issue of Application of Game Theory to the Environmental Protection Problem*, Bulletin of Leningrad University, 1981,Vol 1, № 1, pp. 111–113.

[11] Zakharov, V. V.   *The Dynamic Game-Theoretic Model of Environmental Protection in Multistage*, Differential, Cooperative and Noncooperative Games and Their Applications, Kalinin, 1982, pp. 126–134.

[12] Zakharov, V. V.   *Games with a Gap in Hyperplane*, in Game Theory and Its Applications, Kemerovo, 1983, pp. 22–32.

[13] Zakharov, V. V. and Petrosjan, L. A.   *The Game-Theoretic Approach to the Environmental Protection Problem*, Bulletin of Leningrad University, 1981, Vol 1, $N^{\underline{o}}$ 1, pp. 26–32.

[14] Zubov, V. I.   *Motion Stability. Liapunov's Methods and Their Applications*, M., 1973, p. 272.

[15] Zubov, V. I.   *Modeling of Biological Processes by Differential Equations*, in Issues of Cybernetics, 1975, Vol 25, pp. 3–9.

[16] Zubov, V. I.   *Dynamics of Controlled Systems*, M., 1982, p 286.

[17] Zubov, V. I. and Petrosjan, L. A. *Problem of Optimal Capital Investments Allocation*, Leningrad, 1971, p 21.

[18] Zubov, V. I. and Petrosjan, L. A.   *Mathematical Methods in Planning*, Leningrad, 1982, p 112.

[19] Kiney, R. P. and Raiffa, H.   *Multicriteria Decision-Making: Preferences and Substitutions*, M., 1981, p 560.

[20] Kolmogorov, A. N.   *Qualitative Studies of Mathematical Models for Population Dynamics*, in Issues of Cybernetics, Vol 25, M., 1972, pp. 100–106.

[21] Kondratyev, K. Y.   *Space Exploration of Environment and Natural Resources*, M., 1982, p 63.

[22] Krasovskii, N. N.   *Control of a Dynamical System*, M., 1985, p 518.

[23] Krasovskii, N. N. and Subbotin, A. I.   *Positional Differential Games*, M., 1974, p 456.

[24] Ladizhenskaya, O. A.   *Boundary-Value Problems in Mathematical Physics*, M., 1973, pp. 146–180.

[25] Marchuk, G. I.   *Application of Adjoint Equations to Solution of Problems in Mathematical Physics*, in Advances in Mechanics, 1981, $N^{\underline{o}}$ 1, pp. 7–12.

[26] Marzuk, G. I. *Mathematical Modelling in Environmental Problems*, M., 1982, p 320.

[27] *Control Models for Natural Resources*, Edited by Gurman, V. I., M., 1981, p 264.

[28] Moiseyev, N. N. *Information Theory of Hierarchical Systems*, in Proceedings of the First All-Union Conference on Operations Research, Minsk, 1972, pp. 95–99.

[29] Moiseyev, N. N. *Hierarchical Structures and Theory of Games*, in Proceedings of the USSR Academy of Sciences. Engineering Cybernetics, 1973, $N^{\underline{o}}$ 6, pp. 1–11.

[30] Moiseyev, N. N. *Mathematical Problems in Systems Analysis*, M., 1981, p 487.

[31] Monin, A. S. and Yaglom, A. M. *Statistical Hydrodynamics*, Vol 1, M., 1965, p 638.

[32] Odum, J. *Foundations of Ecology*, M., 1975, p 321.

[33] Owen, G. *Theory of Games*, 1971, p 230.

[34] Petrosjan L. A. *Stability of Solutions in N-Person Differential Games*, in Bulletin of Leningrad University, 1977, $N^{\underline{o}}$ 19, pp. 46–52.

[35] Petrosjan, L. A. *Differential Games of Pursuit*, Leningrad, 1977, p 224.

[36] Petrosjan, L. A. and Danilov, N. N. *Stability of Solutions in Nonzero-Sum Differential Games with Transferable Payoffs,*, in Bulletin of Leningrad University, 1979, $N^{\underline{o}}$ 1, pp. 46–54.

[37] Petrosjan, L. A. and Zakharov, V. V. *Dynamic Game Model of Regional Development Planning*, in Multistage, Differential, Cooperative and Noncooperative Games, Kalinin, 1983, pp. 31–39.

[38] Petrosjan, L. A. and Zakharov, V. V. *An introduction to Mathematical Ecology*, Leningrad, 1986, p 224.

[39] Petrosjan, L. A. and Tomsky, G. V. *Dynamic Games and Their Applications*, Leningrad, 1982, p 252.

[40] Petrosjan, L. A. and Zaccour, R. *A Multistage Supergame of Down-stream Pollution*, in Proceedings of 18 th International Conference of Computers & Industrial Engineering, Shanghai, 1995, pp. 1288–1292

[41] Podinovsky, V. V. and Nogin, V. D. *Pareto-Optimal Solutions of Multicriteria Problems*, M., 1982, p 255.

[42] Poluektov, R. A., Pikh, Y. A. and Shvitov, I. A. *Dynamic Models of Ecological Systems*, Leningrad, 1980, p 289.

[43] Pikh, Y. A. Stability of Solutions of the Lotka-Volterra *Differential Equations*, in Applied Mathematics and Mechanics, 1977, Vol 41, $N^{\underline{o}}$ 2, pp. 262 270.

[44] Pikh, Y. A. *Equilibrium and Stability in the Models of Population Dynamics*, M., 1983, p 184.

[45] Svirezhev, Y. M. and Yelizarov, Y. Y. *Mathematical Modeling of Biological Systems*, M., 1972, p 159.

[46] Svirezhev, Y. M. and Logofet, D. O. *Stability of Biological Communities*, M., 1978, p 352.

[47] Timofeyev, N. N. and Svirezhev, Y. M. *Theory of Trophic Chains and its Related Optimization Problems*, in Issues of Cybernetics, 1979, $N^{\underline{o}}$ 52, pp. 5–18.

[48] Tikhonov, I. F. *One Mathematical Model of Regional Planning*, in Mathematical Methods of Optimization and Control in Complex Systems, Kalinin, 1982, pp. 14–18.

[49] Ecological Systems. *Adaptive Estimate and Control*, Edited by Holling, C. S., M., 1981, p 396.

[50] Csanady, G. *Turbulent Diffusion in the Environment*, Dordrecht, 1973, p 248.

[51] Holling, C. S. *The Functional Response of Predator to Prey Density and its Role in Mimicry and Population Regulation*, Mem. Entomol. Soc., Canada, 1965, $N^{\underline{o}}$ 45, pp. 1–60.

[52] Imbert, I. and Petrosjan, L. *Aplicationes de la Teoria de los Yuegos con N Participantes*, Invest. Oper., 1979, $N^{\underline{o}}$ 28, pp. 3–29.

[53] Imbert, I. and Petrosjan, L.   *Un Modelo Teorico de Yuego con Estructura Romboidal de Direction*, Invest. Oper., 1980, $N^{\underline{o}}$ 29, pp. 3–20.

[54] Lotka, A. J.   *Elements of Physical Biology*, Baltimor, 1925, p 46.

[55] Malthus, T. R.   *An Essay on the Principle of Population*, London, 1803, p 610.

[56] Petrosjan, L. and Rodriges, R.   *Modelo Economico-mathematico para la Plantification del Desarrollo del Complejo Azucarero*, Economia y Desarr., 1982, $N^{\underline{o}}$ 67, pp. 191–206.

[57] Resigno, A.   *The Struggle for Life: Two Species*, in Bulletin of Math. Biophys., 1967, Vol 29, $N^{\underline{o}}$ 2, pp. 377–388.

[58] Rozenzweig, M. L. and Mac Artur, R. H.   *Graphical Representation and Stability Conditions of Predator-Prey Interactions*, Amer. Natur., 1963, Vol 97, $N^{\underline{o}}$ 893, pp. 209–223.

[59] Haurie, A. and Zaccour, G.   *Differential Game Models of Global Environmental Management*, Annals of Dynamic Games, 1994.

[60] Fisher Ronald, D. and Mirman Leonard, J.   *Strategic Dynamic Interactions: Fish Wars*, Journal of Economics, Dynamics and Control, 1992, 16, pp. 267–287.

[61] Kaitala, V. and Pohjola, M.   *Economic Development and Agreeable Redistribution in Capitalism: Efficient Game Equilibria in Two-Class Neoclassical Growth Model*, International Economic Review, 1990, 31, pp.421–438.

[62] Kaitala, V. and Pohjola, M.   *Sustainable International Agreements on Green House Warming: A Game Theory Study*, Miteo, 1993.

[63] Van der Ploeg, F. and De Zeeuw, A. J.   *International Aspects of Pollution Control, Environmental and Resource Economics*, 1992, pp. 117–139.

[64] Petrosjan, L. A.   *Solutions of N-Person Differential Games*, in Dynamic Control, Sverdlovsk, 2, pp. 117–139

[65] Bellman, R.   *Dynamic Programming*, M., 1960.

[66] Pontrjagin, L. S., Boltiansky, V. G., Gamkrelidze, R. V. and Mischenko, E. F.   *Mathematical Theory of Optimal Processes*, M., 1961.

[67] Yeskov, V. A. *Regularization of Dynamic Multicriteria Optimization Problems*, in Differential, Multistage, Noncooperative and Hierarchical Games, Kalinin, 1985.

[68] Tan, T. C. and S.R.d.C. Werlang. *The Bayessian Foundations of Solution Concepts of Games*, Journal of Economic Theory, 45, 1988, pp. 370–391.

[69] Maynard Smith, J. and Price, J. R. *The Logic of Animal Conflict*, Nature, London, 1973, 246, pp. 15–18.

[70] Maynard Smith, J. *Evolution and the Theory of Games*, Cambridge University Press, 1982.

[71] Bishop, D. T., Cannings, C. and Maynard Smith, J. *The War of Attrition With Random Rewards*, Journal of Theor. Biol., 1978, 74, pp. 377–388.

[72] Eric van Damme *Stability and Perfection of Nash Equilibria*, Berlin, Springer-Verlag, 1987.

[73] Charnov, E. L. *The Theory of Sex Allocation*, Princeton University Press, New Jersey, 1982.

[74] Nash, J. F. *Noncooperative Games*, Annals of Mathematics, 1951, 54, pp. 289–295.

[75] Taylor, P. D. and Jonker, L. B. *Evolutionary Stable Strategies and Game Dynamics*, Math. Biosc., 1978, 40, pp. 145–156.

[76] Zeeman, E. C. *Population Dynamics from Game Theory*, 1980, pp. 471–497, in Nitecki, Z. and Robinson C., (eds). Global Theory of Dynamical Systems, Lecture Notes in Math., 819, Springer-Verlag.

[77] Eigen, M. and Schuster, P. *Emergence of the Hypercycle*, Naturwissenschaften, 64, pp. 541–565.

[78] Stepanov, V. V. *A Course in Differential Equations*, M., 1952, State Engineering Pub. House.

[79] Hopfinger, E. *Dynamic Standard Setting for Carbon Dioxide*, Applied Game Theory, 1979, Phisica-Verlag, Wuerzburg, Germany.

[80] Savishenko, N. *Regularizaton of Bargaining Scheme in Pollution Problems*, in Issue of Scientific Works. Pskov, 1994, pp. 26–32.

[81] Petrosjan, L. A. and Zakharov, V. V. *Game-Theoretic Models in Ecology*, in Review of Applied and Industrial Mathematics, 1994, Vol 1, 6, pp. 942–956.

[82] Selten, R. *A Note on Evolutionary Stable Strategies in Extensive Two-Person Games*, Math. Social Sciences, 1983, 5, pp. 269–363.

Index